It Happened One Night • Bringing Up Baby • Franke..... .
Gone With the Wind • Stagecoach • Dracula • Pubic Enemy • The Adventures of Robin Hood
Mr. Smith Goes to Washington • King Kong • The Hunchback of Notre Dame • Wuthering Heights
His Girl Friday • The Philadelphia Story • Rebecca • Maltese Falcon • Double Indemnity • Casablanca
Arsenic and Old Lace • Mildred Pierce • It's a Wonderful Life • The Treasure of Sierra Madre
Gentleman's Agreement • All the Kings Men • Mrs. Miniver • National Velvet • The Lost Weekend
Yankee D   Yesterday
All About   High Noon
From Here   for Murder
The Ten   ver Kwai
Shane • Gia   Like It Hot
The Afric   t of Eden
Stalag 17   Tiffany's
Dr. No • T   r. Zhivago
The Gradu   t Cowboy
Butch Cass   • True Grit
The Magnifi   ockingbird
The Pink P   All Seasons
Easy Rider   own Affair
Cool Hand L   Don't They
The Sand   n • Shaft
The Getaw   koo's Nest
Paper Moo   eat Gatsby
Dirty Harry • Carrie • Rocky • Smokey and the Bandit • Heaven Can Wait • The Deer Hunter • Jaws
Superman • Death Wish • The Goodbye Girl • Animal House • Coming Home • Pretty Baby • Alien
Taxi Driver • The Godfather • Deliverance • The Exorcist • Blazing Saddles • Star Wars • Network
Apocalypse Now • Kramer vs. Kramer • Love Story • Norma Rae • Blue Lagoon • Urban Cowboy
American Gigolo • Raiders of the Lost Ark • An Officer and a Gentleman • Scarface • Tootsie
Fast Times at Ridgemont High • First Blood • Escape from New York • Blade Runner • Scarface
Beverly Hills Cop • The King of Comedy • Terms of Endearment • Footloose • Flashdance
Ghostbusters • The Untouchables • The Breakfast Club • Back to the Future • The Color Purple
Top Gun • Splash • Blue Velvet • Fatal Attraction • Wall Street • The Terminator • The Accused
Dirty Dancing • Die Hard • Rain Man • Working Girl • Big • When Harry Met Sally • Risky Business
Batman • Poltergeist • The Outsiders • Desperately Seeking Susan • Ferris Bueller's Day Off • Witness
Field of Dreams • Predator • Dead Poets Society • The Fabulous Baker Boys • Frances • Platoon
The Silence of the Lambs • The Bonfire of the Vanities • Ghost • Basic Instinct • Thelma & Louise
Pretty Woman • Misery • A League of Their Own • The Hunt for the Red October • Forrest Gump
Pulp Fiction • In the Line of Fire • Dumb & Dumber • Bad Boys • The Shawshank Redemption
Interview with a Vampire • Jurassic Park • Toy Story • Jerry Maguire • Speed • As Good as It Gets
Boogie Nights • Men in Black • Titanic • Shakespeare in Love • American Beauty • Point Break
Se7en • Indecent Proposal • My Cousin Vinny • Kindergarten Cop • Prince of Tides • The Matrix
The Bodyguard • Reservoir Dogs • The Firm • The Fugitive • Groundhog Day • Philadelphia
Sleepless in Seattle • True Lies • Braveheart • Bridges of Madison County • JFK • Get Shorty
Usual Suspects • The English Patient • Evita • Primal Fear • Scream • L.A. Confidential • Fight Club
There's Something About Mary • American Psycho • Charlie's Angels • Bridget Jones's Diary
The Bourne Identity • Gladiator • Monster's Ball • Training Day • Chicago • Gangs of New York
Finding Nemo • Cast   Patriot • Enchanted
Million Dollar Bab **Andrew Kole & Michael Berlin** s • Casino Royale
The Departed • No Country for Old Men • The Wrestler • The Hangover • The Blind Side
Legally Blonde • Moulin Rouge • Spider-Man • Kiss Kiss Bang Bang • Inglorious Bastards • X-Men
Mean Girls • Michael Clayton • Knocked Up • The Curious Case of Benjamin Button • The Fighter
Django Unchained • Silver Linings Playbook • Zero Dark Thirty • Gravity • Dallas Buyers Club
The King's Speech • Salt • 127 Hours • The Avengers • Lincoln • Les Misérables • The Revenant
Manchester by the Sea • Gone Girl • La La Land • Black Panther • Bohemian Rhapsody • Rocketman

*"Casting is sometimes fate and destiny
more than skill and talent."*

— Steven Spielberg

ISBN: 978-0-9990915-2-4

Book Design: Andrea Reider Books
Cover Design: Andrew Kole
Editors: Karen Kass
          Sherie Sylvester

CONTENTS

Coming Attraction

The fact that there isn't an Academy Award for CASTING is quite astonishing if you think about it. Currently, there are twenty-six categories that run the gamut from Best Film to Best Sound Mixing. It is commonly agreed that the top six categories are Best Film, Best Director, Best Actor, Best Actress, followed by Best Supporting Actor and Best Supporting Actress. That means four of the top six categories are directly related to casting.

Critic Roger Ebert said, *"Sometimes it's all about casting."* It's hard to disagree with that statement when you think about how arbitrary the casting of so many iconic roles throughout the history of film came about. Not as infrequently as one might think, actors turned down roles for a variety of reasons, including: dislike of the script, scheduling conflicts, differences in financial compensation, and health issues.

Tom Hanks first came to our attention in *Splash,* but he only got the leading role after six actors, including Chevy Chase, Bill Murray, and Michael Keaton turned it down. After *Splash,* Hanks was cast in *Big,* but not before the part was offered to Robert De Niro, who turned it down when the studio would not meet his quote. And *Forrest Gump* - John Travolta was the first choice, but he turned it down, which lead to Hank's second consecutive Best Actor Oscar.

Jodie Foster's path to stardom was also anything but a straight line. Foster won the role of Iris in *Taxi Driver* after Mariel Hemingway, Carrie Fisher, and Melanie Griffith all turned it down. Foster's first Best Actress Academy Award was for the role of Sarah Tobias in *The Accused.* Due to the gruesome and controversial themes, ten actresses including Jennifer Grey, Ally Sheedy, and Tatum O'Neal turned down the role before Foster was cast. Finally, the casting of Foster as Clarice Starling in *Silence of the Lambs* was a result of Meg Ryan and Michelle Pfeiffer having turned down the role.

Starring WHO? covers nine decades of casting decisions, highlighting the seemingly arbitrary casting of many iconic roles in over 300 movies.

In addition, the book provides an overview of Hollywood for each decade, an opportunity to test your trivia knowledge, and a list of Academy Award winners in all the acting categories beginning in 1930.

Rhett Butler • Scarlett O'Hara • Ashley Wilkes • Melanie Hamilton • Pete Warner
Ellie Andrews • Susan Vance • David Huxley • Robin Hood • Maid Marian
Dorothy • Wizard of Oz • Tin Man • Scarecrow • Dracula • Dallas • Ringo Kid
Anne Darrow • Jack Driscoll • Captain Blood • Marion Kerby • George Kerby
Joe Bonaparte • Jefferson Smith • Saunders • Tom Powers • Matt Doyle • Sondra
Doctor Frankenstein • Quasimodo • Esmeralda • Heathcliff • Cathy Earnshaw
Rhett Butler • Scarlett O'Hara • Ashley Wilkes • Melanie Hamilton • Pete Warner
Ellie Andrews • Susan Vance • David Huxley • Robin Hood • Maid Marian
Dorothy • Wizard of Oz • Tin Man • Scarecrow • Dracula • Dallas • Ringo Kid
Anne Darrow • Jack Driscoll • Captain Blood • Marion Kerby • George Kerby

1930s

Joe Bonaparte • Jefferson Smith • Saunders • Tom Powers • Matt Doyle • Sondra
Doctor Frankenstein • Quasimodo • Esmeralda • Heathcliff • Cathy Earnshaw
Rhett Butler • Scarlett O'Hara • Ashley Wilkes • Melanie Hamilton • Pete Warner
Ellie Andrews • Susan Vance • David Huxley • Robin Hood • Maid Marian
Dorothy • Wizard of Oz • Tin Man • Scarecrow • Dracula • Dallas • Ringo Kid
Anne Darrow • Jack Driscoll • Captain Blood • Marion Kerby • George Kerby
Joe Bonaparte • Jefferson Smith • Saunders • Tom Powers • Matt Doyle • Sondra
Doctor Frankenstein • Quasimodo • Esmeralda • Heathcliff • Cathy Earnshaw
Rhett Butler • Scarlett O'Hara • Ashley Wilkes • Melanie Hamilton • Pete Warner
Ellie Andrews • Susan Vance • David Huxley • Robin Hood • Maid Marian
Dorothy • Wizard of Oz • Tin Man • Scarecrow • Dracula • Dallas • Ringo Kid
Anne Darrow • Jack Driscoll • Captain Blood • Marion Kerby • George Kerby
Joe Bonaparte • Jefferson Smith • Saunders • Tom Powers • Matt Doyle • Sondra
Doctor Frankenstein • Quasimodo • Esmeralda • Heathcliff • Cathy Earnshaw
Rhett Butler • Scarlett O'Hara • Ashley Wilkes • Melanie Hamilton • Pete Warner
Ellie Andrews • Susan Vance • David Huxley • Robin Hood • Maid Marian
Dorothy • Wizard of Oz • Tin Man • Scarecrow • Dracula • Dallas • Ringo Kid
Anne Darrow • Jack Driscoll • Captain Blood • Marion Kerby • George Kerby
Joe Bonaparte • Jefferson Smith • Saunders • Tom Powers • Matt Doyle • Sondra
Doctor Frankenstein • Quasimodo • Esmeralda • Heathcliff • Cathy Earnshaw
Rhett Butler • Scarlett O'Hara • Ashley Wilkes • Melanie Hamilton • Pete Warner
Ellie Andrews • Susan Vance • David Huxley • Robin Hood • Maid Marian
Dorothy • Wizard of Oz • Tin Man • Scarecrow • Dracula • Dallas • Ringo Kid
Anne Darrow • Jack Driscoll • Captain Blood • Marion Kerby • George Kerby
Joe Bonaparte • Jefferson Smith • Saunders • Tom Powers • Matt Doyle • Sondra
Doctor Frankenstein • Quasimodo • Esmeralda • Heathcliff • Cathy Earnshaw
Rhett Butler • Scarlett O'Hara • Ashley Wilkes • Melanie Hamilton • Pete Warner
Ellie Andrews • Susan Vance • David Huxley • Robin Hood • Maid Marian
Dorothy • Wizard of Oz • Tin Man • Scarecrow • Dracula • Dallas • Ringo Kid
Anne Darrow • Jack Driscoll • Captain Blood • Marion Kerby • George Kerby

The Golden Age Begins

When the bottom fell out of the global economy, bankrupting millions of people and prompting mass unemployment, years of hardship and even suicides, Hollywood entered a sort of golden age and became one of the largest businesses in the United States.

Even in the depths of the Great Depression, movies were a weekly escape for many people who loved trading their struggles for a fictional, often dazzling world, if only for a couple of hours. The advent of talking pictures helped re-energize the medium. Desperate for diversion, people began flocking to the cinema in unprecedented numbers.

The assumption that Depression audiences went to the movies to be diverted from their misery by escapist and romantic fare was not entirely accurate. In fact, a new mood of gritty cynicism emerged in Hollywood pictures that matched the grimness of the times and most Depression films were grounded in the social realities of the time.

Films in the early 1930s were full of these wronged heroes, who seemed as overwhelmed by forces outside their control as the down-at-heel punters watching them. Even more popular than these hapless victims were the moviemakers who refused to be cowed by the Depression, and even turned it to their advantage. A new contempt for law and government allowed audiences to revel in the adventures of organized criminals.

In *Little Caesar*, Edward G. Robinson shocked audiences with a no-holds-barred portrayal of a psycho hoodlum, Rico, who guns down a priest on the steps of his church because his preaching made one of Rico's gang feel guilty. Irish-American actor James Cagney followed him, exploding onto the screen as Tom Powers in *Public Enemy*, and breaking another taboo by smashing a grapefruit into Jean Harlow's face.

It turned out that Hollywood, partly through a desperate public need for diversion and partly through its own ingenuity, managed to thrive while the rest of the world was collapsing. This boom was limited. The other great lesson to be drawn from the Great Depression is that if economic slumps go on for long enough, everything is affected.

By 1933, as mass unemployment took hold of America, cinema attendance began to fall by a massive 40%. Attendance would not recover until the late 1930s. By that time, Hollywood had to cope with the strictures of the newly formed League of Decency which had raised a formidable political lobby and attacked films for their immoral content.

From that point on, Hollywood realized it would have to start selling America instead of attacking it. This effort culminated in 1939 when an outstandingly large number of exceptional motion pictures, many of which become honored as all-time classic films, premiered.

Many film historians often rate 1939 as "the greatest in the history of Hollywood," with films such as *Gone with the Wind, The Wizard of Oz, Stagecoach, Wuthering Heights, Mr. Smith Goes to Washington, Goodbye, Mr. Chips, The Hunchback of Notre Dame, Golden Boy, Ninotchka, Of Mice and Men, Gunga Din, Destry Rides Again, Dark Victory, Beau Geste, Love Affair, The Little Princess, Only Angels Have Wings, Stanley and Livingston, Juarez,* and *The Roaring Twenties.*

When looking back, the films of the 1930s launched the careers of many of our favorite movie stars, including: Clark Gable, Errol Flynn, James Cagney, Gary Cooper, Edward G. Robinson, James Stewart, Laurence Olivier, Bette Davis, Cary Grant, Katharine Hepburn, Vivien Leigh, Charlie Chaplin, Mae West, Shirley Temple, Judy Garland, Spencer Tracy, Mickey Rooney, John Wayne, Fred Astaire, Ginger Rodgers, and the Marx Brothers.

The Academy Awards

1930
Best Picture: ***All Quiet On The Western Front***
Best Actor: George Arliss (*Disraeli*)
Best Actress: Norma Shearer (*The Divorcee*)

1931
Best Picture: ***Cimarron***
Best Actor: Lionel Barrymore (*A Free Soul*)
Best Actress: Marie Dressler (*Min and Bill*)

1932
Best Picture: ***Grand Hotel***
Best Actor: Fredric March (*Dr. Jekyll and Mr. Hyde*)
Best Actress: Helen Hayes (*The Sin of Madelon Claudet*)

1933
Best Picture: ***Cavalcade***
Best Actor: Charles Laughton (*The Private Life of Henry VIII*)
Best Actress: Katharine Hepburn (*Morning Glory*)

1934
Best Picture: ***It Happened One Night***
Best Actor: Clark Gable (*It Happened One Night*)
Best Actress: Claudette Colbert (*It Happened One Night*)

1935
Best Picture: ***Mutiny On The Bounty***
Best Actor: Victor McLaglen (*The Informer*)
Best Actress: Bette Davis (*Dangerous*)

1936

Best Picture: ***The Great Ziegfeld***

Best Actor: Paul Muni (*The Story of Louis Pasteur*)

Best Actress: Luise Rainer (*The Great Ziegfeld*)

Best Supporting Actor: Walter Brennan (*Come and Get It*)

Best Supporting Actress: Gale Sondergaard (*Anthony Adverse*)

1937

Best Picture: ***The Life of Emile Zola***

Best Actor: Spencer Tracy (*Captains Courageous*)

Best Actress: Luise Rainer (*The Good Earth*)

Best Supporting Actor: Joseph Schildkraut (*The Life of Emile Zola*)

Best Supporting Actress: Alice Brady (*In Old Chicago*)

1938

Best Picture: ***You Can't Take It With You***

Best Actor: Spencer Tracy (*Boys Town*)

Best Actress: Bette Davis (*Jezebel*)

Best Supporting Actor: Walter Brennan (*Kentucky*)

Best Supporting Actress: Fay Bainter (*Jezebel*)

1939

Best Picture: ***Gone with the Wind***

Best Actor: Robert Donat (*Goodbye, Mr. Chips*)

Best Actress: Vivien Leigh (*Gone with the Wind*)

Best Supporting Actor: Thomas Mitchell (*Stagecoach*)

Best Supporting Actress: Hattie McDaniel (*Gone With the Wind*)

Trivia
Casting Quiz

1. Ruby Keeler came back a star in *42nd Street*. The first choice to play the role of Peggy Sawyer was:
   - a. Vivien Leigh
   - b. Loretta Young
   - c. Bette Davis
   - d. None of the Above

2. Director Mervyn LeRoy was dating this actress at the time and recommended her to play the role of Anytime Annie in *42nd Street.*
   - a. Joan Blondell
   - b. Ginger Rogers
   - c. Ethel Merman
   - d. Carole Lombard

3. In Academy Award winning *It Happened One Night*, the original choice to play Peter Warner was:
   - a. Robert Montgomery
   - b. Spencer Tracy
   - c. Gary Cooper
   - d. None of the Above

4. Claudette Colbert won an Oscar for playing Ellie Andrews in *It Happened One Night.* The role was originally turned down by:
   - a. Loretta Young
   - b. Myrna Loy
   - c. Margaret Sullivan
   - d. All of the Above

5. Before Katharine Hepburn played Susan Vance in *Bringing Up Baby*, this actress was first considered for the role:
   - a. Rosalind Russell
   - b. Carole Lombard
   - c. Olivia de Havilland
   - d. Joan Crawford

6. Cary Grant played the role of Dr. David Huxley in *Bringing Up Baby.* The role was originally offered to:
   - a. Ray Milland
   - b. Ronald Colman
   - c. Fredric March
   - d. All of the Above

7. In *The Adventures of Robin Hood,* the studio's original choice to play the role of Robin Hood was:
   - a. Douglas Fairbanks Jr.
   - b. James Cagney
   - c. Robert Donat
   - d. Ronald Colman

8. In **The Adventures of Robin Hood,** both the roles of Friar Tuck and King Richard were offered to this actor, but he turned them down:
   - a. Charles Laughton
   - b. Douglas Fairbanks Jr.
   - c. Orson Welles
   - d. Ed Wynn

9. In **The Wizard of Oz,** think of Judy Garland as Dorothy marching down the yellow brick road. This actress was the original choice to play Dorothy:
   - a. Deanna Durbin
   - b. Margaret O'Brien
   - c. Shirley Temple
   - d. Always Judy Garland

10. Ray Bolger, who played the Scarecrow in **The Wizard of Oz,** was originally cast in this role:
    - a. The Tin Man
    - b. The Wizard
    - c. The Cowardly Lion
    - d. None of the Above

11. The role of Jefferson Smith in **Mr. Smith Goes to Washington** was originally thought to be played by:
    - a. Henry Fonda
    - b. Gary Cooper
    - c. Ronald Colman
    - d. Cary Grant

12. John Wayne played the Ringo Kid in **Stagecoach.** The role was originally offered to this actor:
    - a. Errol Flynn
    - b. Douglas Fairbanks Jr.
    - c. Gregory Peck
    - d. None of the Above

13. **The Hunchback of Notre Dame** starred Charles Laughton as Quasimodo. However, RKO first offered the role to:
    - a. Bela Lugosi
    - b. Claude Rains
    - c. Orson Welles
    - d. Lon Chaney Jr.

14. This actor was forced by the studio that had him under contract to turn down the role of Rhett Butler in **Gone with the Wind.**
    - a. Gary Cooper
    - b. Ronald Colman
    - c. Errol Flynn
    - d. None of the Above

15. The role of Scarlett O' Hara in **Gone with the Wind** came down to two finalists screen-tested in color. One was Vivien Leigh, the other was:
    - a. Bette Davis
    - b. Katharine Hepburn
    - c. Lana Turner
    - d. Paulette Goddard

IT HAPPENED ONE NIGHT (1934)

Ellie: What are you thinking about?
Peter: By a strange coincidence, I was thinking of you.
Ellie: Really?
Peter: Yeah. I was just wondering what makes dames like you so dizzy.

Plot

A spoiled heiress, running away from her family, is helped by a reporter in need of a story to keep his job, but who then falls for her.

CASTING

Who Starred as Peter Warner?
Clark Gable

Turned Down the Role of Peter Warner
Robert Montgomery • Fredric March

Who Starred as Ellie Andrew?
Claudette Colbert

Turned Down the Role of Ellie Andrews
Myrna Loy • Carole Lombard • Constance Bennett
Miriam Hopkins • Bette Davis • Marion Davies

WHO Trivia

Robert Montgomery turned down the role of Peter Warner, saying it was the worst script he had ever read. After Fredric March also turned down the role, MGM loaned out Clark Gable, who was under contract, to punish him for his affair with Joan Crawford.

Bette Davis wanted the role of Ellie Andrews, but was under contract with Warner Bros. who refused to lend her out. Columbia Pictures refused to loan out Constance Bennett and Marion Davies. Carole Lombard was unable to accept the role because the proposed filming schedule would conflict with her work on *Bolero*.

Initially, Claudette Colbert turned the role down because her first film had been directed by Frank Capra, and it was such a disaster she vowed never to make another film with him. She agreed to appear if her salary was doubled to $50,000, and the filming of her role be completed in four weeks, so she could take her well-planned vacation.

THE ADVENTURES OF ROBIN HOOD (1938)

Robin Hood: Did I upset your plans?
Sir Guy: You've come to Nottingham once too often.
Robin Hood: When this is over, my friend, there'll be no need for me to come again.

Plot

When a treacherous Prince John, in his brother King Richard's absence, usurps the throne and proceeds to oppress the Saxon masses, Sir Robin of Loxley fights back as the leader of a band of outlaws.

CASTING

Who Starred as Robin Hood?
Errol Flynn

Turned Down the Role of Robin Hood
Douglas Fairbanks Jr. • Robert Donat • James Cagney

WHO Trivia

Douglas Fairbanks Jr. turned down the role of Robin Hood because he didn't want to be known for following in his father's footsteps. In the 1922 version of Robin Hood, Douglas Fairbanks Sr. played the lead role. Robert Donat turned down the part for health reasons.

James Cagney then became the studio's "original" choice for Robin Hood. After Cagney walked off the set in a huff, producer Hal B. Wallis delayed the production of the film for three years.

When Wallis was ready to make the film again, he cast Errol Flynn in the lead role against the studio's wishes. It was also Wallis who decided to keep Maid Marian although the original screenwriter wanted to eliminate it. Wallis thought Maid Marian was important in the Robin Hood adventure.

Orson Welles was offered the roles of King Richard and Friar Tuck but Welles turned both of them down. David Niven turned down the role of Will Scarlett.

BRINGING UP BABY (1938)

Susan Vance: There is a leopard on your roof, and it's my leopard, and I have to get it, and to get it I have to sing.

Plot

While trying to secure a $1 million donation for his museum, a man meets the niece of a patron, a madcap adventuress who immediately falls for the straitlaced scientist, setting off ever-growing chaos, including a missing dinosaur bone and a pet leopard that threatens to swallow him whole.

CASTING

Who Starred as Susan Vance?
Katharine Hepburn

Turned Down the Role of Susan Vance
Carole Lombard

Who Starred as David Huxley?
Cary Grant

Turned Down the Role of David Huxley
Ronald Colman • Fredric March • Ray Milland

WHO Trivia?

Director/Producer Howard Hawks signed a contract at RKO for an adaptation of *Gunga Din* in March 1937. When the studio was unable to borrow either Clark Gable or Spencer Tracy from MGM, production of the film was delayed. This delay caused Hawks to look for a new project. In April 1937, he read a funny short story, *Bringing Up Baby*, by Hagar Wilder in *Collier's* magazine, and immediately wanted to make a film from it.

Hagar Wilde's short story differed significantly from the film that Hawks made. In the original story, David and Susan are engaged, but he is not a scientist and there is no dinosaur or museum. However, Susan does get a pet panther named "Baby" from her brother. When Baby escapes into the Connecticut wilderness, David and Susan must find it with the help of Baby's favorite song, "I Can't Give You Anything but Love, Baby."

GONE WITH THE WIND (1939)

Scarlett O'Hara: Where shall I go? What shall I do?
Rhett Butler: Frankly, my dear, I don't give a damn.

Plot
A manipulative southern belle and a roguish gentleman conduct a turbulent and tangled romance during the Civil War and Reconstruction periods.

CASTING

Who Starred as Rhett Butler?
Clark Gable

Turned Down the Role of Rhett Butler
Gary Cooper

Who Starred as Scarlett O'Hara?
Vivien Leigh

Turned Down the Role of Scarlett O'Hara
Norma Shearer

WHO Trivia
The casting of the two lead roles, Rhett Butler and Scarlett O'Hara, was a very complex two-year endeavor.

Producer David O. Selznick considered only four actors for the role of Rhett Butler: Gary Cooper, Errol Flynn, Ronald Colman, and Clark Gable.

Gary Cooper was under contract to Samuel Goldwyn. He refused to loan him out, thus turning down the role for him. Selznick really wanted Clark Gable from the start, but Gable was under contract to MGM, which never loaned him to other studios.

In exchange for distribution rights, Warner Bros.' Jack L. Warner offered a package of Bette Davis, Errol Flynn and Olivia de Havilland for the lead roles. This package was turned down as Selznick was determined to get Gable, and because Bette Davis, being considered for the role of Scarlett, refused to play opposite Errol Flynn.

Eventually, Selznick struck a deal with MGM. In August, 1938, Selznick's father-in-law, MGM chief Louis B. Mayer, gave the go-ahead for Clark Gable to star in the film as well as $1,250,000 in financing. The deal would include paying Gable's weekly salary, and half the film's profits to MGM.

The arrangement to release through MGM meant delaying the start of production until the end of 1938 when Selznick's distribution deal ended with United Artists. Selznick used the delay to build publicity for the film by conducting a nationwide casting call for the role of Scarlett; 1,400 unknown actresses were interviewed. The effort cost $100,000, and was useless for the film, but created priceless publicity.

After the deal was struck with MGM, Selznick met with Norma Shearer, who was MGM's top female star at the time. She quickly turned down the role of Scarlett O'Hara. Katharine Hepburn lobbied hard for the role with the support of her friend, George Cukor, who had been hired to direct; she was vetoed by Selznick who felt she was not right for the part.

Although Margaret Mitchell refused to publicly name her choice to play the role of Scarlett O'Hara, an actress who came closest to winning her approval was Miriam Hopkins, an early frontrunner for the role. The problem was that Hopkins, in her mid-thirties, was considered too old for the part.

Tallulah Bankhead, born in Alabama and an authentic "Southern Belle," became the clear front-runner, but her unsavory personal life made Selznick reluctant to hire her.

By late 1938, four actresses including Jean Arthur and Joan Bennett, were still under consideration; however, only two, Paulette Goddard and Vivien Leigh, were tested in Technicolor. Paulette Goddard almost won the role, but controversy over her marriage to Charlie Chaplin caused Selznick to change his mind at the last moment and give the role to Vivien Leigh.

For the role of Ashley Wilkes, a number of actors auditioned, including: Douglas Fairbanks Jr., Dennis Morgan, Wayne Morris, Melvyn Douglas, Robert Young, and Ray Milland. The role went to Leslie Howard.

Although Olivia de Havilland was always the front-runner for the part of Melanie Hamilton, actresses Janet Gaynor, Fay Wray and Jane Wyman were all seriously considered. It was reported that when Joan Fontaine was asked if she was interested, she said no. It was she who suggested that Olivia de Havilland, her sister, should be cast in the role.

STAGECOACH (1939)

The Ringo Kid: Well, I guess you can't break out of prison and into society in the same week.

Plot
In 1880, a group of strangers headed by stagecoach to Lordsburg, NM, must fight off Geronimo and a band of Apaches to get there alive.

CASTING

Who Starred as The Ringo Kid?
John Wayne

Turned Down the Role of The Ringo Kid
Errol Flynn • Joel McCrea

Who Starred as Dallas?
Claire Trevor

Turned Down the Role of Dallas
Katharine Hepburn

WHO Trivia
Director John Ford asked David O. Selznick to produce the film, but Selznick was only interested if he could have Gary Cooper as The Ringo Kid and Marlene Dietrich as Dallas. They were not available, so Selznick passed.

John Ford then reached out to Errol Flynn and Joel McCrea. Both turned the role down. Ford then asked John Wayne for any suggestions, and Wayne told Ford to talk to Lloyd Nolan. Weeks later, Wayne decided to play the role of The Ringo Kid himself.

John Ford initially wanted Katharine Hepburn, with whom he had previously worked with and had an affair with, to play the role of Dallas; she turned him down. It took thirty years before Wayne and Hepburn finally worked together in *True Grit*.

John Ford wanted Ward Bond to play Buck, the stagecoach driver. However, when Ford found out Bond couldn't drive a "six-up" stagecoach, and there wasn't time to teach him, he gave the role to Andy Devine.

THE WIZARD OF OZ (1939)

Dorothy: Toto, I've a feeling we're not in Kansas anymore.

Plot

A young Kansas girl is cast into a fantasy world and, while trying to return home, she is aided by three unusual companions, a Scarecrow, a Tinman, and a Cowardly Lion, each with a quest of his own.

CASTING

Who Starred as Dorothy?
Judy Garland

Turned Down the Role of Dorothy
Shirley Temple • Deanna Durbin

Who Starred as the Wizard of Oz?
Frank Morgan

Turned Down the Role of the Wizard of Oz
Ed Wynn

Who Starred as the Tin Man?
Jack Haley

Turned Down the Role of the Tin Man
Ray Bolger • Buddy Ebsen

Who Starred as the Scarecrow?
Ray Bolger

Turned Down the Role of the Scarecrow
Buddy Ebsen

WHO Trivia

Mervyn LeRoy always insisted that he wanted to cast Judy Garland to play Dorothy from the start. Evidence suggests that negotiations with 20th Century Fox to loan out Shirley Temple took place. The deal was to exchange Shirley Temple for Clark Gable and Jean Harlow, under contract at MGM, so they could do a film for 20th Century Fox. The tale is almost certainly untrue, as Harlow died in 1937, which was before MGM had even purchased the rights to *The Wizard of Oz*.

In the end, the general consensus was that 20th Century simply refused to loan Shirley Temple out to MGM to play the role of Dorothy.

Despite this, the story appears in many film biographies including Shirley Temple's own autobiography. The documentary, *The Wonderful Wizard of Oz: The Making of a Movie Classic*, states that Mervyn LeRoy was under pressure to cast Temple, then the most popular child star. At an unofficial audition, MGM musical mainstay Roger Edens listened to Temple sing. It has been documented that Edens felt an actress with a different vocal style was needed.

Actress Deanna Durbin, who was under contract to Universal Pictures, was then offered the part of Dorothy. Durbin, at the time, far exceeded Garland in film experience and fan base, but Universal refused to lend her out.

Ray Bolger was originally cast as the Tin Man, and Buddy Ebsen was cast as the Scarecrow. However, Bolger longed to play the Scarecrow and was unhappy with his role as the Tin Man. Eventually, Bolger convinced producer Mervyn LeRoy to recast him in the part he so desired.

Buddy Ebsen did not object since he looked at the role of the Tin Man, from a dancer's, perspective as more challenging. Then, ten days into the shoot, Ebsen suffered a reaction to the aluminum powder makeup he wore; he was hospitalized in critical condition, and subsequently forced to leave the project.

Ebsen was replaced by Jack Haley, who many thought "stole the picture."

Initially, Ed Wynn was offered the role of the Wizard, but turned it down as he thought the part was too small.

W. C. Fields was then cast as the Wizard of Oz. After protracted haggling over Fields' fee, MGM ran out of patience and decided to cast another contract player, Frank Morgan, instead.

Bonus Movies

Dracula (1931)
Universal Studio acquired "Dracula" so that Lon Chaney could play the lead. Unfortunately, due to illness, he was not able to make the film. Paul Muni was then offered the role, but declined; Bela Lugosi was then cast.

Public Enemy (1931)
Originally, Edward Woods was cast as Tom Powers, the lead character, and James Cagney cast as Matt Doyle, the key supporting character. When the Director, William A. Wellman, saw the star power of James Cagney dominating the film, he had the actors switch roles.

Frankenstein (1932)
John Carradine turned down the role of the monster because he felt he was too well trained an actor. Universal, after the success of Dracula, was anxious to follow up with *Frankenstein,* and offered Bela Lugosi the role of the monster. Because he wanted to play Doctor Frankenstein, he turned it down. The part then went to the relatively unknown Boris Karloff.

King Kong (1933)
Much in demand, Jean Harlow refused the lead role of Anne Darrow played by Fay Wray, while Joel McCrea turned down the role of Jack Driscoll, played by Bruce Cabot.

Captain Blood (1935)
When the dashing Robert Donat, who was cast as Captain Blood, did not show up for the first day of shooting, the studio scrambled and asked Brian Aherne to do the film, but he turned them down. This resulted in Errol Flynn being cast in the role that made him a legend.

Lost Horizon (1937)
Director Frank Capra wanted Jean Arthur to play Sondra, the ageless heroine of Shangri-La, but she turned him down. Subsequently, Barbara Stanwyck turned him down, so he offered the role to Jane Wyatt.

Topper (1937)
Producer Hal Roach wanted W.C. Fields and Jean Harlow in the leading roles, but both were unavailable due to commitments on other projects. Roach then cast Cary Grant and Constance Bennett to play the carefree ghost and his wife.

Golden Boy (1939)

Tyrone Power was offered many roles while under contract at Fox, but the head of the studio, Darryl Zanuck, turned them all down. This included the lead role of Joe Bonaparte in *Golden Boy*.

John Garfield was passed over for the leading role, even though the original play was written by his friend, Clifford Odets, expressly for him.

Richard Carlson had been set to star opposite Barbara Stanwyck in the movie version of Odets' play, but was tied up with another play. Stanwyck then championed William Holden, who got the part.

Mr. Smith Goes to Washington (1939)

When Frank Capra came on board as director, the film was to be a sequel to his *Mr. Deeds Goes to Town,* called *Mr. Deeds Goes to Washington*, with Gary Cooper reprising his role as Longfellow Deeds.

Because Cooper was unavailable, Capra saw it immediately as a vehicle for Jimmy Stewart as Jefferson Smith and Jean Arthur as Saunders.

Capra said, "I knew Stewart would make a hell of a Mr. Smith... He looked like the country kid, the idealist."

The Hunchback of Notre Dame (1939)

After hearing the news that RKO was going to remake the original 1923 film, Lon Chaney Jr. sought out the role of Quasimodo. Charles Laughton was set to star as Quasimodo, but when it seemed like the British actor would be unable to work in America due to IRS troubles, Bela Lugosi, Claude Rains and Orson Welles were then considered for the role before RKO offered it to Chaney. Luckily, Laughton managed to overcome his problems and played the part.

Kathryn Adams was supposed to play Esmeralda, but suddenly lost the role to Maureen O'Hara, then 18-years old, when Laughton cabled from Ireland to Hollywood that he was "bringing Esmeralda."

Wuthering Heights (1939)

When Laurence Olivier was cast as Heathcliff, Vivien Leigh said she wanted to play the female lead, Catherine Linton, alongside her then-lover and future husband. Studio executives felt the role could not go to an actress who was largely unknown, and cast Merle Oberon instead.

However, because of Olivier, Vivien Leigh was offered the part of Isabella, which she declined. As it turned out, Leigh was cast in *Gone with the Wind* that same year, winning an Academy Award for Best Actress.

Sam Spade • Brigid O'Shaughnessy • "Fat Man" • Hildy Johnson • Walter Burns
Maxim de Winter • 2nd Maxim de Winter • C.K. Dexter Haven • Mike Connor
Rick Blaine • Ilsa Lund • Mortimer Brewster • Walter Neff • Phyllis Dietrichson
Mildred Pierce • Veda Pierce • George Bailey • Mary Bailey • Henry Potter
Clarence • Phil Green • Fred C. Dobbs • Bob Curtin • Willie Stark • Alvin York
Barry Kane • Paula Anton • George M. Cohan • Mary Cohan • Mrs. Miniver
Velvet Brown • Mr. Brown • Waldo Lydecker • Laura Hunt • Helen St. James
Don Birnam • "Swede" Anderson • Kitty Collins • Don Hewes • Nadine Hale
Sam Spade • Brigid O'Shaughnessy • "Fat Man" • Hildy Johnson • Walter Burns
Maxim de Winter • 2nd Maxim de Winter • C.K. Dexter Haven • Mike Connor

1940s

Rick Blaine • Ilsa Lund • Mortimer Brewster • Walter Neff • Phyllis Dietrichson
Mildred Pierce • Veda Pierce • George Bailey • Mary Bailey • Henry Potter
Clarence • Phil Green • Fred C. Dobbs • Bob Curtin • Willie Stark • Alvin York
Barry Kane • Paula Anton • George M. Cohan • Mary Cohan • Mrs. Miniver
Velvet Brown • Mr. Brown • Waldo Lydecker • Laura Hunt • Helen St. James
Don Birnam • "Swede" Anderson • Kitty Collins • Don Hewes • Nadine Hale
Sam Spade • Brigid O'Shaughnessy • "Fat Man" • Hildy Johnson • Walter Burns
Maxim de Winter • 2nd Maxim de Winter • C.K. Dexter Haven • Mike Connor
Rick Blaine • Ilsa Lund • Mortimer Brewster • Walter Neff • Phyllis Dietrichson
Mildred Pierce • Veda Pierce • George Bailey • Mary Bailey • Henry Potter
Clarence • Phil Green • Fred C. Dobbs • Bob Curtin • Willie Stark • Alvin York
Barry Kane • Paula Anton • George M. Cohan • Mary Cohan • Mrs. Miniver
Velvet Brown • Mr. Brown • Waldo Lydecker • Laura Hunt • Helen St. James
Don Birnam • "Swede" Anderson • Kitty Collins • Don Hewes • Nadine Hale
Sam Spade • Brigid O'Shaughnessy • "Fat Man" • Hildy Johnson • Walter Burns
Maxim de Winter • 2nd Maxim de Winter • C.K. Dexter Haven • Mike Connor
Rick Blaine • Ilsa Lund • Mortimer Brewster • Walter Neff • Phyllis Dietrichson
Mildred Pierce • Veda Pierce • George Bailey • Mary Bailey • Henry Potter
Clarence • Phil Green • Fred C. Dobbs • Bob Curtin • Willie Stark • Alvin York
Barry Kane • Paula Anton • George M. Cohan • Mary Cohan • Mrs. Miniver
Velvet Brown • Mr. Brown • Waldo Lydecker • Laura Hunt • Helen St. James
Don Birnam • "Swede" Anderson • Kitty Collins • Don Hewes • Nadine Hale
Sam Spade • Brigid O'Shaughnessy • "Fat Man" • Hildy Johnson • Walter Burns
Maxim de Winter • 2nd Maxim de Winter • C.K. Dexter Haven • Mike Connor
Rick Blaine • Ilsa Lund • Mortimer Brewster • Walter Neff • Phyllis Dietrichson
Mildred Pierce • Veda Pierce • George Bailey • Mary Bailey • Henry Potter
Clarence • Phil Green • Fred C. Dobbs • Bob Curtin • Willie Stark • Alvin York
Barry Kane • Paula Anton • George M. Cohan • Mary Cohan • Mrs. Miniver
Velvet Brown • Mr. Brown • Waldo Lydecker • Laura Hunt • Helen St. James
Don Birnam • "Swede" Anderson • Kitty Collins • Don Hewes • Nadine Hale

Hollywood
Goes to War

The early years of the 1940s were not promising for the American film industry, especially following the attack on Pearl Harbor by the Japanese and the resultant loss of foreign markets. The movie industry, responded to the national war effort by making movies, and producing many wartime favorites.

The classic propaganda film was the romantic story of self-sacrifice; *Casablanca* told about a disillusioned nightclub owner and a former lover separated by WWII in Paris.

A variety of wartime films presented both the flag-waving heroics and action of the war as well as the realistic, brutal misery of the experience: *Bataan, Objective Burma, Sergeant York and Thirty Seconds Over Tokyo.*

Charlie Chaplin reappeared, directing and starring in his first talking picture, *The Great Dictator*, an anti-fascist lampooning of the Third Reich and Adolf Hitler, rare among American films.

In 1945, the year World War II ended, six of the top ten box office films were musicals. A year later, Hollywood enjoyed its greatest financial year with box office receipts at $4.5 billion.

The genre most characteristic of the era was Film Noir. It reflected the way Hollywood felt as it faced its greatest challenges during the post-war period, darker and more cynical. The genre was already evolving from a series of 1930s gangster films with dark plots, untrustworthy femme fatales, and tough but cynical fatalistic heroes. The first, and considered one of the best ever, was John Huston's directorial debut film, *The Maltese Falcon.*

Director John Ford embarked on his most prolific era with an expanded string of classic Westerns to chronicle America's pioneer past. These films included: *Fort Apache, She Wore a Yellow Ribbon and Rio Grande,* all starring John Wayne, and *My Darling Clementine,* starring Henry Fonda.

Frank Capra, who had won three Best Director Academy Awards in the 1930s, idealized the "common man" in *Meet John Doe*. His Christmas classic, *It's a Wonderful Life*, was a major flop at the time, only to become popularized after repeated Christmas-time television viewings years later.

After causing quite a sensation with his Mercury Theatre on the air performance of H.G. Wells' *The War of the Worlds* in 1938, 23-year-old Orson Welles was given an RKO Studios contract that led to the making of arguably the greatest American film of all time, his innovative masterpiece, *Citizen Kane*, in which he served as director, co-writer and star.

The 1940s was when "liberal" Hollywood crusaded against injustices and inequities in emotional films of social concern: *The Grapes of Wrath* told of the struggle of a displaced, poverty-stricken American migrant family who left Oklahoma's dustbowl for California; the ground-breaking drama of a tormented alcoholic writer in *The Lost Weekend*; a powerful indictment of anti-Semitism in America in *Gentleman's Agreement*; and the rise and fall of a corruptible politician in *All The King's Men*.

The decade also brought on investigations conducted by the House of Representatives' Un-American Activities Committee (HUAC). Beginning in 1947, these investigations were aimed at rooting out suspected Communists and political subversives within the Hollywood film industry and ended up repressing liberal themes in films as well. Over 300 movie industry figures and blacklisted stars had their careers ruined between 1947 and 1952. When the HUAC investigation ended in the mid-1950s, film stars John Garfield, Gregory Peck, Katharine Hepburn, Paul Muni, Edward G. Robinson, Charlie Chaplin, Zero Mostel, Orson Welles, Fredric March, Judy Holliday, Gene Kelly, and Danny Kaye were all affected by the blacklist.

Hollywood found itself with many threatening forces at the close of the 1940s and the start of the next decade, which included the coming of television enticing potential moviegoers to remain at home; blacklisting and McCarthyism; the gradual decline of theater-attending audiences; inflation that raised film production costs; and anti-trust rulings by the government against the studios. Studios would be gradually reduced to production and distribution organizations, forced to give up or divest themselves of their theater holdings, and begin selling film rights to pre-1948 films to television to bolster profits.

The Academy Awards

1940
Best Picture: ***Rebecca***
Best Actor: James Stewart (*The Philadelphia Story*)
Best Actress: Ginger Rogers (*Kitty Foyle*)
Best Supporting Actor: Walter Brennan (*The Westerner*)
Best Supporting Actress: Jane Darwell (*The Grapes of Wrath*)

1941
Best Picture: ***How Green Was My Valley***
Best Actor: Gary Cooper (*Sergeant York*)
Best Actress: Joan Fontaine (*Suspicion*)
Best Supporting Actor: Donald Crisp (*How Green was My Valley*)
Best Supporting Actress: Mary Astor (*The Great Lie*)

1942
Best Picture: ***Mrs. Miniver***
Best Actor: James Cagney (*Yankee Doodle Dandy*)
Best Actress: Greer Garson (*Mrs. Miniver*)
Best Supporting Actor: Van Heflin (*Johnny Eager*)
Best Supporting Actress: Teresa Wright (*Mrs. Miniver*)

1943
Best Picture: ***Casablanca***
Best Actor: Paul Lukas (*Watch on the Rhine*)
Best Actress: Jennifer Jones (*The Song of Bernadette*)
Best Supporting Actor: Charles Coburn (*The More the Merrier*)
Best Supporting Actress: Katina Paxinou (*For Whom the Bell Tolls*)

1944
Best Picture: ***Going My Way***
Best Actor: Bing Crosby (*Going My Way*)
Best Actress: Ingrid Bergman (*Gaslight*)
Best Supporting Actor: Barry Fitzgerald (*Going My Way*)
Best Supporting Actress: Ethel Barrymore (*None But the Lonely Heart*)

1945
Best Picture: ***The Lost Weekend***
Best Actor: Ray Milland (*The Lost Weekend*)
Best Actress: Joan Crawford (*Mildred Pierce*)
Best Supporting Actor: James Dunn (*A Tree Grows in Brooklyn*)
Best Supporting Actress: Anne Revere (*National Velvet*)

1946
Best Picture: ***The Best Years of Our Lives***
Best Actor: Fredric March (*The Best Years of Our Lives*)
Best Actress: Olivia de Havilland (*To Each His Own*)
Best Supporting Actor: Harold Russell (*The Best Years of Our Lives*)
Best Supporting Actress: Anne Baxter (*The Razor's Edge*)

1947
Best Picture: ***Gentleman's Agreement***
Best Actor: Ronald Colman (*A Double Life*)
Best Actress: Loretta Young (*The Farmer's Daughter*)
Best Supporting Actor: Edmund Gwenn (*Miracle on 34th Street*)
Best Supporting Actress: Celeste Holm (*Gentlemen's Agreement*)

1948
Best Picture: ***Hamlet***
Best Actor: Laurence Olivier (*Hamlet*)
Best Actress: Jane Wyman (*Johnny Belinda*)
Best Supporting Actor: Walter Huston (*The Treasure of the Sierra Madre*)
Best Supporting Actress: Claire Trevor (*Key Largo*)

1949
Best Picture: ***All the King's Men***
Best Actor: Broderick Crawford (*All the King's Men*)
Best Actress: Olivia de Havilland (*The Heiress*)
Best Supporting Actor: Dean Jagger (*Twelve O'Clock High*)
Best Supporting Actress: Mercedes McCambridge (*All the King's Men*)

Casting Trivia Quiz

1. Rosalind Russell starred with Cary Grant in **His Girl Friday** after this actress turned down the role:
   - a. Katharine Hepburn
   - b. Irene Dunne
   - c. Ginger Rogers
   - d. All of the Above

2. In **The Philadelphia Story,** Katharine Hepburn always wanted this leading man to play the role of Dexter Haven:
   - a. Errol Flynn
   - b. Gary Cooper
   - c. Clark Gable
   - d. William Powell

3. Producer Hal B. Wallis' first choice to play the role of gumshoe Sam Spade in **The Maltese Falcon** was:
   - a. Humphrey Bogart
   - b. George Raft
   - c. Spencer Tracy
   - d. Alan Ladd

4. Mary Astor played the role of femme fatale Brigid O'Shaughnessy in **The Maltese Falcon.** The role was first offered to:
   - a. Bette Davis
   - b. Barbara Stanwyck
   - c. Joan Crawford
   - d. Geraldine Fitzgerald

5. Despite many rumors to the contrary, this actor was originally committed to play Rick in **Casablanca.**
   - a. Humphrey Bogart
   - c. George Raft
   - c. Ronald Reagan
   - d. David Niven

6. In **Casablanca,** producer Hal Wallis nearly made Sam, the piano player, a woman. He considered this woman for the role:
   - a. Lena Horne
   - b. Hazel Scott
   - c. Ella Fitzgerald
   - d. All of the Above

7. The role of Mortimer Brewster in **Arsenic and Old Lace** was originally intended for:
   - a. Cary Grant
   - b. Bob Hope
   - c. Jack Benny
   - d. James Stewart

8. Billy Wilder wanted this actress to play the role of Phyllis Dietrichson in the film ***Double Indemnity.***
   - a. Barbara Stanwyck
   - b. Lana Turner
   - c. Bette Davis
   - d. Joan Crawford

9. Warner Bros. and director Michael Curtiz originally wanted this actress for the Academy award-winning role of ***Mildred Pierce.***
   - a. Vivien Leigh
   - b. Joan Fontaine
   - c. Olivia De Havilland
   - d. Bette Davis

10. Fred MacMurray played Walter Neff in ***Double Indemnity*** after this actor turned down the role:
    - a. Gregory Peck
    - b. James Cagney
    - c. Spencer Tracy
    - d. All of the Above

11. The role of Mary Bailey in ***It's a Wonderful Life*** played by Donna Reed was originally turned down by:
    - a. Ginger Rogers
    - b. Grace Kelly
    - c. Vivien Leigh
    - d. Margaret Sullavan

12. John Huston's neo-western ***Treasure of Sierra Madre*** starred Humphrey Bogart as Fred C. Dobbs. This actor was considered first:
    - a. George Raft
    - b. Kirk Douglas
    - c. Gregory Peck
    - d. Van Heflin

13. Fred Astaire was brought in to star in ***Easter Parade*** after this actor broke his ankle:
    - a. Donald O'Connor
    - b. Frank Sinatra
    - c. Gene Kelly
    - d. Bing Crosby

14. Broderick Crawford won the Academy Award for Best Actor playing Willie Stark in ***All The King's Men.*** The role was originally offered to:
    - a. Melvin Douglas
    - b. Gary Cooper
    - c. John Wayne
    - d. Spencer Tracy

15. Who turned down the role of Maxim de Winter in ***Rebecca*** before Laurence Olivier came on board:
    - a. Ronald Colman
    - b. Robert Donat
    - c. William Powell
    - d. All of the Above

HIS GIRL FRIDAY (1940)

Hildy: A big fat lummox like you - hiring an airplane to write, "Hildy, don't be hasty, remember my dimple." Walter. It delayed our divorce twenty minutes while the judge went out to watch it.

Walter: I've still got the dimple and in the same place.

Plot

A newspaper editor who uses every trick in the book to keep his ace reporter, and ex-wife, from remarrying.

CASTING

Who Starred as Hildy Johnson?
Rosalind Russell

Turned Down the Role of Hildy Johnson
Jean Arthur • Katharine Hepburn • Claudette Colbert
Ginger Rogers • Irene Dunn • Carole Lombard

WHO Trivia

Director/Producer Howard Hawks had a lot of difficulty casting the role of Hildy Johnson. While the choice of Cary Grant was instantaneous for the role of Walter Burns, the role of Hildy was not easy to fill.

Hawks wanted Carole Lombard, but the cost of hiring Lombard in her new status as a freelancer proved to be far too expensive, and he simply could not afford her. Hawks then turned to Jean Arthur. Arthur was under contract to the studio, but adamantly refused, resulting in the studio suspending her.

Hawks then offered the role to an impressive list of actresses, including: Katharine Hepburn, Claudette Colbert, Margaret Sullavan, Ginger Rogers, and Irene Dunne. They all turned it down with Dunne saying, "the role was too small and needed to be expanded." Finally, Howard Hawks decided to borrow Rosalind Russell from MGM.

An interesting fact about the dialogue was that in most films the rate of verbal dialogue was around 90 words a minute, but in this film, the delivery was clocked at 240 words a minute. This pace was achieved by Hawks encouraging Grant and Russell to add dialogue, funny bits of business, and to step on each other's lines whenever possible.

THE PHILADELPHIA STORY (1940)

C.K. Dexter Haven: The moon is also a goddess, chaste and virginal.
Tracy Lord: Oh, stop using those foul words.

Plot

A socialite's plan to marry a nouveau riche businessman and aspiring politician, gets complicated by the simultaneous arrival into her life of two cynical but romantic men; her ex-husband, and a smitten journalist.

CASTING

Who Starred as C. K. Dexter Haven?
Cary Grant

Turned Down the Role of C. K. Dexter Haven
Clark Gable

Who Starred as Mike Connor?
James Stewart

Turned Down the Role of Mike Connor
Spencer Tracy

WHO Trivia

Katharine Hepburn acquired the film rights to the play, in which she had also starred, as a vehicle for her screen comeback.

The film was Hepburn's first big hit following several flops. These flops made her eligible for Harry Brandt's 1938 compilation of a list of actors considered to be "box office poison."

Hepburn wanted Clark Gable to play Dexter Haven and Spencer Tracy to play Mike Connor, but both had other commitments.

After MGM purchased the film rights from Hepburn, the head of the studio, Louis B. Mayer, very skeptical about Hepburn's box office appeal, took an unusual precaution. Mayer decided to cast two "box office" stars, Cary Grant and Jimmy Stewart, to support Hepburn.

Grant agreed to play the part of Dexter Haven on the condition that he be given top billing, and his $137,000 salary be donated directly to the British War Relief Society.

REBECCA (1940)

2nd Mrs. de Winter: If you don't think we are happy, it would be much better if you didn't pretend. I'll go away. Why don't you answer me?

Maxim de Winter: How can I answer you when I don't know the answer myself? If you say we're happy, let's leave it at that. Happiness is something I know nothing about.

Plot

A naive young woman marries a rich widower, moves into his mansion, and finds the memory of the first wife maintaining a grip on her husband and the servants.

CASTING

Who Starred as Maxim de Winter?
Laurence Olivier

Turned Down the Role of Maxim de Winter
Ronald Colman • Robert Donat • William Powell

Who Starred as 2nd Mrs. de Winter?
Joan Fontaine

Turned Down the Role of 2nd Mrs. de Winter
Olivia de Havilland • Geraldine Fitzgerald
Maureen O'Hara

WHO Trivia

Rebecca is the first movie director Alfred Hitchcock made in Hollywood, and the only one that won an Oscar for Best Picture. However, he did not win for Best Director; John Ford did for *Grapes of Wrath*.

Hitchcock originally cast Ronald Colman as Maxim de Winter, but Colman dropped out due to production code issues about a main character getting away with murder. Robert Donat was Hitchcock's next choice, but he had health issues and had to turn it down. Hitchcock then offered the role to William Powell, but MGM, who had him under contract, raised its loan-out fee, making him too expensive. Laurence Olivier then got the role.

Hitchcock's first choice for the 2nd Mrs. de Winter was Olivia de Havilland, but she turned it down when she found out her sister, Joan Fontaine, was also up for the part. Geraldine Fitzgerald turned it down due to other commitments, and according to her biography, Maureen O'Hara also turned it down.

THE MALTESE FALCON (1941)

Spade: (smiling) You are a liar.
Brigid: I am. I've always been a liar.
Spade: Don't brag about it. Was there any truth at all in that yarn?
Brigid: Some...not very much... I'm so tired, so tired of lying and making up lies, not knowing what is a lie and what's the truth.

Plot
A wisecracking San Francisco private detective has to deal with three unscrupulous adventurers, all of whom are fervently competing to obtain a jewel-encrusted falcon statuette.

CASTING

Who Starred as Sam Spade?
Humphrey Bogart

Turned Down the Role of Same Spade
George Raft

Who Starred as Brigid O'Shaughnessy?
Mary Astor

Turned Down the Role of Brigid O'Shaughnessy
Geraldine Fitzgerald

WHO Trivia
Reportedly, Humphrey Bogart was not the first choice to play Sam Spade. Producer Hal B. Wallis initially offered the role to George Raft who rejected it because he did not want to work with John Huston, an inexperienced director.

The role of the deceitful *femme fatale* Brigid O'Shaughnessy was originally offered to Geraldine Fitzgerald, but went to Mary Astor when Fitzgerald decided to appear in a stage play.

The character of the sinister "Fat Man" Kasper Gutman was based on an overweight British detective who was involved in many sophisticated capers. Hal Wallis suggested Huston screen test Sydney Greenstreet, a veteran stage character actor who had never appeared on film before. Greenstreet, who weighed between 280 and 350 pounds, impressed Huston with his sheer size, distinctive abrasive laugh, bulbous eyes, and manner of speaking.

CASABLANCA (1942)

Rick: My letter of transit? I could use a trip. But it doesn't make any difference about our bet. You still owe me ten thousand francs.

Renault: And that ten thousand francs should pay our expenses.

Rick: Our expenses?

Renault: Mm-hm.

Rick: Louis, I think this is the beginning of a beautiful friendship.

Plot

An American expatriate owner of an upscale club and gambling den in the Moroccan city of Casablanca meets a former lover, with unforeseen complications.

CASTING

Who Starred as Rick Blaine?
Humphrey Bogart

Turned Down the Role of Rick Blaine
George Raft

WHO Trivia

Early in the production development, studio head Jack L. Warner offered the role of Rick Blaine to George Raft, but the actor turned it down. As the script took shape, producer Hal B. Wallis began to envision Humphrey Bogart in the role of Rick Blaine. As Bogart was under contract to Warner Bros., the role was assigned to him by Wallis.

After Bogart was cast, Raft reconsidered his decision and contacted Warner to deliver the news that he had decided to accept the part after all. After consulting with Wallis, who wanted Bogart, Warner decided to support his producer, telling Raft the part was no longer available. Ironically, this was the third of three roles Raft turned down that Bogart took. The other two roles were Roy "Mad Dog" Earle in *High Sierra* and Sam Spade in *The Maltese Falcon*. The three roles contributed greatly to establishing Bogart's legendary career.

Wallis obtained the services of Ingrid Bergman, who was under contract to David O. Selznick, by agreeing to lend Olivia de Havilland to Selznick for the film, *She Walks in Beauty,* scheduled to be shot after *Casablanca* finished filming.

To keep their names in the press, a false story was planted by a studio publicist claiming Ronald Reagan and Ann Sheridan were going to co-star in the film.

ARSENIC AND OLD LACE (1944)

Mortimer: Insanity runs in my family. It practically gallops.

Plot
A man makes a quick trip home to break the news of his unexpected marriage to his two maiden aunts, and finds out his aunts' hobby: poisoning lonely old men and burying them in the cellar.

CASTING

Who Starred as Mortimer Brewster?
Cary Grant

Turned Down the Role of Mortimer Brewster
Bob Hope

Who Starred as Jonathan Brewster?
Raymond Massey

Turned Down the Role of Jonathan Brewster
Boris Karloff

WHO Trivia
Bob Hope was going to play the lead role of Mortimer Brewster, but he could not get a release from his contract with Paramount Pictures.

Director/Producer Frank Capra considered Jack Benny and Ronald Reagan for the role until Cary Grant signed on.

The additional casting for the film was interesting. Boris Karloff played the role of Jonathan Brewster in the Broadway production, and Josephine Hull and Jean Adair portrayed the Brewster sisters, Abby and Martha. Frank Capra wanted the three actors to reprise their roles in the film. Hull and Adair both received an eight-week leave of absence from the stage production to do the film. Karloff did not get a leave of absence because he was the main draw for the play. Karloff was replaced by Raymond Massey for the film.

Capra actually filmed the movie in 1941 because of star Cary Grant's availability, but it was not released until 1944, after the original stage version had finished its run on Broadway.

DOUBLE INDEMNITY (1944)

Walter: It was a hot afternoon, and I can still remember the smell of honeysuckle all along that street. How could I have known that murder can sometimes smell like honeysuckle?

Plot

An insurance salesman, Walter Neff, meets Phyllis Dietrichson, the seductive wife of one of his clients, and they have an affair. She then proposes to kill her husband to receive the proceeds of an accident insurance policy, and he devises a scheme to receive twice the amount based on a double indemnity clause.

CASTING

Who Starred as Walter Neff?
Fred MacMurray

Turned Down the Role of Walter Neff
Alan Ladd • James Cagney • Spencer Tracy
Gregory Peck • George Raft • Dick Powell

WHO Trivia

Barbara Stanwyck was director Billy Wilder's first choice to play the role of Phyllis Dietrichson. Given the nature of the role, she was reluctant, fearing it would hurt her career. Stanwyck said, "I love the script and I love you Billy, but I am a little afraid after all these years of playing heroines to go into an out-and-out killer." Then, Mr. Wilder looked at Stanwyck and said, "Well, are you a mouse or an actress?" And she said, "Well, I hope I'm an actress." He replied, "Then do the part."

The character of Walter Neff was not only a heel; he was a weak and malleable heel, resulting in many Hollywood actors turning the role down. Dick Powell actually wanted the role, but he was under contract to another studio, and the studio wouldn't allow him to be in the movie.

Fred MacMurray was accustomed to playing "happy-go-lucky good guys" in light comedies, and when Wilder first approached him about the Neff role, MacMurray said, "You're making the mistake of your life!" Playing a serious role required acting, he said, "And I can't do it."

As it turned out, MacMurray made a great heel; his performance demonstrated new breadths of his acting talent, causing him to say, "I never dreamed it would be the best picture I ever made."

MILDRED PIERCE (1945)

Veda: Are you sure you want to know?
Mildred: Yes.
Veda: Then I'll tell you. With this money, I can get away from you and your chickens, pies and kitchens and everything that smells of grease. I can get away from this shack and its cheap furniture. And this town and its dollar-days and its women that wear uniforms and its men that wear overalls.
Mildred: I think I'm really seeing you for the first time in my life and you're cheap and horrible.

Plot
A woman become independent and successful after her cheating husband leaves her, but can't win the approval of her spoiled daughter.

CASTING

Who Starred as Mildred Pierce?
Joan Crawford

Turned Down the Role of Mildred Pierce
Bette Davis • Barbara Stanwyck • Rosalind Russell
Ann Sheridan

WHO Trivia
In 1942, after Joan Crawford had been unceremoniously released from MGM, she campaigned for the lead role in *Mildred Pierce*, which most lead actresses did not want because of the implied age as mother of a teenage daughter. Crawford saw the role as the ultimate opportunity to finally climb to the top of her craft.

Director Michael Curtiz wanted Bette Davis to play the title role, but she declined, as did Rosalind Russell and Ann Sheridan. Curtiz then campaigned for Barbara Stanwyck who was not available.

Although from the beginning, Curtiz did not want Crawford to play the part, he ultimately approved her casting after seeing her screen test.

Shirley Temple was considered for the role of the heroine's pretentious, hateful young ingrate of a daughter, Veda, played by Ann Blyth.

IT'S A WONDERFUL LIFE (1946)

Zuzu: Look, Daddy. Teacher says, every time a bell rings an angel
gets his wings.
George: That's right, that's right... Attaboy, Clarence!

Plot

An angel-in-training gives a despondent man a look at what the world
would be like if he had never been born.

CASTING

Who Starred as Mary Bailey?
Donna Reed

Turned Down the Role of Mary Bailey
Jean Arthur • Olivia de Havilland
Ginger Rogers • Ann Dvorak

WHO Trivia

The original story, titled *The Greatest Gift*, was written by Philip Van Doren
Stern in 1939. After it was rejected by several publishers, Stern had it printed
in 1943 as a pamphlet, and mailed to 200 family members and friends for
Christmas. The story came to the attention of RKO Pictures who bought the
film rights, hoping to turn it into a vehicle for Cary Grant, but he went on
to make another Christmas staple, *The Bishop's Wife*.

Director Frank Capra considered Henry Fonda, arguably James Stewart's
best friend, for the lead role of George Bailey. However, Capra really
wanted Stewart, and Fonda was cast in *My Darling Clementine*, which was
filmed at the same time, so no decision needed to be made.

After Jean Arthur turned down the role of Mary Bailey, Capra offered it to
Olivia de Havilland, Jimmy Stewart's girlfriend at the time. She rejected it,
taking the Oscar-winning role in *To Each His Own* instead. Ginger Rogers
then turned it down because she considered it "too bland."

A long list of actors was considered for the role of Henry Potter, including:
Edward Arnold, Charles Bickford, Edgar Buchanan, Raymond Massey, and
Thomas Mitchell, who played Uncle Billy. Lionel Barrymore was ultimately
cast in the role.

GENTLEMAN'S AGREEMENT (1947)

Mrs. Green: You think there's enough anti-Semitism in life already without people reading about it?

Phil Green: No, but this story is doomed before I start. What can I say about anti-Semitism that hasn't been said before?

Mrs. Green: Maybe it hasn't been said well enough. If it had, you wouldn't have had to explain it to Tommy right now.

Plot
A reporter pretends to be Jewish in order to cover a story on anti-Semitism, and personally discovers the true depths of bigotry and hatred.

CASTING

Who Starred as Phil Green?
Gregory Peck

Turned Down the Role of Phil Green
Cary Grant

WHO Trivia
The role of Phil Green was first offered to Cary Grant, but he turned it down. Gregory Peck decided to accept the role, although his agent advised him to refuse, believing his client would be endangering his career.

John Garfield, who was Jewish, took a small supporting role in the film as Peck's longtime childhood friend, Dave Goldman. Had Garfield not been nominated for Best Actor for his role in *Body and Soul*, he might well have earned a nomination for Supporting Actor for *Gentleman's Agreement*.

Producer Darryl Zanuck decided to make a film version of Laura Z. Hobson's novel, after being refused membership in the Los Angeles Country Club, because it was assumed incorrectly that he was Jewish. Before filming commenced, Samuel Goldwyn and a number of other Jewish film executives approached Zanuck, and asked him not to make the film. They feared it would "stir up trouble."

One favorite character in the film was June Havoc as Peck's secretary. Ironically, Havoc's character changed her name to something ethnically neutral to get her job at the very magazine she is working for in the film that is now going to crusade against anti-Semitism.

THE TREASURE OF SIERRA MADRE (1948)

Dobbs: I sure had some cockeyed ideas about prospectin' for gold. It was all in the finding I thought. I thought all you had to do was find it, pick it up, put it in sacks, and carry 'em off to the nearest bank.

Plot

Two American down-and-outers in 1920s Mexico hook up with an old-timer to prospect for gold.

CASTING

Who Starred as Bob Curtin?
Tim Holt

Turned Down the Role of Bob Curtin
Ronald Reagan

WHO Trivia

After a smashing success with his directorial debut film, *The Maltese Falcon*, John Huston started working on this project. The studio had George Raft, Edward G. Robinson, and John Garfield in mind for the three main roles, but World War II intervened.

By the time Huston returned from the war, Humphrey Bogart had become Warner Brothers' biggest star. When Bogart heard that Huston might be making a film of the B. Traven novel, he immediately badgered him for the role of Fred C. Dobbs.

Producer Henry Blanke, initially thrilled at Walter Huston's scene-stealing performance as the character Howard in the film, started to have second thoughts about Walter Huston upstaging the film's star, Humphrey Bogart. Blanke decided to send notes to John Huston telling him to tone down his father's performance.

As it turned out, Walter Huston, won an Oscar for Best Supporting Actor, and John Huston won an Oscar for Best Director.

Ronald Reagan was offered the part of Bob Curtin by director John Huston, but Warner Bros. studio head, Jack L. Warner, refused to let the actor out of *The Voice of the Turtle*, which was scheduled to be made at the same time.

ALL THE KING'S MEN (1949)

Stark: Why have they used every dirty method known to make sure I'm not elected County Treasurer? Well, I'll tell ya why - because they're afraid of the truth, and the truth is this. They're trying to steal your money. Yeah, I said steal. The County Commissioners rejected the low bid on the schoolhouse. Why? Well, they'll tell ya the reason is the job will be done better. The County Commissioners would have you believe that they're interested in public welfare. They're interested, sure, but it's their own.

Plot
The story of a politician's rise from a rural county seat to the governor's mansion. Along the way, loses his initial innocence and becomes as corrupt as the politicians he once fought against.

CASTING

Who Starred as Willie Stark?
Broderick Crawford

Turned Down the Role of Willie Stark
John Wayne

WHO Trivia
Director Robert Rossen originally offered the starring role to John Wayne, who found the proposed film script unpatriotic and indignantly refused the part.

Harry Cohn, the president of Columbia Pictures, wanted Spencer Tracy for the role of Willie Stark. Rossen disagreed, saying that the audience might like Tracy too much. Humphrey Bogart was also considered.

Broderick Crawford, who eventually took the role, won the Academy Award for Best Actor, beating out John Wayne, who had been nominated for his role in *Sands of Iwo Jima*.

In addition to Broderick Crawford winning the award for Best Actor, the film won Best Picture, and Mercedes McCambridge won Best Supporting Actress.

The film is loosely based on the life of Huey P. Long, former Governor of Louisiana and that state's U.S. senator in the mid-1930s. Ironically, using the name Huey P. Long on the set was forbidden.

Bonus Movies

Sergeant York (1941)

The real Alvin York refused several times to authorize a film version of his life story, but finally yielded to persistent efforts in order to finance the creation of an interdenominational bible school. It was contingent on Gary Cooper, and only Gary Cooper, playing the role. Making this film was Cooper's way of contributing to the war effort as he could not serve due to his age and injuries.

Mrs. Miniver (1942)

After first-choice Norma Shearer rejected the title role, refusing to play a mother, Greer Garson was cast. Although she didn't want the part either, she was contractually bound to take it. Ironically, she won the Academy Award for Best Actress, and the film won for Best Picture.

Saboteur (1942)

Gary Cooper turned down director Alfred Hitchcock when he was offered the lead role of Barry Kane. Hitchcock then turned to Henry Fonda, who also declined. Hitchcock then decided to hire Robert Cummings to play the part, while offering the female lead of Patricia "Pat" Martin to Barbara Stanwyck, but she declined. Finally, the role went to Priscilla Lane.

Yankee Doodle Dandy (1943)

Before James Cagney signed on to play the legendary George M. Cohan, dancer Fred Astaire was seriously considered. Joan Crawford turned down the role of Mary Cohan, played by Joan Leslie in her film debut.

Gaslight (1944)

Both Irene Dunne and Hedy Lamarr turned down the role of Paula, which won the Academy Award for Best Actress for Ingrid Bergman

Laura (1944)

Laird Cregar was cast to play Waldo Lydecker, but his premature death paved the way for Clifton Webb to become a movie star in the role. Jennifer Jones, Hedy Lamarr, and Rosalind Russell all turned down the chic mystery woman role ultimately played by Gene Tierney.

National Velvet (1944)

Originally in 1939, an 18-year-old Gene Tierney was going to star as Velvet, with Spencer Tracy as her father, Mr. Brown. When production was delayed,

Tierney went back to Broadway. After Gene Tierney quit, Susanna Foster was set to play the lead, but she ended up turning the role down because there "wasn't any singing in it."

When production started up in 1944, the role of Velvet went to an unknown actress named Elizabeth Taylor, and the role of Mr. Brown to Donald Crisp.

All of Mickey Rooney's scenes were shot first, during the one month allotted by the U.S. Army before Rooney was inducted in June 1944.

The Lost Weekend (1945)
Director Billy Wilder's first choice to play Don Birnam, a chronic alcoholic, was Jose Ferrer, but Paramount insisted that only a matinee idol in the lead could sell the film. Ray Milland was cast, and won the Oscar for Best Actor.

Katharine Hepburn was director Billy Wilder's first choice for the role of the girlfriend of alcoholic Don Birnam, Helen St. James, but Hepburn had signed on to do *Without Love* and declined. The part went to Jane Wyman.

The Killers (1946)
Burt Lancaster was not producer Mark Hellinger's first choice to play the part of "the Swede," but Warner Bros. wouldn't lend out Wayne Morris for the role. *The Killers* was Lancaster's debut film. Other actors considered for the part included: Van Heflin, Sonny Tufts, Jon Hall, and Edmond O'Brien, who was cast in the role of the insurance investigator.

In the role of the femme fatale, Kitty Collins, Hellinger cast Ava Gardner, who up to then had appeared virtually unnoticed in a string of minor films.

The Stranger (1946)
Director Orson Welles wanted actress Agnes Moorehead to portray the investigator, Mr Wilson. "I thought it would be much more interesting to have a spinster lady on the heels of this Nazi." Instead, Edward G. Robinson was cast in the role.

Easter Parade (1948)
Gene Kelly was originally cast to play Don, but broke his ankle. Kelly was replaced by Fred Astaire. Cyd Charisse was up for the role of Nadine, but a torn ligament in her knee forced her to drop out. Ann Miller was subsequently cast in the role.

Margo Channing • Eve Harrington • Billie Dawn • Harry Brock • Joe Gillis
Norma Desmond • Don Lockwood • Cosmo Brown • Kathy Selden • Will Kane
Stanley Kowalski • Blanche DuBois • Charles Allnut • Rose Sayer • Sgt. Walden
Karen Holmes • Pvt. Prewitt • Joe Bradley • Princess Ann • Shane • Joe Starrett
Terry Malloy • Edie Doyle • Charley Malloy • Esther Blodgett • Norman Maine
Tony Wendice • Margot Wendice • Lt. Doug Roberts • "Doc" • Ensign Pulver
Bick Benedict • Jed Rink • Leslie Benedict • Maggie The Cat • Brick Pollitt
Judah Ben-Hur • Messala • Roger O. Thornhill • Eve Kendall • Phillip Vandamm
Moses • Jerry/Daphne • Sugar "Kane" Kowalczyk • Joe/Josephine • Annie Oakley
Guy Harris • Bruno Antony • Sky Masterson • Nathan Detroit • Sarah Brown

1950s

J.J. Sefton • Cal Trask • Jim Stark • Frankie Machine • Shears • Col. Nicholson
Dr. Ben McKenna • Jo McKenna • Gigi • Nellie Forbush • "Scottie" Ferguson
Margo Channing • Eve Harrington • Billie Dawn • Harry Brock • Joe Gillis
Norma Desmond • Don Lockwood • Cosmo Brown • Kathy Selden • Will Kane
Stanley Kowalski • Blanche DuBois • Charles Allnut • Rose Sayer • Sgt. Walden
Karen Holmes • Pvt. Prewitt • Joe Bradley • Princess Ann • Shane • Joe Starrett
Terry Malloy • Edie Doyle • Charley Malloy • Esther Blodgett • Norman Maine
Tony Wendice • Margot Wendice • Lt. Doug Roberts • "Doc" • Ensign Pulver
Bick Benedict • Jed Rink • Leslie Benedict • Maggie The Cat • Brick Pollitt
Judah Ben-Hur • Messala • Roger O. Thornhill • Eve Kendall • Phillip Vandamm
Moses • Jerry/Daphne • Sugar "Kane" Kowalczyk • Joe/Josephine • Annie Oakley
Guy Harris • Bruno Antony • Sky Masterson • Nathan Detroit • Sarah Brown
J.J. Sefton • Cal Trask • Jim Stark • Frankie Machine • Shears • Col. Nicholson
Dr. Ben McKenna • Jo McKenna • Gigi • Nellie Forbush • "Scottie" Ferguson
Margo Channing • Eve Harrington • Billie Dawn • Harry Brock • Joe Gillis
Norma Desmond • Don Lockwood • Cosmo Brown • Kathy Selden • Will Kane
Stanley Kowalski • Blanche DuBois • Charles Allnut • Rose Sayer • Sgt. Walden
Karen Holmes • Pvt. Prewitt • Joe Bradley • Princess Ann • Shane • Joe Starrett
Terry Malloy • Edie Doyle • Charley Malloy • Esther Blodgett • Norman Maine
Tony Wendice • Margot Wendice • Lt. Doug Roberts • "Doc" • Ensign Pulver
Bick Benedict • Jed Rink • Leslie Benedict • Maggie The Cat • Brick Pollitt
Judah Ben-Hur • Messala • Roger O. Thornhill • Eve Kendall • Phillip Vandamm
Moses • Jerry/Daphne • Sugar "Kane" Kowalczyk • Joe/Josephine • Annie Oakley
Guy Harris • Bruno Antony • Sky Masterson • Nathan Detroit • Sarah Brown
J.J. Sefton • Cal Trask • Jim Stark • Frankie Machine • Shears • Col. Nicholson
Dr. Ben McKenna • Jo McKenna • Gigi • Nellie Forbush • "Scottie" Ferguson
Margo Channing • Eve Harrington • Billie Dawn • Harry Brock • Joe Gillis
Norma Desmond • Don Lockwood • Cosmo Brown • Kathy Selden • Will Kane
Stanley Kowalski • Blanche DuBois • Charles Allnut • Rose Sayer • Sgt. Walden
Karen Holmes • Pvt. Prewitt • Joe Bradley • Princess Ann • Shane • Joe Starrett

Movies vs. Television

The 1950s was known for the advent of television, TV dinners, and the rise of drive-in theaters to a peak number of over 4,000 outdoor screens by the end of the decade. Older viewers were prone to stay at home and watch television with almost 11 million homes having a TV set by 1950.

Following World War II, when most of the films were idealized with conventional portrayals of men and women, young people wanted new and exciting symbols of rebellion. Hollywood responded to audience demands. The late 1940s and 1950s saw the rise of the anti-hero, with new stars like Steve McQueen, James Dean, Paul Newman and Marlon Brando.

All of the Hollywood studios, fearful of television's growing impact, forbade their movies and their "movie stars" from appearing on the small screen at all. By the early 1950s, film attendance had declined dramatically. This was attributed to the fact that 50% of all homes had at least one TV set. The Academy Awards were televised for the *first* time by NBC. The broadcast received the largest single audience in television's five-year history.

The studios acknowledged the power of television and scurried to find creative ways to make money from it; Hollywood studios were beginning to produce more hours of content for television than for feature films.

By the mid 1950s, television had become affordable and a permanent fixture in most American homes. More than half of Hollywood's productions were made in color to take Americans away from their black and white television sets and bring them back into the movie theaters. Simultaneously, major studios began to sell older black-and-white movies to television for broadcast and viewing. The first feature film to be broadcast on television was *The Wizard of Oz* in 1956.

With television geared towards family audiences, the movies explored realistic adult themes and stronger or previously taboo subjects, such as veiled hints at homosexuality in *Strangers on a Train;* voyeurism in *Rear Window*; class differences in *A Place in the Sun*; the atrocities of Nazi war crimes were addressed in *Judgment at Nuremberg*; race relations, and interracial marriage in *Guess Who's Coming to Dinner*; the plight of a man unjustly accused of a crime in *The Wrong Man*; and drug addiction in *The Man With the Golden Arm*.

Westerns flooded the screens, *High Noon, Shane, The Searchers, Gunfight at the O.K. Corral*, and *Last Train from Gun Hill*. Bookending the decade were two iconic Howard Hawks' westerns, *Red River* and *Rio Bravo*.

To compete for an audience, Disney Studios returned to feature length 'story' animations with films such as *Lady and the Tramp, Peter Pan, Cinderella*, and *Sleeping Beauty*— four of the top six grossing films of the decade.

At the same time, lavish, classic musicals, mostly from MGM, emerged filling the big screen: *Annie Get Your Gun, Singin' In The Rain, Kiss Me Kate, Oklahoma, Guys and Dolls, The King and I* and *Porgy and Bess*.

The decade also ushered in the age of rock and roll, and an entirely new and younger film market was created. *Rock Around the Clock* that featured disc jockey Alan Freed and Bill Haley & The Comets. The influences of rock 'n' roll surfaced in *Blackboard Jungle*, the first major Hollywood film to use rock and roll on its soundtrack. This new young audience attended Drive-ins theaters which mostly showed exploitative B-movies such as *The Blob*.

Meanwhile, the studio "star system" began to lose some of its power and grip on movie stars as well, and the decline would steadily spread into the next decade. Many of the stars began moving from studio to studio for individual pictures, ushering in the age of the independent superstar.

By 1959, the production of films in the US dropped to about 250 films a year from over 500 films a decade earlier; only 42 million people were attending films on a weekly basis, as compared to more than double that amount at the end of the previous decade. Studios realized that television was here to stay, and began to adjusted its technology by expanding into technicolor, stereo sound and new widescreen formats.

The Academy Awards

1950
Best Picture: ***All About Eve***
Best Actor: Jose Ferrer (*Cyrano de Bergerac*)
Best Actress: Judy Holliday (*Born Yesterday*)
Best Supporting Actor: George Sanders (*All About Eve*)
Best Supporting Actress: Josephine Hull (*Harvey*)

1951
Best Picture: ***An American in Paris***
Best Actor: Humphrey Bogart (*The African Queen*)
Best Actress: Vivien Leigh (*A Streetcar Named Desire*)
Best Supporting Actor: Karl Malden (*A Streetcar Named Desire*)
Best Supporting Actress: Kim Hunter (*A Streetcar named Desire*)

1952
Best Picture: ***The Greatest Show on Earth***
Best Actor: Gary Cooper (*High Noon*)
Best Actress: Shirley Booth (*Come Back, Little Sheba*)
Best Supporting Actor: Anthony Quinn (*Viva Zapata*)
Best Supporting Actress: Gloria Grahame (*The Bad and the Beautiful*)

1953
Best Picture: ***From Here to Eternity***
Best Actor: William Holden (*Stalag 17*)
Best Actress: Audrey Hepburn (*Roman Holiday*)
Best Supporting Actor: Frank Sinatra (*From Here to Eternity*)
Best Supporting Actress: Donna Reed (*From Here to Eternity*)

1954
Best Picture: ***On the Waterfront***
Best Actor: Marlon Brando (*On the Waterfront*)
Best Actress: Grace Kelly (*The Country Girl*)
Best Supporting Actor: Edmond O'Brien (*The Barefoot Contessa*)
Best Supporting Actress: Eva Marie Saint (*On The Waterfront*)

1955

Best Picture: ***Marty***
Best Actor: Ernest Borgnine (*Marty*)
Best Actress: Anna Magnani (*The Rose Tattoo*)
Best Supporting Actor: Jack Lemmon (*Mister Roberts*)
Best Supporting Actress: Jo Van Fleet (*East of Eden*)

1956

Best Picture: ***Around the World in 80 Days***
Best Actor: Yul Brynner (*The King and I*)
Best Actress: Ingrid Bergman (*Anastasia*)
Best Supporting Actor: Anthony Quinn (*Lust for Life*)
Best Supporting Actress: Dorothy Malone (*Written on the Wind*)

1957

Best Picture: ***The Bridge on the River Kwai***
Best Actor: Alec Guinness (*The Bridge on the River Kwai*)
Best Actress: Joanne Woodward (*The Three Faces of Eve*)
Best Supporting Actor: Red Buttons (*Sayonara*)
Best Supporting Actress: Miyoshi Umeki (*Sayonara*)

1958

Best Picture: ***Gigi***
Best Actor: David Niven (*Separate Tables*)
Best Actress: Susan Hayward (*I Want to Live*)
Best Supporting Actor: Burl Ives (*The Big Country*)
Best Supporting Actress: Wendy Hiller (*Separate Tables*)

1959

Best Picture: ***Ben-Hur***
Best Actor: Charlton Heston (*Ben-Hur*)
Best Actress: Simone Signoret (*Room at the Top*)
Best Supporting Actor: Hugh Griffith (*Ben-Hur*)
Best Supporting Actress: Shelley Winters (*The Diary of Anne Frank*)

Casting
Trivia Quiz

1. William Holden played Joe Gillis in **Sunset Boulevard** after this actor walked away from the production after two weeks of shooting:
   - a. Montgomery Clift
   - b. Gene Kelly
   - c. James Stewart
   - d. Marlon Brando

2. This actress was originally cast as Margo Channing in **All About Eve** but a ruptured disc before filming started forced her to withdraw:
   - a. Joan Crawford
   - b. Donna Reed
   - c. Olivia De Havilland
   - d. Claudette Colbert

3. This actor turned down the role of Don Lockwood, played by Gene Kelly, in **Singing in the Rain.**
   - a. Donald O'Connor
   - b. Gordon McRae
   - c. Howard Keel
   - d. John Raitt

4. Before James Dean was cast in **Rebel Without a Cause** this actor did a screen test in New York for the role of Jim Stark:
   - a. Tab Hunter
   - b. Marlon Brando
   - c. Anthony Perkins
   - d. Paul Newman

5. The role of Blanche DuBois in **A Streetcar Named Desire** was offered to this actress before Vivien Leigh got the role:
   - a. Elizabeth Taylor
   - b. Anne Baxter
   - c. Olivia de Havilland
   - d. Joan Fontaine

6. Marlon Brando played Stanley Kowalski in **A Streetcar Named Desire** on Broadway and in the film. This actor was first offered the film role:
   - a. Robert Mitchum
   - b. Gregory Peck
   - c. Burt Lancaster
   - d. Tyrone Power

7. Jack Lemmon played Jerry/Daphne in Billy Wilder's **Some Like It Hot** after this actor said no because he didn't want to dress in drag:
   - a. Jerry Lewis
   - b. Danny Kaye
   - c. Bob Hope
   - d. Anthony Perkins

8. In ***From Here to Eternity,*** Donna Reed won an Oscar for her role of Alma after this actress turned down the role:
   - a. Rita Hayworth
   - b. Gloria Grahame
   - c. Joan Fontaine
   - d. Kim Stanley

9. Producer Stanley Kramer first offered the role of Will Kane in the western classic, ***High Noon,*** to this actor:
   - a. John Wayne
   - b. Henry Fonda
   - c. Gregory Peck
   - d. Burt Lancaster

10. Gregory Peck co-starred with Audrey Hepburn in ***Roman Holiday.*** Peck's role as Joe Bradley was first offered to:
    - a. Cary Grant
    - b. Paul Newman
    - c. James Stewart
    - d. Charlton Heston

11. ***Ben Hur,*** winner of eleven Oscars, had Charlton Heston in the title role after this actor turned down the role:
    - a. Paul Newman
    - b. Montgomery Clift
    - c. Kirk Douglas
    - d. Tony Curtis

12. Alfred Hitchcock wanted this actress as the intended victim Margot Wendice in ***Dial M for Murder*** before Grace Kelly accepted the role:
    - a. Donna Reed
    - b. Deborah Kerr
    - c. Janet Leigh
    - d. Ava Gardner

13. James Mason was nominated for an Oscar as the unsympathetic alcoholic Norman Maine in ***A Star is Born*** after this actor turned down the role:
    - a. Humphrey Bogart
    - b. Frank Sinatra
    - c. Errol Flynn
    - d. All of the Above

14. George Stevens' originally cast this actor in the classic lead role in ***Shane*** before Alan Ladd was cast:
    - a. Gary Cooper
    - b. Paul Newman
    - c. Montgomery Clift
    - d. James Dean

15. Paul Newman was nominated for an Oscar for his portrayal of Brick Pollitt in ***Cat on a Hot Tin Roof*** after this actor turned down the role:
    - a. Ben Gazzara
    - b. Robert Mitchum
    - c. Elvis Presley
    - d. All of the Above

ALL ABOUT EVE (1950)

Margo: Fasten your seatbelts, it's going to be a bumpy night.

Plot
A calculating ingenue insinuates herself into the company of an aging stage actress and her circle of theater friends to establish herself as an actress.

CASTING

Who Starred as Margo Channing?
Bette Davis

Turned Down the Role of Margo Channing
Barbara Stanwyck • Claudette Colbert • Ingrid Bergman

Who Starred as Eve Harrington?
Anne Baxter

Turned Down the Role of Eve Harrington
Jeanne Crain

WHO Trivia
Among the actresses originally considered to play Margo Channing were Marlene Dietrich, dismissed as "too German," Susan Hayward, who was rejected as "too young," and Gertrude Lawrence, who was ruled out when her lawyer insisted she not have to drink or smoke in the film, and that the script be rewritten to allow her to sing a torch song.

Producer Darryl F. Zanuck favored Barbara Stanwyck, but she was not available. He then considered Tallulah Bankhead and Joan Crawford. Eventually, the role went to Claudette Colbert, but she had to withdraw after she sustained an injury shortly before filming began.

Director Joseph Mankiewicz then offered the role to Ingrid Bergman, who turned it down. She had just fallen in love with Roberto Rossellini, and didn't want to leave Europe. Finally, Mankiewicz decided to cast Bette Davis.

Jeanne Crain was cast as Eve Harrington, but she got pregnant and withdrew. A number of actresses were considered before Anne Baxter was cast, including: June Allyson, Ann Blyth, Donna Reed and Elizabeth Taylor.

BORN YESTERDAY (1950)

Paul: You were great tonight. Didn't you think you were great?
Billie: Oh, yeah. We really tricked them, didn't we?
Paul: What's the matter?
Billie: Well, if you saw a great ventriloquist, who would you compliment?... the dummy?
Paul: You're not a dummy.

Plot
An uncouth, loudmouth junkyard tycoon descends upon Washington D.C. to buy himself a congressman or two, bringing with him his uneducated mistress. To make her more presentable, he hires a tutor to teach her proper etiquette with unexpected results.

CASTING

Who Starred as Billie Dawn?
Judy Holliday

Turned Down the Role of Billie Dawn
Rita Hayworth • Gloria Grahame

WHO Trivia
The film was based on the play by Garson Kanin, which starred Judy Holliday and Paul Douglas. Holliday initially refused to reprise her popular Broadway role for the film, which was okay with Columbia's Harry Cohn as he wasn't sold on her acting ability.

Cohn pursued Rita Hayworth, but she decided to marry Aly Kahn, and wasn't available. It was then reported Gloria Grahame was to be borrowed from RKO for the lead, but the studio refused to lend her out

Supposedly, Kanin convinced Cohn to cast Judy Holliday in *Adam's Rib,* soon to start production, in a part he wrote particularly for her. Holliday's performance garnered critical acclaim and convinced Cohn of her comedic abilities. Cohn's "late faith" was rewarded by Holliday's Academy Award for Best Actress and the success of the film.

Columbia negotiated with Paul Douglas to reprise his Broadway role, but decided to cast Broderick Crawford.

SUNSET BOULEVARD (1950)

Joe: You're Norma Desmond.... You used to be in silent pictures. You used to be big.

Norma: I am big. It's the pictures that got small.

Plot

A faded movie star tries to entrap an unsuspecting down-on-his-luck screen-writer into her fantasy world in which she dreams of making a triumphant return to the screen.

CASTING

Who Starred as Joe Gillis?
William Holden

Turned Down the Role of Joe Gillis
Montgomery Clift • Fred MacMurray

Who Starred as Norma Desmond?
Gloria Swanson

Turned Down the Role of Norma Desmond
Pola Negri • Norma Shearer • Greta Garbo • Mae Murray

WHO Trivia

Montgomery Clift was signed to play Joe Gillis, but just before the start of filming, he withdrew, claiming his role of a young man involved with an older woman was too close to the one he had played in *The Heiress*. It was suggested that the real reason Clift dropping the film was that he was having an affair with much older, very wealthy, former actress, Libby Holman. Clift was scared the press would start prying, and didn't want to bring attention to the situation.

Director Billy Wilder contacted Pola Negri by telephone for the role of Norma Desmond, but had a difficult time understanding her heavy Polish accent. Wilder then asked Norma Shearer, but she rejected the role due to both her retirement and distaste for the film. Wilder then approached Greta Garbo who expressed no interest.

According to one often-told but discredited anecdote, Mae Murray was offended by the film and commented, "None of us floozies was that nuts."

A STREETCAR NAMED DESIRE (1951)

Stanley: Stella. Hey, STELLA!

Plot

A fragile southern belle, after encountering a series of personal blows, leaves her aristocratic background to seek refuge with her sister and brother-in-law in a dilapidated tenement in New Orleans.

CASTING

Who Starred as Stanley Kowalski?
Marlon Brando

Turned Down the Role of Stanley Kowalski
Robert Mitchum • John Garfield

Who Starred as Blanche DuBois?
Vivien Leigh

Turned Down the Role of Blanche DuBois
Olivia de Havilland • Jessica Tandy

Who Starred as Stella Kowalski?
Kim Hunter

Turned Down the Role of Stella Kowalski
Bette Davis • Patricia Neal
Joan Fontaine • Anne Baxter

WHO Trivia

Although Jessica Tandy originated the role of Blanche DuBois on the stage, Elia Kazan, who directed the film, wanted someone with star power for it. After Olivia de Havilland turned down the role, he offered it to Vivien Leigh.

The same was true for the role of Stanley Kowalski. John Garfield turned it down because he didn't want to be overshadowed by the female lead. RKO refused to let Robert Mitchum, under contract, play the part.

A unique fact about the final film cast was that nine members of the original Broadway cast, including Marlon Brando, Kim Hunter, and Karl Malden repeated their roles in the film.

HIGH NOON (1952)

Kane: It's no good. I've got to go back, Amy.
Amy: Why?
Kane: This is crazy. I haven't even got any guns.
Amy: Then let's go on. Hurry.
Kane: No, that's what I've been thinkin'. They're making me run. I've never run from anybody before.
Amy: I don't understand any of this.
Kane: Well, I haven't got time to tell ya.
Amy: Then don't go back, Will.
Kane: I've got to. That's the whole thing.

Plot

A marshal finds out that his entire town refuses to help him when he is compelled to face a returning deadly enemy.

CASTING

Who Starred as Will Kane?
Gary Cooper

Turned Down the Role of Will Kane
John Wayne • Gregory Peck • Marlon Brando
Montgomery Clift • Charlton Heston • Kirk Douglas
Burt Lancaster • Henry Fonda

WHO Trivia

John Wayne was originally offered the lead role of Will Kane, but turned it down because he felt writer Carl Foreman's story was an obvious allegory against blacklisting, which he actively supported.

After Wayne turned it down, producer Stanley Kramer offered the role to Gregory Peck, who declined because he felt the role was too similar to his role the year before in *The Gunfighter*. After Peck turned it down, a Who's Who of actors turned down the role, including: Charlton Heston, Marlon Brando, Montgomery Clift, Kirk Douglas, and Burt Lancaster.

Henry Fonda was considered for the role, but missed out because he had been "gray-listed" in the industry due to his political beliefs. Finally, Gary Cooper was cast, winning the Academy Award for Best Actor.

SINGIN' IN THE RAIN (1952)

Don: Hey Cos, do something, call me a cab.
Cosmo: OK, you're a cab.

Plot

A silent film production company and cast make a difficult transition in their first movie with sound.

CASTING

Who Starred as Don Lockwood?
Gene Kelly

Turned Down the Role of Don Lockwood
Howard Keel

Who Starred as Cosmo Brown?
Donald O'Connor

Turned Down the Role of Cosmo Brown
Oscar Levant

Who Starred as Kathy Selden?
Debbie Reynolds

Turned Down the Role of Kathy Selden
Judy Garland • June Allyson • Ann Miller

WHO Trivia

Debbie Reynolds' background was as a gymnast, not a dancer, when she made *Singin' in the Rain*.

As the story goes, Gene Kelly apparently insulted Reynolds for her lack of dance experience, greatly upsetting her. Fred Astaire found Reynolds crying under a piano. Hearing what had happened, Astaire volunteered to help her with her dancing. Kelly later admitted that he had not been kind to Reynolds, and was surprised she was still willing to talk to him after his criticism of her.

After shooting the "Good Morning" routine, which had taken from 8:00 a.m. until 11:00 p.m., Reynolds' feet were bleeding. Years later, she was quoted as saying that *"Singin' in the Rain* and childbirth were the two hardest things I ever had to do in my life."

FROM HERE TO ETERNITY (1953)

Pvt. Prewitt: A man don't go his own way, he's nothing.
Sgt. Warden: Maybe back in the days of the pioneers a man could go his own way, but today you got to play ball.

Plot

Set in 1941 in Hawaii in the months leading up to the attack on Pearl Harbor, the film deals with the tribulations of three soldiers.

CASTING

Who Starred as Sgt. Warden?
Burt Lancaster

Turned Down the Role of Sgt. Warden
Tyrone Power

Who Starred as Karen Holmes?
Deborah Kerr

Turned Down the Role of Karen Holmes
Joan Crawford • Joan Fontaine

Who Starred as Alma 'Lorene' Burke?
Donna Reed

Turned Down the Role of Alma 'Lorene' Burke
Shelley Winters

WHO Trivia

The casting controversy of *From Here to Eternity* was legendary.

Harry Cohn, the head of Columbia Pictures, had his own ideas as to the cast. If he had gotten his way, it would have been as follows: Robert Mitchum as Sgt. Warden, instead of Burt Lancaster; Aldo Ray as Prewitt, instead of Montgomery Clift; Rita Hayworth as Karen Holmes, instead of Deborah Kerr; Julie Harris as Lorene, instead of Donna Reed; and Eli Wallach as Maggio, instead of Frank Sinatra.

Tyrone Power turned down the role of Sgt. Warden because he was committed to a play at the time. In an effort to change his mind, they offered his wife, Linda Christian, the role of Lorene, but Power decided to still do the play.

Harry Cohn resisted the idea of casting Montgomery Clift as Private Prewitt, "He was no soldier, no boxer and probably a homosexual." The problem for Cohn was that director Fred Zinnemann refused to make the film without Clift. He also stood firm on having the final say on all casting.

Eventually, Cohn gave in and was rewarded when the film garnered eight Academy Awards, including: Best Picture, Best Director, Supporting Actor (Frank Sinatra) and Supporting Actress (Donna Reed), a role turned down by Shelley Winters because she had just given birth.

Joan Crawford turned down the Karen Holmes role because she didn't like the costumes, and Joan Fontaine regretted that family problems compelled her to also turn down the role. Eli Wallach had already accepted the Maggio role, but lost it to Sinatra for reasons still a mystery.

One favorite urban myth is that Frank Sinatra got the role in the film by means of his alleged Mafia connections, which was also thought to be the basis for a subplot in *The Godfather.* Another explanation for Sinatra's casting was that his then-wife, Ava Gardner, persuaded studio head Harry Cohn's wife to use her influence with her husband. Eventually, Cohn did cast Sinatra for a mere $8,000 because his stock in Hollywood was so low.

Sinatra would later comment that he thought his performance of heroin addict Frankie Machine in *The Man with the Golden Arm* was more deserving of an Oscar than his role as Maggio.

William Holden, who won the Best Actor Oscar for *Stalag 17* said that he felt either Lancaster or Clift (both were nominated) should have won.

ROMAN HOLIDAY (1953)

Princess Ann: Is this the elevator?
Joe Bradley: This is my ROOM!

Plot

A romantic comedy about a bored and sheltered princess who escapes her guardians and falls in love with an American newsman in Rome.

CASTING

Who Starred as Joe Bradley?
Gregory Peck

Turned Down the Role of Joe Bradley
Cary Grant

Who Starred as Princess Ann?
Audrey Hepburn

Turned Down the Role of Princess Ann
Elizabeth Taylor • Jean Simmons

WHO Trivia

Director/Producer William Wyler first offered the role to Cary Grant, but he turned it down believing he was too old to play Audrey Hepburn's love interest, though he played opposite her ten years later in *Charade*.

Gregory Peck's contract gave him solo star billing with highly-regarded newcomer, Audrey Hepburn, listed much less prominently in the credits. Halfway through the filming, Peck suggested to Wyler that he elevate Hepburn to equal billing, an almost unheard-of gesture in Hollywood.

Wyler had initially wanted either Elizabeth Taylor or Jean Simmons for the role of Princess Ann, but both were unavailable.

The original writer, Dalton Trumbo, was blacklisted as one of the legendary Hollywood Ten, and therefore could not receive credit for the screenplay, even when the film won the Academy Award for Best Screenplay.

Instead, Trumbo's friend, Ian Hunter, took credit and accepted the Oscar. Hunter received a $50,000 payment which he gave to Trumbo.

SHANE (1953)

Shane: I'm alright, Joey. You go home to your mother and your father. And grow up to be strong and straight. And Joey, take care of them, both of them.

Joey: He'd never have been able to shoot you - if you'd have seen him.

Shane: Bye, little Joe.

Joey: He never even would have cleared the holster, would he, Shane?... Pa's got things for you to do, and Mother wants you. I know she does. Shane. Shane!... Come back! Bye, Shane.

Plot

A Southern gunfighter, seeking to escape his secret past by getting a job as a ranch hand to a family of homesteaders, must return to his roots when a cattle rancher needs to get rid of the homesteaders.

CASTING

Who Starred as Shane?
Alan Ladd

Turned Down the Role of Shane
Montgomery Clift

Who Starred as Joe Starrett?
Van Heflin

Turned Down the Role of Joe Starrett
William Holden

Who Starred as Jack Wilson?
Jack Palance

Turned Down the Role of Jack Wilson
Jack Elam

WHO Trivia

Director George Stevens originally cast Montgomery Clift as Shane and William Holden as Joe Starrett. When both decided to do other films, *Shane* was nearly abandoned before Stevens asked studio head, Y. Frank Freeman, who was under contract to the studio. Upon looking at a list of available actors, Stevens cast Alan Ladd, Van Heflin and Jean Arthur within three minutes.

The iconic scene in which Shane gives Joey a demonstration of his ability with a gun took 116 takes to get right.

ON THE WATERFRONT (1954)

Charley: Oh, I had some bets down for you. You saw some money.
Terry: You don't understand. I coulda had class. I coulda been a contender. I coulda been somebody, instead of a bum, which is what I am. Let's face it. It was you, Charley.

Plot
An ex-prizefighter turned longshoreman struggles to stand up to his corrupt union bosses.

CASTING

Who Starred as Edie Doyle?
Eva Marie Saint

Turned Down the Role of Edie Doyle
Grace Kelly • Janice Rule

Who Starred as Charley Malloy?
Rod Steiger

Turned Down the Role of Charley Malloy
Lawrence Tierney

WHO Trivia
The part of Terry Malloy was originally written for John Garfield who died before the film was made.

Frank Sinatra signed for the lead role with a "handshake deal," but no formally signed contract, after Marlon Brando initially turned it down because of director Elia Kazan's testimony before the House Un-American Activities Committee. Producer Sam Spiegel knew Kazan still favored Brando for the role and enlisted Jay Kanter, Brando's agent, to persuade him to change his mind.

Grace Kelly, preferring to make *Rear Window* instead of *On the Waterfront*, turned down the role of Edie Doyle. Janice Rule, the brilliant, unconventional actress turned down the role because she was appearing on Broadway to great acclaim in the play, *Picnic*.

The role of Terry's older brother Charley "the Gent" Malloy, was originally offered to Lawrence Tierney. When the producers refused to meet his quote, the role went to Rod Steiger.

A STAR IS BORN (1954)

Esther Blodgett: Hello, Mr. Maine. You turn up in the strangest places.
Norman Maine: Don't I now?
Esther Blodgett: And you're cold sober.
Norman Maine: Well, you'd better make the most of it!

Plot

A movie star helps a young singer/actress find fame, as age and alcoholism send his own career into a downward spiral.

CASTING

Who Starred as Norman Maine?
James Mason

Turned Down the Role of Norman Maine
Cary Grant • John Hodiak • Marlon Brando
Montgomery Clift • Richard Burton • Stewart Granger
Errol Flynn • Gregory Peck • Tyrone Power
James Stewart • Gary Cooper • Henry Fonda

WHO Trivia

Director George Cukor originally wanted Cary Grant, who initially accepted the role of Norman Maine. Although Grant agreed that it was "the role of a lifetime," he changed his mind. Cukor then suggested either Humphrey Bogart or Frank Sinatra. Both were rejected by studio head, Jack L. Warner. Judy Garland suggested John Hodiak, her co-star in *The Harvey Girls*, but he was unavailable.

When Montgomery Clift and Richard Burton both turned down the role of Maine, it left Stewart Granger as the front runner for the role. He backed out when he was unable to adjust to Cukor's habit of acting out scenes as a form of direction. After that, the part was turned down by a Who's Who of leading men.

Finally, Cukor offered Marlon Brando the role of Maine while he was making *Julius Caesar*. Brando's response, "Why would you come to me? I'm in the prime of my life... If you're looking for some actor to play an alcoholic has-been, he's sitting right over there." He then pointed to James Mason.

When the Oscar for Best Actress went to Grace Kelly instead of Judy Garland, Groucho Marx called it "the biggest robbery since Brink's."

DIAL M FOR MURDER (1954)

Margot: Do you really believe in the perfect murder?
Mark: Mmm, yes, absolutely. On paper, that is. And I think I could, uh, plan one better than most people, but I doubt if I could carry it out.
Tony: Oh?... Why not?
Mark: Well, because in stories things usually turn out the way the author wants them to, and in real life they don't... always.

Plot

An ex-tennis pro finds out his unfaithful wife had an affair and decides to murder her, but, when things go wrong, he improvises a brilliant plan B, framing her for first degree murder instead.

CASTING

Who Starred as Tony Wendice?
Ray Milland

Turned Down the Role of Tony Wendice
Cary Grant • William Holden

Who Starred as Margot Wendice?
Grace Kelly

Turned Down the Role of Margot Wendice
Deborah Kerr • Olivia de Havilland

WHO Trivia

Director Alfred Hitchcock's dream cast included Deborah Kerr as Margot Wendice and William Holden as Tony Wendice. Both were busy making other movies and had to turn the roles down

Hitchcock then offered Cary Grant the role of Tony but Grant did not want to play a villain, a role Ray Milland was happy to play.

Olivia de Havilland was offered the role of Margot, but the studio would not meet her asking price so, she turned it down.

For his role as Inspector Hubbard, John Williams won the 1953 Tony Award for Best Featured Actor in the stage production for *Dial M for Murder*; he re-created the role in the film.

Mr. Roberts (1955)

Captain Morton: *(on loudspeaker, referring to his missing palm tree)* All right, who did it? Who did it? You are going to stand sweating at those battle stations until someone confesses! It's an insult to the honor of this ship! The symbol of our cargo record has been destroyed, and I'm going to find out who did if it takes all night!

Plot

In the waning days of World War II, the United States Navy cargo ship Reluctant and her crew are stationed in the "backwater" areas of the Pacific when trouble ensues after the crew members are granted liberty.

CASTING

Who Starred as Lt. Doug Roberts?
Henry Fonda

Turned Down the Role of Lt. Doug Roberts
Marlon Brando • William Holden

Who Starred as "Doc"?
William Powell

Turned Down the Role of "Doc"
Spencer Tracy

WHO Trivia

After Marlon Brando and William Holden both turned down the leading role of Lt. Douglas Roberts, director John Ford got whom he really wanted, Henry Fonda.

Fonda had been reluctant to reprise the title role that he originated on Broadway, for which he won a Tony Award in 1948. It was his relationship with John Ford that changed his mind.

Ironically, during filming, Ford and Fonda had a falling out over the interpretation of the script. The falling out led to Ford punching Fonda in the mouth, virtually ending their sixteen-year personal friendship and professional relationship. Ford left the film before it was finished. Though Ford apologized to Fonda afterward, Fonda only appeared in one more Ford film after that, *How the West Was Won*, in a segment not directed by Ford.

Jack Lemmon got the role of Ensign Pulver after Harry Cohn, the head of Columbia Pictures, agreed to loan him to Ford.

GIANT (1956)

Leslie Benedict: Tell me as soon as we're in Texas.
"Bick" Benedict: Well, that's Texas you been looking at... For the last eight hours.

Plot

When Texas rancher Bick Benedict visits a Maryland farm to buy a prize horse, he meets and falls in love with the owner's daughter Leslie. They are married immediately and return to his ranch where the story of their family and its rivalry with a cowboy, and later oil tycoon, unfolds across two generations.

CASTING

Who Starred as Jett Rink?
James Dean

Turned Down the Role of Jett Rink
Alan Ladd

Who Starred as Leslie Benedict?
Elizabeth Taylor

Turned Down the Role of Leslie Benedict
Ava Gardner • Audrey Hepburn

WHO Trivia

Director/Producer George Stevens considered the following for the lead role of Bick Benedict before offering it to Rock Hudson: Clark Gable, John Wayne, Gary Cooper, William Holden, Henry Fonda, Charlton Heston, James Stewart, Burt Lancaster, Kirk Douglas, and Errol Flynn.

After Ava Gardner and Audrey Hepburn both turned down the role of Leslie, Stevens gave Hudson a choice between Elizabeth Taylor and Grace Kelly to play his leading lady; Hudson chose Taylor.

Stevens favored Alan Ladd, his star of *Shane* who was in the midst of a career decline, to play oilman Jett Rink. Ladd turned the role down, and it was given to James Dean after Stevens considered a number of other actors for the role.

After James Dean's death late in production, Nick Adams was brought in to overdub some of Dean's lines, which were nearly inaudible.

THE TEN COMMANDMENTS (1956)

Moses: Thus sayeth the Lord God of Israel: "Let my people go!"

Plot
The Egyptian Prince, Moses, learns of his true heritage as a Hebrew and his divine mission as the deliverer of his people.

CASTING

Who Starred as Moses?
Charlton Heston

Turned Down the Role of Moses
William Boyd

WHO Trivia
Director/Producer Cecil B. DeMille initially wanted William Boyd to play the role of Moses. Boyd, best known as the cowboy, "Hopalong Cassidy," turned it down out of respect for DeMille, fearing his identification as "Hoppy" would hurt the film.

Charlton Heston, who worked with DeMille on *The Greatest Show on Earth,* was given the part after he impressed DeMille with his knowledge of ancient Egypt during his audition.

Heston was also chosen to be the voice of God in the form of a burning bush, toned down to a softer and lower register. Heston's newborn son, Fraser, was cast as Baby Moses after DeMille found out Heston's wife was pregnant. Fraser was three months old during filming.

The part of Nefretiri was considered "the most sought-after role of the year" in 1954. DeMille initially liked Audrey Hepburn for the part, but dismissed her because of her figure, which was too slim for the character's Egyptian gowns.

After Grace Kelly turned down the role of Sephora, Anne Baxter, was a contender for it. Instead, DeMille decided to cast Baxter as Nefretiri and Yvonne De Carlo as Sephora.

Merle Oberon and Claudette Colbert were both considered for the role of Bithiah. DeMille chose Jayne Meadows, who then declined the role, leaving DeMille to cast Nina Foch in the part.

THE BRIDGE ON THE RIVER KWAI (1957)

Saito: Do you know what will happen to me if the bridge is not built on time?

Col. Nicholson: I haven't the foggiest.

Saito: What would you do if you were me?

Col. Nicholson: I suppose if I were you, I'd have to kill myself.

Plot

After settling his differences with a Japanese P.O.W. camp commander, a British colonel cooperates to oversee his men's construction of a railway bridge for their captors, while oblivious to a plan by the Allies to destroy it.

CASTING

Who Starred as Shears?
William Holden

Turned Down the Role of Shears
Cary Grant • Rock Hudson

Who Starred as Colonel Nicholson?
Alec Guinness

Turned Down the Role of Colonel Nicholson
Laurence Olivier • Charles Laughton

WHO Trivia

The initial screenplay by Carl Foreman was written with Humphrey Bogart in mind for the role of Commander Shears, but Bogart was contractually committed to another film and had to turn the role down.

Producer Sam Spiegel's first choice for the role of Shears was Cary Grant. When offered the part, Grant turned it down. Rock Hudson then turned down the role choosing to make *A Farewell to Arms* instead. Eventually, realizing the film needed a movie star, Spiegel cast William Holden.

Spiegel tried to persuade Spencer Tracy to play the part of Col. Nicholson. Tracy told Spiegel emphatically that an Englishman must play the part. Spiegel offered the role of Nicholson to Sir Laurence Olivier who turned it down to direct *The Princess and the Showgirl*. Charles Laughton was then cast, but he dropped out because he couldn't stand the climate in Ceylon. Alec Guinness, who had initially turned down the role, changed his mind and replaced him, ironically winning an Academy Award for Best Actor.

CAT ON A HOT TIN ROOF (1958)

Brick: You'll make out fine. Your kind always does.
Maggie: Oh, I'm more determined than you think. I'll win all right.
Brick: Win what? What is, uh, the victory of a cat on a hot tin roof?
Maggie: Just stayin' on it, I guess. As long as she can.

Plot
An alcoholic ex-football player drinks his days away and resists the affections of his wife. His reunion with his father, who is dying of cancer, jogs a host of memories and revelations for both father and son.

CASTING

Who Starred as Brick Pollitt?
Paul Newman

Turned Down the Role of Brick Pollitt
Ben Gazzara • Elvis Presley
Montgomery Clift • Robert Mitchum

Who Starred as Maggie The Cat?
Elizabeth Taylor

Turned Down the Role of Maggie The Cat
Carroll Baker

WHO Trivia
Ben Gazzara who played Brick in the stage production rejected the film role as did Elvis Presley, Montgomery Clift and Robert Mitchum.

James Dean was set to play the part, but died before production began.

Carroll Baker was offered the role of Maggie The Cat, but after turning down three films in a row, Warner Bros. decided to punish Baker by refusing to loan her out to MGM. Lana Turner, Grace Kelly, and Ava Gardner were considered for the role. It is said that Marilyn Monroe actually sought out the role. Eventually, Elizabeth Taylor was cast as Maggie The Cat.

Production began on March 12, 1958. By March 19, Taylor had contracted a virus which kept her off the shoot. On March 21, she canceled plans to fly with her husband Mike Todd to New York, where he was to be honored the following day. The plane crashed, and all passengers, including Todd, died. Beset with grief, Taylor remained off the film until April 14, when she returned to the set in a much thinner and weaker condition.

BEN-HUR (1959)

Judah Ben-Hur: I would do anything for you, Messala, except betray my own people.

Messala: In the name of all the gods, Judah, what do the lives of a few Jews mean to you?

Plot

A Jewish prince is betrayed and sent into slavery by a Roman friend, but later regains his freedom and returns for revenge.

CASTING

Who Starred as Judah Ben-Hur?
Charlton Heston

Turned Down the Role of Judah Ben-Hur
Burt Lancaster • Paul Newman
Kirk Douglas • Rock Hudson

Who Starred as Messala?
Stephen Boyd

Turned Down the Role of Messala
Charlton Heston • Stewart Granger • Robert Ryan

WHO Trivia

The film was originally intended to be made in 1956 with Marlon Brando in the lead role and Stewart Granger as Messala, but production was delayed. When the production resumed, Burt Lancaster turned down the role of Moses because he found the script boring and belittling to Christianity.

Paul Newman turned down the role because he said he didn't have the legs to wear a tunic. MGM then offered $750,000 to Universal if they would loan out Rock Hudson, who refused the role, choosing the lead in *A Farewell to Arms* instead.

Kirk Douglas was offered the role of Messala, but turned it down because he wanted to play Judah Ben-Hur.

Director William Wyler originally wanted Heston for the role of Messala, but had to find another actor after he casted Heston to play Judah Ben-Hur. That actor turned out to be Stephen Boyd.

NORTH BY NORTHWEST (1959)

Thornhill: Mother, this is your son, Roger Thornhill... No, no, Mother.
I have not been drinking. No, no. These two men, they
poured a whole bottle of bourbon into me... No, they
didn't give me a chaser.

Plot

An advertising executive is mistaken for a spy and is pursued across the
country while looking for a way to survive.

CASTING

Who Starred as Eve Kendall?
Eva Marie Saint

Turned Down the Role of Eve Kendall
Kim Novak • Grace Kelly • Sophia Loren

WHO Trivia

In order to reduce the budget, MGM suggested their own actors under
contract, Gregory Peck and Cyd Charisse, for the leading roles of Roger O.
Thornhill and Eve Kendall. Director Alfred Hitchcock refused, citing that in
his contract he had final say over the principal cast.

While filming *Vertigo,* Hitchcock described some of the plot of this project
to James Stewart, who assumed Hitchcock meant to cast him in the lead role
of Roger Thornhill; Stewart was eager to play it.

Actually, Hitchcock wanted Cary Grant for the role of Thornhill. By the time
Hitchcock realized the misunderstanding with Stewart, he thought rejecting
Stewart would cause problems in the future. Hitchcock decided to delay the
production until Stewart was safely committed to another movie. The result
was that Stewart had to turn down the role of Roger Thornhill, which left
Hitchcock free to offer it to his number one choice, Cary Grant.

Initially, Hitchcock wanted Kim Novak for the role of Eve Kendall, but
she was not available. He then turned to Grace Kelly, now the Princess of
Monaco, but she turned him down. Cary Grant suggested Sophia Loren. She
also turned down the role. Finally, Eva Marie Saint was cast.

When Yul Brynner proved to be unavailable to play baddie Phillip Vandamm;
Hitchcock cast James Mason in the role.

SOME LIKE IT HOT (1959)

Jerry/Daphne:	Well, I have a terrible past. For three years now, I've been living with a saxophone player.
Osgood:	I forgive you.
Jerry/Daphne:	I can never have children!
Osgood:	We can adopt some.
Jerry/Daphne:	But you don't understand, Osgood! *(Whips off his wig, changes to manly voice)* Uhhh, I'm a man!
Osgood:	*(Looks at him then turns back, unperturbed)* Well, nobody's perfect!

Plot

After accidentally witnessing the Saint Valentine's Day Massacre, two musicians disguise themselves as women and flee with an all-female band.

CASTING

Who Starred as Jerry/Daphne?
Jack Lemmon

Turned Down the Role of Jerry/Daphne
Frank Sinatra • Jerry Lewis

WHO Trivia

Director/Producer/Writer Billy Wilder first spotted Tony Curtis while he was making Houdini, and thought he'd be perfect for the role of Joe/Josephine. Curtis was the first actor Wilder cast.

Wilder originally wanted Frank Sinatra as Jerry/Daphne, but Sinatra turned it down. Wilder then offered the role to Jerry Lewis, who also turned it down saying he didn't want to dress in drag. Wilder then wanted Jack Lemmon for the role, but United Artists pressured him to cast a bigger box-office name.

At the same time, Wilder always had Mitzi Gaynor in mind for the role of Sugar Kane Kowalczyk, never thinking such a big star as Marilyn Monroe would take the part. When Monroe made it known that she really wanted the part of Sugar, Wilder knew he had to have her. They had worked together four years earlier on *The Seven Year Itch*.

Once Marilyn Monroe signed on, Wilder was able to cast Jack Lemmon in the role that got him his first Academy Award nomination.

Bonus Movies

Annie Get Your Gun (1950)

When Judy Garland was fired during filming, Betty Grable lobbied producer Darryl F. Zanuck to loan her to MGM, but he refused. Betty Hutton was then cast in the role. director After director Busby Berkeley was fired, he was replaced by Charles Walters who was also fired and replaced by George Sidney.

Strangers on a Train (1951)

Director Alfred Hitchcock said that he originally wanted Willian Holden for the Guy Haines role, played by Farley Granger, but Holden declined.

"Holden would have been all wrong — too sturdy, too put off by Bruno", wrote critic Roger Ebert. "Granger is softer and more elusive, more convincing as he tries to slip out of Bruno's conversational web instead of flatly rejecting him."

In the casting of Anne Morton, Warner Brothers got what they wanted when they assigned Ruth Roman, under contract to the studio, to the project, in spite of Hitchcock's objections. Perhaps it was the circumstances of her forced casting, but Roman became the target of Hitchcock's scorn throughout the production. Farley Granger diplomatically described it as Hitchcock's "disinterest" in the actress, and said, "Hitchcock always had to have one person in each film he could harass."

The African Queen (1952)

The first version of the film in 1938 had David Niven and Bette Davis in the lead roles, but financing never materialized. Two years later, Bette Davis was paired with John Mills, but again the film never happened. A year later, RKO proposed Charles Laughton and his wife Elsa Lanchester in the lead roles. Once again, nothing materialized.

Then in 1947, Bette Davis was offered the lead again, with James Mason as her counterpart, but Davis had to turn it down because she was pregnant, causing Mason to drop out because he wanted to do it with Davis, or not do the film at all.

Finally, in 1951, the film was shot, starring Humphrey Bogart, in his only Oscar winning role and Katharine Hepburn. Bette Davis was still interested in playing Rose Sayer, but the cast was set.

Stalag 17 (1953)

Charlton Heston was originally considered for the lead role of J.J. Sefton, but when the script was altered to make the character less heroic, Heston dropped out.

Kirk Douglas was next in line, but he turned down the role, making their third choice, William Holden, the choice to play the role. John Ericson who played Sefton in the original stage version, was not considered a big enough name for the film version.

East of Eden (1955)

Age played a major role in the casting. Director Elia Kazan first toyed with the idea of Marlon Brando as Cal and Montgomery Clift as Aron, but at 30 and 34 years old, respectively, they were simply too old to play teenage brothers.

Paul Newman, one year younger than Brando, was a finalist for the part of Cal, which was eventually played by James Dean, six years younger than Newman.

Guys and Dolls (1955)

In 1952, Paramount announced this film would be made with Bob Hope and Bing Crosby in the leading roles. After the film was delayed, Samuel Goldwyn considered casting Dean Martin and Jerry Lewis. Again, the film was shelved.

Finally, when the film did go into production, it was Marlon Brando who was cast as Sky Masterson over Gene Kelly and Frank Sinatra. Sinatra was in the film, but in the role of Nathan Detroit. Grace Kelly turned down the role of Salvation Army do-gooder Sarah Brown, which was played by Jean Simmons.

Rebel Without a Cause (1955)

All three leading actors died prematurely and under very tragic circumstances: James Dean in an automobile accident in 1955, Sal Mineo was stabbed to death in 1976, and Natalie Wood drowned in 1981.

According to a biography of Natalie Wood, she almost did not get the role of Judy because director Nicholas Ray thought she didn't fit the role of the wild teenage character.

Then, while on a night out with friends, she got into a car accident, causing Ray to rush to the hospital. While in delirium, Wood overheard the doctor murmuring, calling her a "goddamn juvenile delinquent"; she yelled to Ray, "Did you hear what he called me, Nick? He called me a goddamn juvenile delinquent! Do I get the part now?"

The Man Who Knew Too Much (1956)

Director Alfred Hitchcock again cast James Stewart to be his protagonist as he considered the actor a creative partner.

Alfred Hitchcock requested blonde Doris Day to play the main female role, "Jo" Conway McKenna, based on her performance in *Storm Warning*. Producer Herbert Coleman was reluctant to cast Day, whom he only knew as a singer. Coleman strongly suggested that a more serious blonde actress like Lana Turner, Grace Kelly, or Kim Novak be cast in the role.

Coleman then suggested casting a brunette, like Jane Russell, Gene Tierney, or Ava Gardner. Finally, Hitchcock insisted on Doris Day and she was cast.

The Man With the Golden Arm (1956)

John Garfield was originally attached to star as Frankie Machine, but died before production began. The studio then decided to offer the role to Marlon Brando and Frank Sinatra at the same time, with Sinatra accepting before Brando could even respond.

Lauren Bacall turned down the role of Zosh Machine because the studio wouldn't meet her quote. Eleanor Parker was cast in the role.

Gigi (1958)

Audrey Hepburn turned down the lead role of Gigi, exhausted after playing the role on Broadway. Leslie Caron was then cast in the role.

Dirk Bogarde was first choice to play Gaston, but couldn't get out of his British Rank Organization contract in order to go to Hollywood, thus leaving the role to Louis Jourdan.

South Pacific (1958)

The producers' original plan was to have Ezio Pinza and Mary Martin, the two leads of the original Broadway cast, reprise their roles for the film, but Pinza died suddenly in May, 1957. Had he lived to perform in the film, the producers would have cast Martin.

Doris Day was then offered the role of Nellie, but she turned it down when the studio would not meet her quote. Audrey Hepburn, Janet Leigh, Jane Powell, Debbie Reynolds, and Elizabeth Taylor were all considered. Ultimately, Mitzi Gaynor was cast because of her prior work in musical films.

Vertigo (1958)

Miles

Alfred Hitchcock originally wanted to cast Lana Turner as Judy, but she "wanted too much loot." Vera Mills, under contract to Columbia, was then cast. But she got pregnant and became unavailable. Columbia head Harry Cohn agreed to lend Kim Novak to *Vertigo* if James Stewart would agree to co-star with Novak in *Bell, Book, and Candle,* plus $250,000.

This movie was unavailable for three decades because its rights, along with four other movies, were bought back by Alfred Hitchcock, and left as part of his legacy to his daughter. The four other films: *Rope* (1948), *Rear Window* (1954), *The Trouble with Harry* (1955), and *The Man Who Knew Too Much* (1956) were all released with *Vertigo* around 1984.

Rio Bravo (1959)

Director Howard Hawks offered Montgomery Clift the role of Dude, the alcoholic deputy, but Clift turned down the opportunity to work with his Red River co-star John Wayne. Dean Martin was cast instead.

Holly Golightly • Paul Varjak • "Fast Eddie" Felson • Sarah Packard
Minnesota Fats • Maria • Tony • James Bond • Dr. No • T. E. Lawrence
Prince Faisal • Sherif Ali • The Man With No Name • Humbert Humbert
Lolita • Dr. Zhivago • Lara • Victor Komarovsky • Maria Von Trapp
Captain Von Trapp • Major Reisman • Archie Maggott • Benjamin Braddock
Mrs. Robinson • Elaine Robinson • Rosemary Woodhouse • Guy Woodhouse
Fanny Brice • Nicky Arnstein • Bob • Carol • Ted • Alice • Butch Cassidy
Sundance Kid • Ratso Rizzo • Joe Buck • Rooster Cogburn • Mattie Ross
Danny Ocean • Vin Tanner • Spartacus • Apple Annie • Prof. Harold Hill
Marian the Librarian • Anne Sullivan • Helen Keller • Inspector Clouseau

1960s

Atticus Finch • John F. Kennedy • Mary Poppins • Sol Nazerman • Loana
Sir Thomas Moore • Lancey Howard • Alfie • Jake Holman • Clyde Barrow
Bonnie Parker • Lucas Jackson • Dragline • Richard Hickock • Perry Smith
Barbarella • Felix Unger • Oscar Madison • George Hanson • Thomas Crown
Max Bialystock • Leibkind • Gloria Beatty • Robert Syverton • Pike Bishop
Holly Golightly • Paul Varjak • "Fast Eddie" Felson • Sarah Packard
Minnesota Fats • Maria • Tony • James Bond • Dr. No • T. E. Lawrence
Prince Faisal • Sherif Ali • The Man With No Name • Humbert Humbert
Lolita • Dr. Zhivago • Lara • Victor Komarovsky • Maria Von Trapp
Captain Von Trapp • Major Reisman • Archie Maggott • Benjamin Braddock
Mrs. Robinson • Elaine Robinson • Rosemary Woodhouse • Guy Woodhouse
Fanny Brice • Nicky Arnstein • Bob • Carol • Ted • Alice • Butch Cassidy
Sundance Kid • Ratso Rizzo • Joe Buck • Rooster Cogburn • Mattie Ross
Danny Ocean • Vin Tanner • Spartacus • Apple Annie • Prof. Harold Hill
Marian the Librarian • Anne Sullivan • Helen Keller • Inspector Clouseau
Atticus Finch • John F. Kennedy • Mary Poppins • Sol Nazerman • Loana
Sir Thomas Moore • Lancey Howard • Alfie • Jake Holman • Clyde Barrow
Bonnie Parker • Lucas Jackson • Dragline • Richard Hickock • Perry Smith
Barbarella • Felix Unger • Oscar Madison • George Hanson • Thomas Crown
Max Bialystock • Leibkind • Gloria Beatty • Robert Syverton • Pike Bishop
Holly Golightly • Paul Varjak • "Fast Eddie" Felson • Sarah Packard
Minnesota Fats • Maria • Tony • James Bond • Dr. No • T. E. Lawrence
Prince Faisal • Sherif Ali • The Man With No Name • Humbert Humbert
Lolita • Dr. Zhivago • Lara • Victor Komarovsky • Maria Von Trapp
Captain Von Trapp • Major Reisman • Archie Maggott • Benjamin Braddock
Mrs. Robinson • Elaine Robinson • Rosemary Woodhouse • Guy Woodhouse
Fanny Brice • Nicky Arnstein • Bob • Carol • Ted • Alice • Butch Cassidy
Sundance Kid • Ratso Rizzo • Joe Buck • Rooster Cogburn • Mattie Ross

A Reflection of the Country

The films of this decade reflected tremendous cultural and social changes occurring in American society. It was a turbulent decade identified by the Cuban Missile Crisis, assassination of JFK, Vietnam protests, the Beatles, color television, riots in Watts, Sesame Street, the first microchip and first Barbie doll, man walking on the moon, and Woodstock.

The 1960s saw the traditional Hollywood studio era disappearing. Both foreign and domestic business conglomerates acquired more and more studios, and with the high cost of making films in Hollywood, studios decreased production in the United States and increased moviemaking outside the country.

In 1962, the major studios became financiers and distributors of foreign made films, like *Dr. Zhivago*, *A Man For All Seasons*, and *Lawrence of Arabia*.

In 1963, the worst year in history for major film production in the United States, only 121 feature films were released. The next year, 361 foreign films were released in the United States, as opposed to 141 films produced in America and released.

With movie audiences declining due to the dominance of television, Hollywood film companies began to diversify, getting into the record and publishing business, and the production of series for television. Made-for-TV movies became a regular feature of network programming.

By the mid-60s, the average movie ticket price was less than a dollar, the average film budget was slightly over one and a half million dollars, and studio-bound "contract stars" were no longer. Even with that trend, Hollywood was not giving up on producing great movies and believed the major motion picture still had life.

The 1960s gave us some great comedies: Jerry Lewis as *The Nutty Professor*; super sleuth, Inspector Clouseau premiered in *The Pink Panther*; former blacklisted Zero Mostel starred in *The Producers*, and *A Funny Thing Happened on the Way to the Forum*.

Westerns had a revival beginning in 1960 with *The Magnificent Seven*. In 1964, Clint Eastwood starred in the first of *The Man With No Name* films, reinventing the genre with profitable Italian-made "spaghetti westerns."

Elvis Presley made his film debut in *Love Me Tender*, following it up by releasing over a dozen Presley movies by 1964. George Roy Hill ended the decade with *Butch Cassidy and the Sundance Kid*.

Though musicals had declined in popularity, three were among the screen's greatest spectacles: *West Side Story, My Fair Lady* and *The Sound of Music*. Alfred Hitchcock opened the decade with his shocking thriller, *Psycho*, his masterpiece of both horror and effective psychological tension. The first James Bond film, *Doctor No*, kicked off the franchise, while the Beatles joined the British film invasion with *A Hard Day's Night*.

What stands out most when looking at the 1960s impact on the film industry is that censorship eased its grip on content. A new freedom of language, subject matter and permissiveness was expressed in such films as: *The Apartment, Days of Wine and Roses, Butterfield 8*, and *La Dolce Vita*.

Director Elia Kazan's *Splendor in the Grass*, a love story between two high school students in a small Kansas town, featured Hollywood's first on-screen, open-mouthed kiss between Natalie Wood and newcomer Warren Beatty. *To Kill a Mockingbird* was an adaptation of Harper Lee's novel about a 1930s small-town, widowed southern lawyer who defended a falsely accused black man against charges of the rape of a white woman. Stanley Kubrick's *Lolita* dealt with the sensitive topic of pedophilia, and producer/director Otto Preminger's political courtroom drama *Advise & Consent* involved homosexuality.

In November 1968, a new *voluntary* ratings code replacing the decades-old Production Code was announced. Ratings were to be enforced by theaters, distributors and exhibitors, with four categories: "G" (general audiences or suitable for all ages), "M" (suggested for mature audiences, soon changed to "PG" for 'parental guidance' suggested), "R" (restricted audiences - no one under age 16 admitted without an accompanying adult) and "X" (for those 16 years and older, "not suitable for children.") It was a new beginning.

The Academy Awards

1960
Best Picture: ***The Apartment***
Best Actor: Burt Lancaster (*Elmer Gantry*)
Best Actress: Elizabeth Taylor (*Butterfield 8*)
Best Supporting Actor: Peter Ustinov (*Spartacus*)
Best Supporting Actress: Shirley Jones (*Elmer Gantry*)

1961
Best Picture: ***West Side Story***
Best Actor: Maximilian Schell (*Judgment at Nuremberg*)
Best Actress: Sophia Loren (*Two Women*)
Best Supporting Actor: George Chakiris (*West Side Story*)
Best Supporting Actress: Rita Moreno (*West Side Story*)

1962
Best Picture: ***Lawrence of Arabia*** ✰
Best Actor: Gregory Peck (*To Kill a Mockingbird*)
Best Actress: Anne Bancroft (*The Miracle Worker*)
Best Supporting Actor: Ed Begley (*Sweet Bird of Youth*)
Best Supporting Actress: Patty Duke (*The Miracle Worker*)

1963
Best Picture: ***Tom Jones***
Best Actor: Sidney Poitier (*Lilies of the Field*)
Best Actress: Patricia Neal (*Hud*)
Best Supporting Actor: Melvyn Douglas (*Hud*)
Best Supporting Actress: Margaret Rutherford (*The V.I.P.s*)

1964
Best Picture: ***My Fair Lady***
Best Actor: Rex Harrison (*My Fair Lady*)
Best Actress: Julie Andrews (*Mary Poppins*)
Best Supporting Actor: Peter Ustinov (*Topkapi*)
Best Supporting Actress: Lila Kedrova (*Zorba the Greek*)

1965

Best Picture: ***The Sound of Music***

Best Actor: Lee Marvin (*Cat Ballou*)

Best Actress: Julie Christie (*Darling*)

Best Supporting Actor: Martin Balsam (*A Thousand Clowns*)

Best Supporting Actress: Shelley Winters (*A Patch of Blue*)

1966

Best Picture: ***A Man for All Seasons***

Best Actor: Paul Scofield (*A Man for All Seasons*)

Best Actress: Elizabeth Taylor (*Who's Afraid of Virginia Woolf*)

Best Supporting Actor: Walter Matthau (*The Fortune Cookie*)

Best Supporting Actress: Sandy Dennis (*Who's Afraid of Virginia Woolf*)

1967

Best Picture: ***In the Heat of the Night***

Best Actor: Rod Steiger (*In the Heat of the Night*)

Best Actress: Katharine Hepburn (*Guess Who's Coming to Dinner*)

Best Supporting Actor: George Kennedy (*Cool Hand Luke*)

Best Supporting Actress: Estelle Parsons (*Bonnie and Clyde*)

1968

Best Picture: ***Oliver***

Best Actor: Cliff Robertson (*Charlie*)

Best Actress: Katharine Hepburn (*The Lion in Winter*)

Barbara Streisand (*Funny Girl*)

Best Supporting Actor: Jack Albertson (*The Subject Was Roses*)

Best Supporting Actress: Ruth Gordon (*Rosemary's Baby*)

1969

Best Picture: ***Midnight Cowboy***

Best Actor: John Wayne (*True Grit*)

Best Actress: Maggie Smith (*The Prime of Miss Jean Brodie*)

Best Supporting Actor: Gig Young (*They Shoot Horses, Don't They?*)

Best Supporting Actress: Goldie Hawn (*Cactus Flower*)

Casting Trivia Quiz

1. Paul Newman was nominated for an Oscar for his role as pool shark "Fast Eddie" Felson in **The Hustler** after the role was turned down by:
   - a. Steve McQueen
   - b. Marlon Brando
   - c. Bobby Darin
   - d. William Holden

2. **West Side Story** featured Richard Beymer as Maria's star-crossed lover, Tony, as this actor turned down the role:
   - a. Richard Chamberlain
   - b. Warren Beatty
   - c. Tab Hunter
   - d. Elvis Presley

3. This actor was the original choice to play James Bond in **Dr. No**, but he would only commit to one film and not to the potential series:
   - a. Cary Grant
   - b. Dean Martin
   - c. Steve Reeves
   - d. None of the above

4. In Barbra Streisand's classic, **Funny Girl,** the role of Nicky Arnstein, played by Omar Sharif, was originally offered to:
   - a. James Garner
   - b. Marlon Brando
   - c. David Janssen
   - d. Frank Sinatra

5. In **The Cincinnati Kid,** Lancey Howard was played by Edward G. Robinson, but the role was originally intended for:
   - a. Yul Brynner
   - b. Spencer Tracy
   - c. James Mason
   - d. Errol Flynn

6. In **The Graduate,** Mrs. Robinson was played by Anne Bancroft after this actress turned down the role:
   - a. Doris Day
   - b. Ava Gardner
   - c. Sophia Loren
   - d. Jean Simmons

7. Dustin Hoffman played Benjamin Braddock in **The Graduate** after the role was turned down by this soon-to-be major movie star:
   - a. Robert Redford
   - b. Steve McQueen
   - c. Warren Beatty
   - d. Al Pacino

8. In **The Thomas Crown Affair,** Steve McQueen starred as the title character after the role was originally turned down by:
   - a. Paul Newman
   - b. Ronald Reagan
   - c. Cary Grant
   - d. Sean Connery

9. In **Butch Cassidy and the Sundance Kid,** the role of the Sundance, made Robert Redford a star. The role was originally offered to:
   - a. Jack Lemmon
   - b. Tony Curtis
   - c. Gregory Peck
   - d. Paul Newman

10. Lee Marvin played the lead role of Major Reisman in the WWII action film, **The Dirty Dozen.** The role was turned down by this actor:
   - a. John Wayne
   - b. Kirk Douglas
   - c. Robert Ryan
   - d. Jack Palance

11. Gene Wilder played Leo Bloom, in Mel Brooks' **The Producers** opposite Zero Mostel as Max Bialystock, but the role was originally turned down by:
   - a. Jack Lemmon
   - b. Dustin Hoffman
   - c. Peter Sellers
   - d. Harpo Marx

12. When **The Producers** puts on the worst show ever, *Springtime for Hitler,* Kenneth Mars played Franz Liebkind. The role of Liebkind was going to be played by this rising star before he dropped out:
   - a. Robert DeNiro
   - b. Warren Beatty
   - c. Dustin Hoffman
   - d. Charles Grodin

13. Omar Sharif played the lead role in the classic **Dr. Zhivago** after the role had been turned down by:
   - a. Paul Newman
   - b. Max von Sydow
   - c. Peter O'Toole
   - d. All of the Above

14. In **Easy Rider,** George Hanson is played by Jack Nicholson. The role was first offered to:
   - a. Al Pacino
   - b. Robert De Niro
   - c. Rip Torn
   - d. Elvis Presley

15. Robert Blake and Scott Wilson played the killers in Richard Brooks' drama, **In Cold Blood.** Columbia wanted this duo to play the roles:
   - a. Robert De Niro & Al Pacino
   - b. Paul Newman & Steve McQueen
   - c. James Caan & Robert Duvall
   - d. Telly Savalas & George Kennedy

BREAKFAST AT TIFFANY'S (1961)

Holly: Thursday! It can't be! It's too gruesome!
Paul: What's so gruesome about Thursday?
Holly: Nothing, except I can never remember when it's coming up.

Plot

A New York socialite becomes interested in a young man who has moved into her apartment building, but her past threatens to get in her way.

CASTING

Who Starred as Holly Golightly?
Audrey Hepburn

Turned Down the Role of Holly Golightly
Marilyn Monroe • Shirley MacLaine • Kim Novak

Who Starred as Paul Varjak?
George Peppard

Turned Down the Role of Paul Varjak
Steve McQueen

WHO Trivia

Writer Truman Capote was very excited when Marilyn Monroe was cast as Holly Golightly; Capote considered her perfect for the role. Lee Strasberg, her drama coach at the time, advised Monroe that playing a "lady of the evening" would be bad for her image. Monroe changed her mind and turned down the role of Holly Golightly. Shirley MacLaine and Kim Novak also turned it down.

Finally, the role was offered to Audrey Hepburn, who wasn't comfortable with director John Frankenheimer. Hepburn insisted he be replaced, and he was with Blake Edwards.

In his autobiography, Tony Curtis talks about really wanting to play the role of writer Paul Varjak. Curtis asked his friend, director Blake Edwards, to cast him. This caused a problem because Mel Ferrer, Audrey Hepburn's husband, didn't want her to make a movie with Curtis, so Edwards said no.

Steve McQueen was offered the role of Paul Varjak while he was under contract for the television show, *Wanted: Dead or Alive*. He had to turn it down allowing George Peppard to take the part.

THE HUSTLER (1961)

"Fast Eddie": Well, you don't leave much when you miss, do ya, Fat Man?

Minnesota Fats: That's what the game's all about.

Plot

An up-and-coming pool player plays a longtime champion in a marathon high-stakes match.

CASTING

Who Starred as "Fast Eddie" Felson?
Paul Newman

Turned Down the Role of "Fast Eddie" Felson
Tony Curtis • Jack Lemmon • Paul Newman

Who Starred as Sarah Packard?
Piper Laurie

Turned Down the Role of Sarah Packard
Kim Novak

WHO Trivia

Tony Curtis and Jack Lemmon turned down the role of "Fast Eddie" Felson. According to Bobby Darin's agent, Martin Baum, Paul Newman's agent turned down the part of "Fast Eddie" because Newman was unavailable, committed to star opposite Elizabeth Taylor in *Two for the Seesaw*. Director Robert Rossen then offered Bobby Darin the part of "Fast Eddie."

When Elizabeth Taylor was forced to drop out of *Two for the Seesaw* because of shooting overruns on *Cleopatra*, Newman was freed up to take the lead role of "Fast Eddie." Taylor was replaced by Shirley MacLaine, and Newman by Robert Mitchum when *Two for the Seesaw* finally went into production. Nobody associated with the production officially notified Darin or his representatives that he had been replaced; they found out from a member of the public at a charity horse race.

Jackie Gleason was hustling pool when he was 14 years old, and did all of his pool shots himself. Newman, on the other hand, knew nothing about the sport, but pool legend Willie Mosconi worked with him; Newman did most of his own pool shots in the movie.

WEST SIDE STORY (1961)

Tony: I didn't believe hard enough.
Maria: Loving is enough.
Tony: Not here. They won't let us be.

Plot
The film adaptation of the same-titled musical play about two lovers heavily entangled in two rival New York City gangs.

CASTING

Who Starred as Maria?
Natalie Wood

Turned Down the Role of Maria
Audrey Hepburn • Diane Baker

Who Starred as Tony?
Richard Beymer

Turned Down the Role of Tony
Elvis Presley

WHO Trivia
A major controversy developed because Carol Lawrence, who played Maria in the stage version and won a Tony Award for her performance, was passed over because of her age; she was 29. Audrey Hepburn was offered the film role, turning it down because she was pregnant. Diane Baker also turned it down.

Elvis Presley was offered the role of Tony. His manager, Colonel Tom Parker, turned it down because Elvis would only sing six of twelve songs in the film, and because he would not have exclusive rights to the soundtrack.

Tab Hunter, then 30, and Burt Reynolds, then 25, were considered, but they were dismissed because of their age. Additionally, Reynolds was considered "too tough" for the part. Richard Chamberlain auditioned, but was deemed "too mature." Russ Tamblyn impressed Robert Wise, the producer, when he auditioned and was given the supporting role of Riff.

When considering Warren Beatty for the role of Tony, Robert Wise viewed a clip from *Splendor in the Grass* that included Natalie Wood. The producers decided Natalie Wood was perfect for Maria, but that Warren Beatty was not suitable for the role of Tony.

DR. NO (1962)

James Bond: I admire your courage, Miss ...?
Sylvia Trench: Trench. Sylvia Trench. I admire your luck, Mr. ...?
James Bond: Bond... James Bond.

Plot

James Bond's investigation of a missing colleague in Jamaica leads him to the island of the mysterious Dr. No and a scheme to end the U.S. space program. It was the first film in the James Bond series.

CASTING

Who Starred as James Bond?
Sean Connery

Turned Down the Role of James Bond
Cary Grant • Richard Johnson • Steve Reeves
Patrick McGoohan • Stephen Boyd

WHO Trivia

Producers Albert Broccoli and Harry Saltzman originally came to an oral agreement with Cary Grant for the role of James Bond, but Grant would only commit to one feature film; the producers decided to go after someone who could be part of a series.-

Richard Johnson was the next choice, but he also turned it down because of the required three-picture commitment. Steve Reeves, the body builder, was offered the role for $100,000, but turned it down because he was making $250,000 playing *Hercules*. Patrick McGoohan, on the strength of his portrayal of spy John Drake in the television series *Danger Man*, was offered the role, but turned it down, as did Stephen Boyd.

Ultimately, the producers turned to Sean Connery for five films. It is often reported that Connery won the role through a contest, "Find James Bond."

In his autobiography, *"When the Snow Melts,"* Cubby Broccoli said Roger Moore had been considered, but was thought to be "too young, perhaps a shade too pretty." In Moore's autobiography, *My Word Is My Bond,* he says he was never approached to play the role of Bond at that time.

Noel Coward turned down the role of Dr. No, played by Joseph Wiseman.

LAWRENCE OF ARABIA (1962)

Lawrence: Sherif Ali, so long as the Arabs fight tribe against tribe, so long will they be a little people, a silly people, greedy, barbarous, and cruel, as you are.

Plot
Loosely based on the life of T.E. Lawrence, a flamboyant and controversial British military figure, and his conflicted loyalties during wartime service.

CASTING

Who Starred as T.E. Lawrence?
Peter O'Toole

Turned Down the Role of T.E Lawrence
Marlon Brando

Who Starred as Prince Faisal?
Alec Guinness

Turned Down the Role of Prince Faisal
Lawrence Olivier

Who Starred as Sherif Ali?
Omar Sharif

Turned Down the Role of Sherif Ali
Horst Buchholz • Alain Delon

WHO Trivia
After Marlon Brando turned down the lead role of Lawrence, Albert Finney, virtually unknown at the time, was director David Lean's choice to play the role. He was cast, and principal photography began. But Finney was fired after two days and replaced by Peter O'Toole

The role of Prince Faisal was to be portrayed by Laurence Olivier. When he dropped out, Alec Guinness who had performed in other David Lean films, got the part of Prince Faisal.

The casting for Sherif Ali was bizarre. Horst Buchholz had to turn it down due to his commitment to the film, *One Two Three*. Second choice Alain Delon turned it down for medical reasons. Finally, Maurice Ronet was cast, but had to be replaced due to language difficulties. Omar Sharif, who was previously cast as Lawrence's guide, Tafas, was then shifted to play the part.

LOLITA (1962)

Lolita: Hey, let's tell mother.
Humbert: Tell mother what?
Lolita: You know what.
Humbert: No, I don't think that would be very funny.
Lolita: I wonder what she'd do? Hmm?

Plot
A middle-aged college professor of literature becomes sexually obsessed with a 14-year-old nymphet.

CASTING

Who Starred as Prof. Humbert Humbert?
James Mason

Turned Down the Role of Prof. Humbert Humbert
Marlon Brando • Cary Grant
Laurence Olivier • David Niven

Who Starred as Lolita?
Sue Lyon

Turned Down the Role of Lolita
Jill Haworth • Joey Heatherton • Tuesday Weld

WHO Trivia
Director Stanley Kubrick's first choice for the role of Humbert Humbert was James Mason, but he initially declined due to a Broadway engagement. After Laurence Olivier refused the part, Producer James Harris suggested David Niven who accepted, but then withdrew for fear the sponsors of his TV show would object. Mason then withdrew from his play and got the part.

Jill Haworth was asked to take the role of Lolita, but she was under contract to Otto Preminger, and he refused to allow it. Joey Heatherton's father refused to let his daughter star in the film, and Tuesday Weld turned the role down. Finally, the role was given to Sue Lyon, who was 14 at the time of filming.

Owing to the MPAA's restrictions at the time, the film toned down the more provocative aspects of the novel, sometimes leaving much to the audience's imagination. Kubrick later commented that if he had realized how severe the censorship limitations were going to be, he probably would never have even attempted to make the film.

A FISTFUL OF DOLLARS (1964)

Don Miguel: That's the right idea? You didn't misunderstand?
Joe: I get the wrong idea only when it suits me.
Ramon: You are well informed, eh?
Joe: A man's life in these parts often depends on a mere scrap of information. Your brother's own words.
Ramon: Tell me. Why are you doing this for us?
Joe: (Holds out his hand)
Five hundred dollars.

Plot
A wandering gunfighter playing two rival families against each other in a town torn apart by greed, pride, and revenge.

CASTING

Who Starred as Man With No Name?
Clint Eastwood

Turned Down the Role of Man With No Name
James Coburn • Charles Bronson
Richard Harrison • Eric Fleming

WHO Trivia
Director Sergio Leone first offered the role of the 'Man with No Name' to James Coburn who was too expensive. Charles Bronson turned it down, describing it as the "worst script I have ever seen."

Leone's next choice, Richard Harrison, also declined the role, but pointed Leone in the direction of the television show *Rawhide*. Leone then offered the part to *Rawhide* star, Eric Fleming, who turned it down, but suggested his co-star Clint Eastwood. The rest as they say is history. Eastwood was paid $15,000 for the role.

A Fistful of Dollars was intended by Leone to reinvent the western genre. In his opinion, American westerns had become stagnant, overly preachy, and not believable. Despite the fact even Hollywood began to gear down production of such films, Leone knew that there was still a significant market in Europe for westerns. The film initiated the popularity of the Spaghetti Western genre. Leone followed up with *For A Few Dollars More* and *The Good, the Bad, and the Ugly,* also starring Clint Eastwood. All three films were released in the United States, catapulting Eastwood into stardom.

DR. ZHIVAGO (1965)

Lara: You know, you often look at me as if you knew me.
Zhivago: I have seen you before. Four years ago. Christmas Eve.

Plot
The life of a Russian physician and poet, who although married to another, falls in love with a political activist's wife and experiences hardship during World War I and the October Revolution.

CASTING

Who Starred as Dr. Zhivago?
Omar Sharif

Turned Down the Role of Dr. Zhivago
Peter O'Toole

Who Starred as Lara?
Julie Christie

Turned Down the Role of Lara
Jane Fonda

Who Starred as Viktor Komarovsky?
Rod Steiger

Turned Down the Role of Viktor Komarovsky
Marlon Brando • James Mason

WHO Trivia
Peter O'Toole, star of Lawrence of Arabia, was David Lean's choice for Zhivago, but O'Toole turned the part down. Omar Sharif, having worked with Lean in *Lawrence of Arabia,* requested to be cast in the role of Pasha, and was quite surprised when Lean suggested he play the lead role.

Producer Carlo Ponti was fixated on his wife, Sophia Loren, to play "Lara," but Lean was able to convince Ponti that Loren was not right for the role of Lara, saying she was "too tall" - while confiding in screenwriter Robert Bolt he could not accept Loren as a virgin for the early parts of the film. Jane Fonda turned down the role of Lara because she didn't want to go to Spain for nine months. She changed her mind weeks later, but Julie Christie was already signed.

Initially, James Mason was cast as Viktor Komarovsky, but Mason changed his mind. Rod Steiger replaced him.

THE SOUND OF MUSIC (1965)

Captain: You are the twelfth in a long line of governesses who have come here to look after my children since their mother died. I trust you will be an improvement on the last one. She stayed only two hours.

Maria: What's wrong with the children, sir?

Captain: Oh, there's nothing wrong with the children. Only the governesses.

Plot

A woman leaves an Austrian convent to become a governess to a naval officer widower and his seven children.

CASTING

Who Starred as Maria?
Julie Andrews

Turned Down the Role of Maria
Grace Kelly • Doris Day • Audrey Hepburn

WHO Trivia

Screenwriter Ernest Lehman's only choice for Maria was Julie Andrews. When director/producer Robert Wise joined the project, he made a list of his choices for the role, which included Andrews, Grace Kelly, and Shirley Jones. Wise and Lehman then went to Disney Studios to view footage from the not yet released, *Mary Poppins*. Minutes into the film, Wise told Lehman, "Let's go sign this girl before somebody else sees this film and grabs her!"

Wise had a more difficult time casting the role of Captain Von Trapp. Wise had seen Christopher Plummer on Broadway and wanted him for the role, but he turned down the offer several times. Plummer finally accepted after being assured he could work with Lehman to improve the character.

Before casting Plummer, Robert Wise did consider Bing Crosby, Yul Brynner, Richard Burton, and Sean Connery for the role.

The casting of the children involved over 200 auditions in the United States and England. Some of the child actors included: Liza Minnelli, Mia Farrow, Patty Duke, Kim Darby, Shelley Fabares, Lesley Ann Warren, Teri Garr, Richard Dreyfuss, Kurt Russell, and Sharon Tate.

THE DIRTY DOZEN (1967)

The Soldier's Plan: **One**: Down to the road block, we've just begun. **Two**: The guards are through. **Three**: The Major's men are on a spree. **Four**: Major and Wladislaw go through the door. **Five**: Pinkley stays in the drive. **Six**: The Major gives the rope a fix. **Seven**: Wladislaw throws the hook to heaven. **Eight**: Jiménez has a date. **Nine**: The other guys go up the line. **Ten**: Sawyer and Gilpin are in the pen. **Eleven**: Posey guards points five and seven. **Twelve**: Wladislaw and the Major go down to delve. **Thirteen**: Franko goes up without being seen. **Fourteen**: Zero-hour, Jiménez cuts the cable, Franko cuts the phone. **Fifteen**: Franko goes in where the others have been. **Sixteen**: We all come out like it's Halloween.

Plot
During World War II, a rebellious Army Major is assigned a dozen convicted murderers to train and lead on a suicide mission.

CASTING

Who Starred as Major Reisman?
Lee Marvin

Turned Down the Role of Major Reisman
John Wayne

Who Starred as Archie Maggott?
Telly Savalas

Turned Down the Role of Archie Maggott
Jack Palance

WHO Trivia
The cast included many World War II U.S. veterans, including Lee Marvin, Charles Bronson, Telly Savalas, Ernest Borgnine, and Clint Walker.

John Wayne turned down the role of Reisman because he objected to the adultery present in the original script; the character was having a relationship with an Englishwoman whose husband was fighting on the Continent.

Jack Palance refused the role of Archie Maggott. He wanted the script to be rewritten, so his character would not be presented as a racist.

THE GRADUATE (1967)

Benjamin: Mrs. Robinson, you're trying to seduce me!... Aren't you?

Plot
A disillusioned college graduate finds himself torn between his older lover and her daughter.

CASTING

Who Starred as Benjamin Braddock?
Dustin Hoffman

Turned Down the Role of Benjamin Braddock
Burt Ward • Charles Grodin • Warren Beatty

Who Starred as Mrs. Robinson?
Anne Bancroft

Turned Down the Role of Mrs. Robinson
Doris Day • Patricia Neal
Geraldine Page • Natalie Wood

Who Starred as Elaine Robinson?
Katharine Ross

Turned Down the Role of Elaine Robinson
Natalie Wood • Patty Duke
Faye Dunaway • Sally Field

WHO Trivia
Director Mike Nichols' initial choice for the role of Benjamin Braddock was Burt Ward; he accepted the offer. However, Ward was locked into the *Batman* television show; the company producing it, Fox Television, wouldn't let him do the movie.

Charles Grodin was then offered the role, but he turned it down because the producers wouldn't meet his quote.

Before Dustin Hoffman was cast, Robert Redford and Warren Beatty were among the other top choices. Beatty was occupied with *Bonnie and Clyde*, and turned it down. Redford tested for the part of Benjamin, but Nichols thought Redford did not possess the underdog quality Benjamin needed.

Dustin Hoffman was already cast as Liebkind in the film, *The Producers*. According to Mel Brooks, late on the night before shooting began, Hoffman begged Brooks to let him out of his commitment if he was able to get the starring role in *The Graduate* for which he had an audition the next day. Brooks was aware of the film, which co-starred his wife, Anne Bancroft. Brooks was skeptical Hoffman would get the role, so he agreed. When Hoffman got the role, Brooks kept his word, and replaced Hoffman with Kenneth Mars.

Director Mike Nichols' first choice for Mrs. Robinson was French actress Jeanne Moreau. The idea behind this was that in the French culture, the "older" women tended to "train" the younger men in sexual matters. Moreau wasn't interested, so Nichols began his search.

Doris Day turned down the role because the required nudity offended her. Patricia Neal turned down the film; she recently had recovered from a stroke and did not feel ready to accept such a major role. Geraldine Page also turned it down. Natalie Wood turned down both the role of Mrs. Robinson and that of Elaine.

Joan Crawford inquired about playing the part, while Lauren Bacall, Audrey Hepburn, and Angela Lansbury wanted the role as well.

Ava Gardner sought the role, and reportedly called Nichols saying, "I want to see you! I want to talk about this Graduate thing!" Nichols did not seriously consider her for the role; he wanted a younger woman, but did meet with Gardner in her hotel. Nichols later recounted "she sat at a little French desk with a telephone, and went through every movie star cliché. Finally she said, "'All right, let's talk about your movie. First of all, I strip for nobody.'"

Other actresses Nichols considered for the part included: Angie Dickinson, Deborah Kerr, Susan Hayward, Eva Marie Saint, Lana Turner, Sophia Loren, Rosalind Russell, and Anne Baxter.

The casting of Elaine was also difficult. Patty Duke turned down the role because she did not want to work at the time. Faye Dunaway turned it down, in favor of Bonnie and Clyde. Sally Field and Shirley MacLaine also refused the role. Candice Bergen, Carroll Baker, Goldie Hawn and Jane Fonda all auditioned.

For the role of Mr. Robinson, Gene Hackman was originally cast but, just before filming began, the director decided he was too young and replaced him. Howard Duff, Brian Keith, Gregory Peck, and Walter Matthau were all considered for the role that Murray Hamilton eventually played.

The following auditioned for the role of Mr. Braddock: Christopher Plummer, Kirk Douglas, Jack Lemmon, Karl Malden, Yul Brynner, and Ronald Reagan. Eventually, William Daniels was cast in the role.

ROSEMARY'S BABY (1968)

Rosemary: I look awful.

Guy: What are you talking about? You look great. It's that haircut that looks awful.

Plot

After a young couple move into an apartment surrounded by peculiar neighbors and occurrences, the wife becomes mysteriously pregnant, and paranoia over the safety of her unborn child begins to control her life.

CASTING

Who Starred as Rosemary Woodhouse?
Mia Farrow

Turned Down the Role of Rosemary Woodhouse
Faye Dunaway • Tuesday Weld • Jane Fonda

Who Starred as Guy Woodhouse?
John Cassavetes

Turned Down the Role of Guy Woodhouse
Robert Redford • Warren Beatty
Burt Reynolds • Robert Wagner

WHO Trivia

Director Roman Polanski saw Rosemary as a robust, full-figured, girl-next-door type. He originally wanted Tuesday Weld, who turned down the role, or his then-fiancée Sharon Tate. Since the book had not yet reached best-seller status, producer Robert Evans was unsure the title alone would guarantee an audience for the film, and felt a bigger name was needed for the lead, so he had Patty Duke audition.

Polanski suggested Mia Farrow, who didn't have any major film credits. Her role as Allison MacKenzie in the television series Peyton Place, and her unexpected marriage to Frank Sinatra had made her a household name; Farrow won the role over Patty Duke.

Robert Redford was the first choice for the role of Guy Woodhouse, but he passed to make *Downhill Racer* instead. Warren Beatty and Burt Reynolds also turned down the role. Robert Wagner was then offered the role, but was starring in the television show *It Takes a Thief*, and ABC would not loan him out to make the film. Polanski then hired John Cassavetes.

FUNNY GIRL (1968)

Nick: I'd be happy to wait while you change.

Fanny: I'd have to change too much; nobody could wait that long.

Plot

The life and career of Broadway and film star and comedienne Fanny Brice and her stormy relationship with entrepreneur and gambler Nicky Arnstein.

CASTING

Who Starred as Nicky Arnstein?
Omar Sharif

Turned Down the Role of Nicky Arnstein
Sean Connery

WHO Trivia

Producer Ray Stark's only choice to portray Fannie Brice on screen was the actress who originated the role on Broadway, Barbra Streisand.

Columbia Pictures executives wanted Shirley MacLaine in the role. MacLaine and Streisand were good friends; both actresses rolled their eyes at the idea. Stark insisted if Streisand were not cast, he would not allow a film to be made, and the studio agreed to his demand.

Jules Styne wanted Frank Sinatra for the role of Nicky Arnstein, but the actor was willing to appear in the film only if the role was expanded and new songs were added for the character. Streisand respected Sinatra's talent, but didn't like him personally, so she vetoed the idea. Stark agreed with Streisand. He thought Sinatra was too old and preferred someone with more class like Cary Grant, even though Grant was eleven years older than Sinatra. Marlon Brando and Gregory Peck were also considered.

Egyptian Omar Sharif was cast after director William Wyler noticed Sharif having lunch in the studio commissary. When the Six-Day War between Israel and Egypt broke out, studio executives considered replacing Sharif, but both Wyler and Streisand threatened to quit if they did. When asked about the controversy, Streisand replied, "You think Cairo got upset? You should see the letter I got from my Aunt Rose!"

BOB & CAROL & TED & ALICE (1969)

Carol: I didn't do it because you did it!

Bob: Why then? Oh, why, God Almighty!

Carol: I did it because I wanted to do it!

Bob: Why?

Carol: Because I wanted to do it! I-I-I just wanted to see if I could do it.

Bob: Why in my house? Why in my bed?

Carol: Well, Bob, it just seems like a convenient thing... You were not going to be here.

Bob: He's not in my pajamas, is he?

Plot

A lighthearted view of middle-aged love and friendship when two couples engage in a mate-sharing foursome.

CASTING

Who Starred as Bob Sanders?
Robert Culp

Turned Down the Role of Bob Sanders
Warren Beatty • Steve McQueen • Robert Redford

Who Starred as Carol Sanders?
Natalie Wood

Turned Down the Role of Carol Sanders
Jane Fonda

Who Starred as Alice Henderson?
Dyan Cannon

Turned Down the Role of Alice Henderson
Faye Dunaway • Tuesday Weld

WHO Trivia

Writer/Director Paul Mazursky tested actors Richard Benjamin, James Caan, Peter Falk, and Elliott Gould for the role of Ted Henderson. The only actor Mazursky offered the role to was Gould, who received an Academy Award nomination for Best Supporting Actor.

Butch Cassidy & the Sundance Kid (1969)

Butch: I'll jump first.
Sundance: Nope.
Butch: Then you jump first.
Sundance: No, I said!
Butch: What's the matter with you?!
Sundance: I can't swim!
Butch: Why, you crazy... the fall'll probably kill ya!

Plot

When they rob a train once too often, two outlaws find a special posse trailing them no matter where they run. Their solution - flee to Bolivia.

CASTING

Who Starred as the Sundance Kid?
Robert Redford

Turned Down the Role of the Sundance Kid
Jack Lemmon • Steve McQueen • Warren Beatty

WHO Trivia

"The Sundance Kid and Butch Cassidy" was the original title of the script. Writer William Goldman had Steve McQueen and Paul Newman read the script at approximately the same time, and both agreed to do it with McQueen playing The Sundance Kid. When McQueen dropped out, the names reversed in the title, as Newman was the box office star.

The role of the Sundance Kid was offered to Jack Lemmon. He turned it down because of a scheduling conflict with filming *The Odd Couple*. Lemmon also did not like riding horses. Warren Beatty turned the role down claiming the film was too similar to Bonnie and Clyde. Marlon Brando was seriously considered to team with Paul Newman for one of the roles, but turned it down due to his commitment to *Burn*.

According to William Goldman, when he first wrote the script, only one studio wanted to buy it, 20th Century Fox, and that was with the proviso that the two lead characters did not flee to South America. When Goldman protested because that was what actually happened, the head of the studio responded, "I don't give a shit. All I know is John Wayne don't run away."

MIDNIGHT COWBOY (1969)

Ratso: HEY! I'm walkin' here! I'm walkin' here!
(bangs hand on car)
Up yours, you son-of-a-bitch! You don't talk to me that way!
Get outta here!
(to Joe)
Don't worry about that. Actually, that ain't a bad way to pick
up insurance, you know.

Plot

A naive male prostitute and his sickly friend struggle to survive on the
streets of New York City.

CASTING

Who Starred as Ratso Rizzo?
Dustin Hoffman

Turned Down the Role of Ratso Rizzo
Robert Blake

Who Starred as Joe Buck?
Jon Voight

Turned Down the Role of Joe Buck
Lee Majors

WHO Trivia

Robert Blake was the first choice to play Ratso Rizzo, but he didn't think the
part was "sexy" enough, so he turned it down.

Lee Majors was cast as Joe Buck, but had to pull out when his television
series, *The Big Valley,* was renewed for another season.

Before Dustin Hoffman auditioned, he knew that his all-American image
could easily cost him the role. To prove he could do it, he asked the casting
director to meet him on a street corner in Manhattan, and in the meantime,
dressed himself in filthy rags.

The casting director arrived at the appointed corner and waited, barely
noticing the "beggar" less than ten feet away who was accosting people for
spare change. At last, the beggar walked up to him and revealed his true
identity.

TRUE GRIT (1969)

Ned: What's your intention, Rooster?

Rooster: I mean to kill you in one minute, Ned, or see you hang at Fort Smith... Which'll it be?

Ned: I call that bold talk for a one-eyed fat man!

Rooster: Fill your hand, you son of a bitch!

Plot

A young girl enlists the aid of a crusty U.S. Marshal to hunt down the man who murdered her father.

CASTING

Who Starred as Mattie Ross?
Kim Darby

Turned Down the Role of Mattie Ross
Mia Farrow • Sondra Locke • Tuesday Weld

Who Starred as Texas Ranger La Boeuf?
Glen Campbell

Turned Down the Role of Texas Ranger La Boeuf
Elvis Presley

WHO Trivia

Mia Farrow was originally cast as Mattie. Prior to filming, she made a film with Robert Mitchum, who advised her not to work with director Henry Hathaway because he was "cantankerous." Farrow asked producer Hal B. Wallis to replace him with Roman Polanski, who had directed her in *Rosemary's Baby,* but Wallis refused, and Farrow quit the film.

After Sondra Locke and Tuesday Weld both turned down the role, John Wayne recommended Karen Carpenter, whom he had met at a talent show. The producers decided against her because she had no acting experience.

Finally, after also considering Sally Field, the role went to Kim Darby.

Elvis Presley was the original choice for Texas Ranger La Boeuf, but the producers turned him down when his manager, Colonel Tom Parker, demanded top-billing over John Wayne and Kim Darby. Glen Campbell was then cast instead.

Bonus Movies

Ocean's 11 (1960)

Director Gilbert Kay, who heard the idea from a gas station attendant, first told Peter Lawford of the basic story of the film. Lawford eventually bought the rights in 1958, with the idea of casting William Holden as Danny Ocean.

When Lawford first told Frank Sinatra of the story, Sinatra joked, "Forget the movie, let's pull the job!" Sinatra then became interested and brought the "Rat Pack" into the project.

The Magnificent Seven (1960)

Producer/Director John Sturges was eager to cast Steve McQueen in the picture, having just worked with him on the 1959 film, *Never So Few*, but McQueen could not get a release from actor/producer Dick Powell who controlled McQueen's hit TV series *Wanted Dead or Alive*.

On the advice of his very clever agent, McQueen, an experienced race car driver, staged a car accident. He claimed he could not work on his series because he had suffered a whiplash injury, and had to wear a neck brace. During the interval required for his recuperation, McQueen was free to appear in *The Magnificent Seven*.

Spartacus (1960)

The development of *Spartacus* was partly instigated by Kirk Douglas' failure to win the title role in William Wyler's *Ben-Hur*.

A friend gave him a copy of the novel *Spartacus* to read. Because it had a similar theme as Ben-Hur, Kirk Douglas optioned the book using his own money. Universal Studios eventually agreed to finance the film after Douglas persuaded Laurence Olivier, Charles Laughton, and Peter Ustinov to act in it with him.

Yul Brynner was also planning his own Spartacus film for United Artists, but with Dalton Trumbo's screenplay being completed in two weeks, Universal and Douglas won the "Spartacus" race.-

Pocket Full of Miracles (1961)

Jean Arthur, Shirley Booth, Helen Hayes, and Katharine Hepburn all turned down the role of Apple Annie. Finally, Bette Davis was cast.

The Miracle Worker (1962)

Despite the fact Anne Bancroft had won the Tony for Best Performance by a Leading Actress in a Play, United Artists executives wanted, in the film adaptation, a bigger name cast as Anne Sullivan.

United Artists offered to budget the film at $5 million if Elizabeth Taylor was cast, but only $500,000 if director Arthur Penn insisted on using Bancroft. Arthur Penn, who had directed the stage production, remained loyal to his star. The move paid off, and Bancroft won an Oscar for her role in the film.

Also, despite the fact Patty Duke had played Helen Keller in the play, she almost did not get the part. The reason was that Duke, 15 years old at the time, was too old to portray a seven-year-old girl, but after Bancroft was cast as Anne in the movie, Duke was chosen to play Helen.

The Music Man (1962)

Frank Sinatra was the studio's first choice to play Harold Hill before Robert Preston was cast in his signature role. Barbara Cook lost the role of Marian the Librarian to Shirley Jones, even though Cook had won a Tony on Broadway for the role. Cook had never done a movie, while Jones was considered a movie star. Jay North, famous for the television show, *Dennis the Menace,* lost out playing Winthrop to Ronnie Howard.

To Kill a Mockingbird (1962)

Rock Hudson was Universal's first choice to play the politically progressive Southern lawyer, widower, and father Atticus Finch. Instead, Gregory Peck was cast in the role, winning the Academy Award for Best Actor.

It's a Mad, Mad, Mad, Mad World (1963)

Although the film was a star-laden production, a number of stars turned down roles including: Bob Hope, Stan Laurel, Red Skelton, George Burns, Ed Wynn, Jackie Mason, and Judy Holliday.

The Pink Panther (1963)

Peter Ustinov turned down the role of Inspector Clouseau, which was originally a minor part that Peter Sellers, in his signature role, went on to play in the film and the sequels.

PT 109 (1963)

Warren Beatty was the personal choice of John and Jackie Kennedy to play John F. Kennedy in the film based on his experiences in the Navy, but the director, Leslie H. Martinson, refused to cast him believing he was too unstable. Instead, he cast Cliff Robertson in the role.

Mary Poppins (1964)

Julie Andrews, who was making her film debut after a successful stage career, got the prime role of *Mary Poppins,* but only after Jack L. Warner decided to cast Audrey Hepburn as Eliza Doolittle in the screen adaptation of *My Fair Lady,* even though Andrews had originated the role on Broadway.

When Disney first approached Andrews about the role of Mary Poppins, Andrews was three months pregnant, and was not sure she should take it. Disney assured her that filming would not begin until after she had given birth, so she accepted the role.

Ironically, Julie Andrews later beat out Audrey Hepburn for Best Actress at the Golden Globes for their respective roles. Andrews would also win the Oscar for Best Actress for her role as Mary Poppins. During her acceptance speech, Julie Andrews specifically thanked Jack L. Warner.

The Pawnbroker (1964)

Sidney Lumet, who took over the film after Arthur Hiller was fired, initially had misgivings about Rod Steiger being cast in the lead role of Sol Nazerman, and preferred James Mason for the role. He even had a meeting with comedian Groucho Marx who very much wanted to play the role.

The Unsinkable Molly Brown (1964)

According to a friend of director Chuck Walters, "His first choice for the lead role was Shirley MacLaine, but Debbie Reynolds campaigned to unseat her and get the role. Debbie and Chuck were buddies, so she played that card big time! Reynolds even called MacLaine directly to talk her out of accepting the role. MacLaine had tons of other offers, so she graciously stepped aside. That made it possible for Reynolds to play the role and garner her only nomination as Best Actress."

The Cincinnati Kid (1965)

Spencer Tracy was originally cast as Lancey Howard, but ill health forced him to withdraw from the film, and Edward G. Robinson was cast.

A Man for All Seasons (1966)

After Richard Burton turned down the role of Sir Thomas Moore, executives at Columbia Studios wanted director Fred Zinnemann to cast Laurence Olivier. However, Zinnemann was adamant that Paul Scofield recreate his stage performance in the film. Zinnemann's casting decision proved to be correct when Scofield won the Academy Award for Best Actor.

Alfie (1966)

Despite having played the role of Alfie on Broadway, Terence Stamp categorically declined to reprise the role on film. Stamp and casting agents approached his good friend and then roommate, Michael Caine, who was not one to then snub a role about a common man. Caine received major acclaim for the breakthrough role of his career.

Several well-known English actors, including Richard Harris, Laurence Harvey, James Booth and Anthony Newley turned down the title role because of the then-taboo subject matter.

One Million Years B.C. (1966)

Before Raquel Welch was cast in the role that catapulted her career, and featured her in the poster, Ursula Andress turned down the role.

The Sand Pebbles (1966)

Steve McQueen received his only Academy Award nomination for the role of Jake Holman in Robert Wise's epic film. Paul Newman turned down the role to work for Alfred Hitchcock on *Torn Curtain*.

Bonnie and Clyde (1967)

Producer Warren Beatty originally wanted the "runtish" Bob Dylan to play Clyde Barrow, but eventually took the role himself.

When casting the role of Bonnie Parker, Warren Beatty is quoted as saying, "Faye wasn't my first choice. We'd been turned down or were considering a lot of actresses for the role, including: Jane Fonda, Tuesday Weld, Natalie Wood, Sharon Tate, Ann-Margret, Leslie Caron, Julie Christie, Carol Lynley, Jean Hale, and Sue Lyon. And then I met Faye."

Cool Hand Luke (1967)

While the script was being developed, the leading role of Lucas "Luke" Jackson was initially considered for Jack Lemmon or Telly Savalas. After hearing about the project, Paul Newman asked if he could play the role.

George Kennedy turned in an Academy Award-winning performance as the leader of the prisoners, Dragline. During the nomination process, worried about the box office success of *Camelot* and *Bonnie and Clyde*, Kennedy invested $5,000 in trade advertising to promote himself. Kennedy later stated that thanks to the award his salary was "multiplied by ten," adding "the happiest part was that I didn't have to play only villains anymore."

In Cold Blood (1967)

Aspiring to recreate a documentary aesthetic for the film, Brooks deliberately cast actors who were relatively unknown. Columbia Pictures originally wanted Paul Newman and Steve McQueen to play Richard Hickock and Perry Smith respectively, but Brooks refused as he felt their star status would render their performances less believable to audiences.

Around 500 contenders were considered for the two roles. Robert Blake was ultimately cast as Smith and Scott Wilson as Hickock. Blake had been a child actor and appeared in numerous films prior to this film, but was not well-known as an adult actor. The film marked Scott Wilson's second feature and first major role. Wilson was recommended for the part by Sidney Poitier with whom he co-starred in *In the Heat of the Night*.

The Producers (1967)

From the start, Mel Brooks wanted Zero Mostel to play Max Bialystock, feeling he was an energetic actor who could convey such an egotistical character. The script was sent to Mostel's lawyer, but the attorney hated it, and never showed it to Mostel.

Eventually, Brooks sent the script through Mostel's wife, Kathryn Harkin. While Mostel did not like the prospect of playing "a Jewish producer going to bed with old women on the brink of the grave," his wife liked the script so much, she eventually convinced him to accept the role. Mostel allowed his pent-up hostilities towards all the sources of his professional disappointments to spill over into his performance as Bialystock, making his a bitter, hate-filled, and often angry interpretation.

Barbarella (1968)

Several actresses were approached before Jane Fonda was cast as Barbarella. Dino De Laurentis' first choice was Virna Lisi; his second was Brigitte Bardot, who was not interested in a sexualized role. His third choice was Sophia Loren, who was pregnant and felt that she would not be suitable for the role.

Fonda was uncertain about the film, but Vadim convinced her by saying science fiction was a rapidly-evolving genre. Before filming Barbarella, Fonda was the subject of two sex scandals: the first when her nude body was displayed across an eight-story billboard promoting the premiere of *Circle of Love* in 1965, and the second when several candid nude photos from Vadim's closed set for *The Game Is Over* were sold to Playboy the following year.

The Odd Couple (1968)

The Odd Couple was originally produced for Broadway, and the original cast starred Art Carney as Felix and Walter Matthau as Oscar. For the film version, Matthau reprised his role as Oscar, and Felix was portrayed by Jack Lemmon, who had never played the character before.

At one point, Frank Sinatra (as Felix) and Jackie Gleason (as Oscar) were reportedly considered for the film version. Dick Van Dyke and Tony Randall were also among those considered for the role of Felix, and Mickey Rooney was considered for the role of Oscar.

The Thomas Crown Affair (1968)

Sean Connery had been the original choice for the title role, but turned it down. A decision he later said he regretted.

Easy Rider (1969)

According to Terry Southern's biographer, the part of George Hanson had been written for Southern's friend, actor Rip Torn. When Torn met with Hopper and Fonda at a New York restaurant in early 1968 to discuss the role, Hopper began ranting about the "rednecks" he had encountered on his scouting trip to the South. Torn, a Texan, took exception to some of Hopper's remarks, and the two almost came to blows, resulting in Torn withdrawing from the project. He was replaced by Jack Nicholson.

Jay Leno interviewed Dennis Hopper about *Easy Rider* on *The Tonight Show*. During the interview, Hopper alleged Rip Torn pulled a knife on him during the altercation, prompting Torn to sue Hopper successfully for defamation.

They Shoot Horses, Don't They? (1969)

Julie Christie and Barbra Streisand turned the role of the embittered dance marathon contestant, Gloria Beatty, the role that earned Jane Fonda an Academy Award Nomination.

During the early shooting of the film, director Sidney Pollack was dissatisfied with Michael Sarrazin's performance in the role of Robert Syverton, and considered replacing him with either Robert Redford or Warren Beatty.

The Wild Bunch (1969)

A number of actors, Charlton Heston, Burt Lancaster, Robert Mitchum, Sterling Hayden, Richard Boone, Gregory Peck, and James Stewart turned down writer/director Sam Peckinpah for the lead role of Pike Bishop, eventually played by William Holden. Lee Marvin had accepted the role, but pulled out after he was offered more money to star in *Paint Your Wagon*.

General George S. Patton • David Sumner • Amy Sumner • "Popeye" Doyle
"Dirty Harry" Callahan • Sally Bowles • Vito Corleone • Michael Corleone
Sonny Corleone • Ed Gentry • Lewis Medlock • "Moze" Pray • Addie Loggins
Chris MacNeil • Regan MacNeil • Father Karras • Father Merrin • Sheriff Bart
"The Waco Kid" • Paul Kersey • Chief Brody • Quint • Matt Hooper
Jay Gatsby • Daisy Buchanan • Esther Hoffman • John Norman Howard
Howard Beale • Diana Christenson • Max Schumacher • Louise Schumacher
Rocky • Adrian • Mickey • Travis Bickle • Iris • Betsy • Charles Palantine
Roy Neary • Ronnie Neary • Jillian Guiler • Luke Skywalker • Han Solo
Princess Leia • Ben Obi-Wan Kenobi • Elliot Garfield • Paula McFadden

1970s

Bluto • Otter • Boon • D-Day • Dave Jennings • Sally Hyde • Luke Martin
Violet • Bellocq • Hattie • Superman/Clark Kent • Lex Luthor • Ripley
Captain Dallas • Kane • Colonel Kurtz • Captain Willard • Lt. Colonel Kilgore
Ted Kramer • Joanna Kramer • Ada Quonsett • Oliver Barrett IV • Shaft
Bree Daniels • John Klute • "Doc" McCoy • Carol McCoy • Jeremiah Johnson
"Sam the Lion" • Harry Coombes • Tonto • Lenny Bruce • Randle McMurphy
Nurse Ratched • Carrie • Julia • "Bandit" • "Frog" • Sheriff Buford T. Justice
Joe Pendleton/Leo Farnsworth/Tom Jarrett • Julia Farnsworth • Mr. Jordan
Michael Vronsky • Joe Gideon • "Chance the Gardener" • Tracy • Norma Rae
General George S. Patton • David Sumner • Amy Sumner • "Popeye" Doyle
"Dirty Harry" Callahan • Sally Bowles • Vito Corleone • Michael Corleone
Sonny Corleone • Ed Gentry • Lewis Medlock • "Moze" Pray • Addie Loggins
Chris MacNeil • Regan MacNeil • Father Karras • Father Merrin • Sheriff Bart
"The Waco Kid" • Paul Kersey • Chief Brody • Quint • Matt Hooper
Jay Gatsby • Daisy Buchanan • Esther Hoffman • John Norman Howard
Howard Beale • Diana Christenson • Max Schumacher • Louise Schumacher
Rocky • Adrian • Mickey • Travis Bickle • Iris • Betsy • Charles Palantine
Roy Neary • Ronnie Neary • Jillian Guiler • Luke Skywalker • Han Solo
Princess Leia • Ben Obi-Wan Kenobi • Elliot Garfield • Paula McFadden
Bluto • Otter • Boon • D-Day • Dave Jennings • Sally Hyde • Luke Martin
Violet • Bellocq • Hattie • Superman/Clark Kent • Lex Luthor • Ripley
Captain Dallas • Kane • Colonel Kurtz • Captain Willard • Lt. Colonel Kilgore
Ted Kramer • Joanna Kramer • Ada Quonsett • Oliver Barrett IV • Shaft
Bree Daniels • John Klute • "Doc" McCoy • Carol McCoy • Jeremiah Johnson
"Sam the Lion" • Harry Coombes • Tonto • Lenny Bruce • Randle McMurphy
Nurse Ratched • Carrie • Julia • "Bandit" • "Frog" • Sheriff Buford T. Justice
Joe Pendleton/Leo Farnsworth/Tom Jarrett • Julia Farnsworth • Mr. Jordan
Michael Vronsky • Joe Gideon • "Chance the Gardener" • Tracy • Norma Rae

The Hollywood Blockbuster

Although the decade began with Hollywood experiencing yet another financial and artistic upheaval, there was no shortage of creativity within the film industry. Restrictions on language, content, sexuality, and violence had changed, and even as the studio system was collapsing, a new wave of young filmmakers filled the void.

The 1970s gave us the end of the Vietnam War, Watergate, the Kent State massacre, and President Nixon's resignation, films reflected these moments highlighted by *All The President's Men, and Coming Home*.

It was a series of commercial hits that drew audiences back into the movie houses including: *Star Wars, Jaws, The Exorcist, The Godfather, Grease, Close Encounters of the Third Kind, Smokey and the Bandit, The Sting, Alien, Saturday Night Fever,* and *Rocky*.

The growth of cable TV was regarded as a threat to advertiser-supported broadcast television networks, independent stations, and movie theaters. Cable's debut included a hockey game and the first commercial-free airing of *Sometimes a Great Notion*. HBO inaugurated its cable service nation-wide with the live transmission of the Ali vs. Frazier fight in October 1975, becoming the first successful, satellite-delivered pay cable service in the United States. A new era of program delivery was born.

The arrival of home recording technology, initially considered a threat to movies because consumers could tape off the air, was re-evaluated once studios discovered lucrative sales and rentals from taped versions of their commercially released movies. These changes came at a price however, as theater attendance would begin to drastically decline in the next decade.

In the 1970s, the focus was on box office receipts and the production of action, youth-oriented blockbuster films with dazzling special effects high-lighted by two films: *Jaws* and *Star Wars*. When *Jaws* premiered in 1975, it was the highest grossing film in history, only to be replaced by *Star Wars* two years later. Both films grossed over 100 million dollars with the average ticket price under three dollars.

The 1970s launched a new generation of movie stars, who were more skilled as "character actors," and could adapt their screen images to play a number of diverse roles. Robert De Niro, Jack Nicholson, Gene Hackman, Al Pacino and Dustin Hoffman exemplified this new generation.

Producer Roger Corman was heralded (years later) for hiring "novices" like Francis Ford Coppola, Martin Scorsese, Jonathan Demme, James Cameron, and Peter Bogdanovich; giving them their first career-breaking employment opportunities to make personally relevant films. His support revived the notion of the *auteur,* - that the director was most influential and responsible for creating a film's ultimate form.

With respect to the types of films being made, Steve McQueen's success in *Bullitt* generated a cycle of "rogue cop" films, such as *Dirty Harry* with emerging star Clint Eastwood, *Serpico* starring Al Pacino, and *The French Connection* with Gene Hackman.

Woody Allen joined the ranks of the 'New Hollywood' young directors with *Take the Money and Run,* a mockumentary spoof of gangster films. This film was followed by the political comedy, *Bananas,* and a series of films culminating with his semi-autobiographical love story, *Annie Hall,* with Diane Keaton as the unconventional, kooky, anxious title character.

After his breakthrough film in the 1960s, *The Producers,* Mel Brooks directed the raunchy western *Blazing Saddles,* and his first commercial hit, the horror film spoof, *Young Frankenstein,* followed, which mirrored Hitch-cock's themes and styles.

Musicals were once again big box-office starting with the Broadway hit, *Fiddler on the Roof,* followed by *The Wiz,* and Bob Fosse's *Cabaret.* Other musicals *All That Jazz, The Rose, Godspell, Jesus Christ, Superstar, Tommy, Saturday Night Fever, Grease* and *The Buddy Holly Story* filled the screen and theater seats with audiences both young and old. Martin Scorsese attempted to capitalize on Liza Minnelli's star-glamour and classic musicals of the past with his failed expressionistic musical *New York, New York.*

The 1970s started the trend toward bigger and more expensive films for the younger audiences with more of an emphasis on special effects than on story or plot. Richard Donner's *Superman,* the most expensive film of the decade, at $55 million, translates to approximately $400 million in 2019.

The Academy Awards

1970
Best Picture: ***Patton***
Best Actor: George C. Scott (*Patton*)
Best Actress: Glenda Jackson (*Women in Love*)
Best Supporting Actor: John Mills (*Ryan's Daughter*)
Best Supporting Actress: Helen Hayes (*Airport*)

1971
Best Picture: ***The French Connection***
Best Actor: Gene Hackman (*The French Connection*)
Best Actress: Jane Fonda (*Klute*)
Best Supporting Actor: Ben Johnson (*The Last Picture Show*)
Best Supporting Actress: Cloris Leachman (*The Last Picture Show*)

1972
Best Picture: ***The Godfather***
Best Actor: Marlon Brando (*The Godfather*)
Best Actress: Liza Minnelli (*Cabaret*)
Best Supporting Actor: Joel Grey (*Cabaret*)
Best Supporting Actress: Eileen Heckart (*Butterflies Are Free*)

1973
Best Picture: ***The Sting***
Best Actor: Jack Lemmon (*Save the Tiger*)
Best Actress: Glenda Jackson (*A Touch of Class*)
Best Supporting Actor: John Houseman (*The Paper Chase*)
Best Supporting Actress: Tatum O'Neal (*Paper Moon*)

1974
Best Picture: ***The Godfather Part II***
Best Actor: Art Carney (*Harry and Tonto*)
Best Actress: Ellen Burstyn (*Alice Doesn't Live Here Anymore*)
Best Supporting Actor: Robert De Niro (*The Godfather Part 11*)
Best Supporting Actress: Ingrid Bergman (*Murder on the Orient Express*)

1975
Best Picture: ***One Flew Over the Cuckoo's Nest***
Best Actor: Jack Nicholson (*One Flew Over the Cuckoo's Nest*)
Best Actress: Louise Fletcher (*One Flew Over the Cuckoo's Nest*)
Best Supporting Actor: George Burns (*The Sunshine Boys*)
Best Supporting Actress: Lee Grant (*Shampoo*)

1976
Best Picture: ***Rocky***
Best Actor: Peter Finch (*Network*)
Best Actress: Faye Dunaway (*Network*)
Best Supporting Actor: Jason Robards (*All the President's Men*)
Best Supporting Actress: Beatrice Straight (*Network*)

1977
Best Picture: ***Annie Hall***
Best Actor: Richard Dreyfuss (*The Goodbye Girl*)
Best Actress: Diane Keaton (*Annie Hall*)
Best Supporting Actor: Jason Robards (*Julia*)
Best Supporting Actress: Vanessa Redgrave (*Julia*)

1978
Best Picture: ***The Deer Hunter***
Best Actor: Jon Voight (*Coming Home*)
Best Actress: Jane Fonda (*Coming Home*)
Best Supporting Actor: Christopher Walken (*The Deer Hunter*)
Best Supporting Actress: Maggie Smith (*California Suite*)

1979
Best Picture: ***Kramer vs. Kramer***
Best Actor: Dustin Hoffman (*Kramer vs. Kramer*)
Best Actress: Sally Field (*Norma Rae*)
Best Supporting Actor: Melvyn Douglas (*Being There*)
Best Supporting Actress: Meryl Streep (*Kramer vs. Kramer*)

Casting Trivia Quiz

1. George C. Scott won an Oscar for playing **Patton** after this actor turned it down:
   - a. Robert Mitchum
   - b. Burt Lancaster
   - c. Rod Steiger
   - d. All of the Above

2. Before Burt Reynolds was cast as Lewis Medlock in **Deliverance**, this actor turned the role down:
   - a. Steve McQueen
   - b. Charlton Heston
   - c. Marlon Brando
   - d. All of the Above

3. Popeye Doyle will always be thought of as Gene Hackman, chasing drugs in New York City in **The French Connection**, but this actor turned down the role first:
   - a. Al Pacino
   - b. Peter Boyle
   - c. Paul Newman
   - d. All of the Above

4. **Dirty Harry** is a defining film for Clint Eastwood, but the role of Detective Harry Callahan was first turned down by:
   - a. John Wayne
   - b. Paul Newman
   - c. George C. Scott
   - d. All of the Above

5. Marlon Brando will always be Don Vito Corleone in **The Godfather,** but before he won the role, it was turned down by:
   - a. Laurence Olivier
   - b. Anthony Quinn
   - c. George C. Scott
   - d. Ernest Borgnine

6. This actor was given the role of Michael Corleone in **The Godfather** before Al Pacino got the role:
   - a. Warren Beatty
   - b. James Caan
   - c. Martin Sheen
   - d. Dustin Hoffman

7. Ellen Burstyn stars as beleaguered mother Chris MacNeil in the William Freidkin classic, **The Exorcist**. The role was first offered to:
   - a. Jane Fonda
   - b. Audrey Hepburn
   - c. Anne Bancroft
   - d. All of the Above

8. Before Gene Wilder was cast as "The Waco Kid" in **Blazing Saddles**, this actor was offered the role:
   a. John Wayne
   b. Burt Lancaster
   c. Kirk Douglas
   d. All of the Above

9. Charles Bronson had a **Death Wish** as Paul Kersey for the men who harmed his family. The original choice for the role was:
   a. Jon Voight
   b. James Coburn
   c. Jack Lemmon
   d. Rod Steiger

10. In the film **Jaws**, before Roy Scheider was cast as Sheriff Brody, this actor turned down the role:
    a. Charlton Heston
    b. Harrison Ford
    c. Robert Duvall
    d. None of the Above

11. Before Robert De Niro was cast as Travis Bickle in **Taxi Driver**, this actor turned the role down:
    a. Al Pacino
    b. Burt Reynolds
    c. Jack Nicholson
    d. All of the Above

12. Peter Finch won an Oscar for his portrayal of deranged anchorman Howard Beale in **Network.** This actor turned down the role:
    a. James Stewart
    b. George C. Scott
    c. Henry Fonda
    d. All of the Above

13. In the 1976 reboot of **A Star is Born,** this actor tuned down the role of John Norman Howard before it went to Kris Kristofferson:
    a. Neil Diamond
    b. Elvis Presley
    c. James Taylor
    d. All of the Above

14. Princess Leia, a leader of the Rebel Alliance in **Star Wars**, was played by Carrie Fisher. The role was originally turned down by:
    a. Ellen Burstyn
    b. Teri Garr
    c. Jodie Foster
    d. Amy Irving

15. Before Martin Sheen was cast as Captain Willard in **Apocalypse Now**, this actor turned down the role:
    a. Steve McQueen
    b. Clint Eastwood
    c. Al Pacino
    d. All of the Above

PATTON (1970)

Patton: I want you to remember that no bastard ever won a war by dying for his country. He won it by making the other poor, dumb bastard die for his country. Men, all this stuff you've heard about America not wanting to fight, wanting to stay out of the war, is a lot of horse dung. Americans, traditionally, love to fight.

Plot
Biographical film of the World War II phase of the career of controversial General George S. Patton.

WHO Trivia
Burt Lancaster turned down the lead role of General George S. Patton because of a lifelong adherence to progressive politics. In contrast, John Wayne eagerly sought out the role, but was turned down by producer Frank McCarthy.

Rod Steiger turned the role down. He later stated that he regretted his decision. Lee Marvin also declined the role. When Robert Mitchum turned it down, he suggested George C. Scott would be a much better choice.

During filming, Scott refused to film the famous speech in front of the American flag when he learned that the speech was going to come at the opening of the film. He felt that, if they put that scene at the beginning, the rest of his performance could not live up to that scene.

Director Franklin J. Schaffner, in order get Scott to do the scene, lied to Scott, telling him the scene would be put at the end of the film.

That lie had nothing to do with the fact that when Scott won the Academy Award for Best Actor, he famously refused to accept it, claiming competition between actors was unfair and a "meat parade."

STRAW DOGS (1971)

Amy: David, give Niles to them. That's what they want. They just
            want him. Give them Niles, David!
David: They'll beat him to death.
Amy: I don't care! Get him out!
David: You really don't care, do you?
Amy: No, I don't.
David: No. I care. This is where I live. This is me.
            I will not allow violence against this house.

Plot
A young American and his English wife come to rural England and face
increasingly vicious local harassment.

CASTING

Who Starred as David Sumner?
Dustin Hoffman

Turned Down the Role of David Sumner
Beau Bridges • Stacy Keach • Sidney Poitier
Jack Nicholson • Donald Sutherland

Who Starred as Amy Sumner?
Susan George

Turned Down the Role of Amy Sumner
Judy Geeson • Jacqueline Bisset • Diana Rigg
Helen Mirren • Charlotte Rampling • Hayley Mills

WHO Trivia
Dustin Hoffman agreed to do the film because the character, a pacifist
unaware of his feelings and potential for violence, intrigued him.

After Susan George was selected for the role of Amy, Hoffman had a
disagreement with director Sam Peckinpah, feeling his character would
never marry such a "Lolita-ish" kind of girl. Peckinpah wasn't swayed, and
cast George, an unknown actress at that time.

The character, Henry Niles, had a limp that was not part of the script, but
was due to the fact David Warner had broken his leg before production
began. Warner was able to walk with a cane by the time production started,
therefore the limp. The injury made Warner uninsurable, thus uncredited
in the film.

THE FRENCH CONNECTION (1971)

"Popeye" Doyle: This is Doyle. I'm sittin' on Frog One.
Mulderig: Yeah, I know that. We got the Westbury covered like a tent.
"Popeye" Doyle: The Westbury my ass! I got him on the shuttle at Grand Central. Now what the hell's going on up there?

Plot

The story of detectives Jimmy "Popeye" Doyle and Buddy "Cloudy" Russo, in pursuit of wealthy French heroin smuggler Alain Charnier.

CASTING

Who Starred as Det. "Popeye" Doyle?
Gene Hackman

Turned Down the Role of Det. "Popeye" Doyle
Jimmy Breslin • Steve McQueen • Peter Boyle
Lee Marvin • James Caan • Robert Mitchum • Rod Taylor

WHO Trivia

Director William Friedkin had problems with casting choices from the start. Strongly opposed to the studio choice of Gene Hackman for the lead, he wanted Paul Newman, but the latter was too expensive. Steve McQueen, potentially also too expensive, turned the role down because he didn't want to do another police film after *Bullitt*. Peter Boyle declined the role after disapproving of the violent theme. Lee Marvin, James Caan, and Robert Mitchum all turned down the role. Jackie Gleason was considered, but was box office poison after his film *Gigot* had flopped several years before.

Still not wanting Gene Hackman, Friedkin cast Jimmy Breslin, a New York columnist, who had never acted before, as Doyle. Breslin quickly revealed himself as a horrible actor, and didn't know how to drive, a requirement for the car chase scene, so Friedkin ultimately fired him.

Friedkin almost settled on Rod Taylor, who had actively pursued the role, and another choice the studio approved. Not sold on Taylor, Friedkin decided to go with Hackman. Ironically, after the Breslin disaster, Hackman did much of the driving in the infamous car chase scene himself.

DIRTY HARRY (1971)

"Dirty Harry":   I know what you're thinking: 'Did he fire six shots or only five? Well, to tell you the truth, in all this excitement, I've kinda lost track myself. But being this is a .44 Magnum, the most powerful handgun in the world, and would blow your head clean off, you've got to ask yourself one question... 'Do I feel lucky?'... Well, do you, punk?"

Plot
A San Francisco cop with little regard for rules, but who always gets results, tracks down a serial killer, loosely based on the real-life Zodiac Killer.

CASTING

Who Starred as "Dirty Harry"?
Clint Eastwood

Turned Down the Role of "Dirty Harry"
John Wayne • Frank Sinatra
Burt Lancaster • Robert Mitchum
George C. Scott • Steve McQueen • Paul Newman

WHO Trivia
Although Detective Harry Callahan is arguably Clint Eastwood's signature role, he was not a top contender for the role. Seven A-list actors turned it down before it was offered to him.

John Wayne was the first to turn the role down. Frank Sinatra was then attached, but after years of unsuccessfully trying to get the project off the ground, Sinatra finally left it. Burt Lancaster and Robert Mitchum then turned down the role. George C. Scott was offered the part, but the script's violent nature led him to turn it down.

The producers considered younger actors including Steve McQueen, but he refused to make another "cop movie" after *Bullitt*. After Paul Newman turned the role down, believing the character was too "right-wing" for him, he suggested the film would be a good vehicle for Clint Eastwood.

Audie Murphy was going to play the role of Scorpio, the serial killer, but he died before filming began. James Caan was considered, but in the end the role went to unknown Andy Robinson.

CABARET (1972)

Sally: I suppose you're wondering what I'm doing, working at a place like the Kit Kat Club.

Brian: Well, it is a rather unusual place.

Sally: That's me, darling. Unusual places, unusual love affairs. I am a most strange and extraordinary person.

Plot

A female girlie club entertainer in Weimar Republic-era Berlin romances two men while the Nazi Party rises to power around them.

CASTING

Who Starred as Sally Bowles?
Liza Minnelli

Turned Down the Role of Sally Bowles
Faye Dunaway • Jill Ireland • Barbra Streisand

WHO Trivia

When this project was in its earliest planning stages, Julie Christie was offered the role of Sally Bowles to play opposite her then-boyfriend, Warren Beatty, as bisexual gigolo, Brian.

Before Liza Minnelli was cast as Sally Bowles, and won the Academy Award for Best Actress, Faye Dunaway turned the role down, as did Jill Ireland, whose husband, Charles Bronson, rejected it in her name. Julie Andrews, Ann-Margret, Jane Fonda, Shirley MacLaine, and Natalie Wood were all considered for the role.

Producer Cy Feuer had cast Joel Grey as the Master of Ceremonies reprising his stage role, long before Fosse was attached, so he was given the option of using Grey or walking away from the production.

Before Michael York was cast as Brian, Malcolm McDowell, David Hemmings, Timothy Dalton, Jeremy Irons, and Tim Curry were considered for the role.

Billy Wilder and Gene Kelly both turned down offers to direct *Cabaret* before Bob Fosse accepted it.

THE GODFATHER (1972)

Don Vito Corleone: You look terrible. I want you to eat. I want you to rest a while. And in a month from now, this Hollywood bigshot's gonna give you what you want.

Johnny Fontane: It's too late, they start shooting in a week.

Don Vito Corleone: I'm gonna make him an offer he can't refuse.

Plot
The aging patriarch of an organized crime dynasty transfers control of his empire to his reluctant son .

CASTING

Who Starred as Don Vito Corleone?
Marlon Brando

Turned Down the Role of Don Vito Corleone
Laurence Olivier

Who Starred as Michael Corleone?
Al Pacino

Turned Down the Role of Michael Corleone
James Caan • Warren Beatty • Jack Nicholson
Robert Redford • Dustin Hoffman • Martin Sheen

Who Starred as Sonny Corleone?
James Caan

Turned Down the Role of Sonny Corleone
Carmine Caridi

WHO Trivia
Author Mario Puzo wanted Marlon Brando to portray Don Vito Corleone from the beginning. He even sent a letter to Brando in which Puzo stated Brando was the "only actor who can play the Godfather." Despite Puzo's wishes, the executives at Paramount were against having Brando, partly due to the poor performance of his recent films and also his short temper.

Director Francis Ford Coppola favored Marlon Brando or Laurence Olivier, but Olivier's agent turned it down claiming Olivier was sick, although he went on to star in *Sleuth* that same year. Studio executives pushed for Ernest Borgnine. Others considered were: George C. Scott, Anthony Quinn, and Orson Welles.

After months of debate between Coppola and Paramount over Brando, the two finalists for the role were Borgnine and Brando. Coppola did not want to offend Brando, so Coppola told Brando he wanted to come to Brando's California residence to test equipment for other screen tests, and that he needed Brando's help. Doing his own make-up for the "test" audition tape, Brando stuck cotton balls in his cheeks, and put shoe polish in his hair to darken it.

Back at the studio, Coppola placed Brando's "test" audition tape in the middle of the videos of the audition tapes. As the Paramount executives went through the tapes, they were so impressed with Brando's efforts they allowed Coppola to cast Brando for the role under two conditions – if Brando accepted a lower salary, and put up a bond to ensure he would not cause any delays in production.

As the start of filming approached, the role of Michael Corleone had not yet been cast. Al Pacino was Coppola's favorite for the role, but Paramount executives wanted a popular actor, either Warren Beatty or Robert Redford. Coppola didn't think either was a good fit for the role, instead offering the role to Jack Nicholson who turned it down, thinking it wasn't right for him.

There was a rumor Burt Reynolds was considered to play Michael Corleone. Some say he was actually cast but Marlon Brando wouldn't act alongside him. After James Caan auditioned, Paramount executives, in concert with Coppola, gave him the part of Michael. The role of Sonny Corleone was given to Carmine Caridi. Coppola still pushed for Pacino to play Michael after the fact. Robert Evans, the head of the studio, eventually conceded, allowing Pacino to have the role of Michael as long as Caan played Sonny. Evans preferred Caan over Caridi because Caan was seven inches shorter than Caridi, which was closer to Pacino's height.

Despite winning the role of Michael Corleone, Pacino was contracted to star in MGM's *The Gang That Couldn't Shoot Straight*. The two studios agreed on a settlement. Pacino was signed three weeks before shooting began.

Originally, Robert De Niro, was given the part of Paulie in *The Godfather*. After Pacino quit *The Gang That Couldn't Shoot Straight*, De Niro auditioned for and got Pacino's role in *The Gang That Couldn't Shoot Straight*, and left *The Godfather*. Later, De Niro went on to star in *Godfather Part II* as the younger Vito Corleone.

DELIVERANCE (1972)

Ed: What are we gonna do, Lewis? You're the guy with the answers. What the hell do we do now?

Lewis: Now you get to play the game.

Ed: Lewis, you're wrong.

Plot

Four suburban professional men from Atlanta, Georgia go on a weekend canoe and camping trip into the dangerous American back-country.

CASTING

Who Starred as Ed Gentry?

Jon Voight

Turned Down the Role of Ed Gentry

Gene Hackman • Lee Marvin • Jack Nicholson

Who Starred as Lewis Medlock?

Burt Reynolds

Turned Down the Role of Lewis Medlock

Steve McQueen • Charlton Heston • Marlon Brando

WHO Trivia

Warner Bros. wanted to cast either Steve McQueen or Charlton Heston as Lewis, but both passed on the film.

Director/Producer John Boorman wanted Lee Marvin and Marlon Brando to play Ed and Lewis, respectfully. After reading the script, Marvin said he was too old and wouldn't be able to handle the physically difficult river scenes. Brando said he would think about it.

After Henry Fonda turned down the role of Ed, Gene Hackman was offered the role, but he wanted to play Lewis; Boorman did not agree.

Finally, Jack Nicholson agreed to play Ed as long as Brando played Lewis. However, the actors' combined fees totaled more than $1 million, half the movie's budget. This forced Boorman to cast cheaper actors, Burt Reynolds, who thought the role would advance his career, and Jon Voight, whose stock was low at the time.

PAPER MOON (1973)

Addie: I want my two hundred dollars.

Moze: I don't have your two hundred dollars no more.

Addie: If you don't give me my two hundred dollars I'm gonna tell a policeman how you got it and he'll make you give it to me.

Moze: But I don't have it!

Addie: Then get it!

Plot

During the Great Depression, a con man finds himself saddled with a young girl who may or may not be his daughter, and the two forge an unlikely partnership.

CASTING

Who Starred as Moses "Moze" Pray?
Ryan O'Neal

Turned Down the Role of Moses "Moze" Pray
Paul Newman

Who Starred as Addie Loggins?
Tatum O'Neal

Turned Down the Role of Addie Loggins
Nell Potts

WHO Trivia

The film project was originally associated with John Huston and was to star Paul Newman and his daughter, Nell Potts, but when Huston left the project, the Newmans became dissociated from the film.

Peter Bogdanovich was looking for a project when his ex-wife and frequent collaborator, Polly Platt, recommended Joe David Brown's script, based on the novel *Addie Pray*. Platt also suggested that eight-year-old Tatum O'Neal audition for the role, although she had no acting experience. Bogdanovich had recently worked with Tatum's father Ryan O'Neal on *What's Up, Doc?*, decided to cast them as the leads.

Bogdanovich didn't like the title of the novel, *Addie Pray*, but wasn't convinced *Paper Moon* was right, so he asked his mentor, Orson Welles, who replied, "That title is so good, you shouldn't even make the picture, just release the title." Welles also suggested shooting the film in black and white.

THE EXORCIST (1973)

Father/Dr. Karras: Hello, Regan. I'm a friend of your mother's. I'd like to help you.

Regan: *(in possessed voice)* You might loosen these straps then.

Father/Dr. Karras: I'm afraid you might hurt yourself, Regan.

Regan: I'm not Regan.

Father/Dr. Karras: Well then, let's introduce ourselves. I'm Damien Karras.

Regan: And I'm the devil. Now kindly undo these straps!

Plot

After discovering the demonic possession of her 12-year-old daughter, her desperate mother attempts to save her back through an exorcism conducted by two priests.

CASTING

Who Starred as Chris MacNeil?
Ellen Burstyn

Turned Down the Role of Chris MacNeil
Audrey Hepburn • Anne Bancroft • Jane Fonda
Geraldine Page • Barbra Steisand

Who Starred as Regan MacNeil?
Linda Blair

Turned Down the Role of Regan MacNeil
Anissa Jones • Denise Nickerson • Jamie Lee Curtis

WHO Trivia

The casting for *The Exorcist*, the first and only horror film to be nominated for Best Picture, until *Get Out* in 2017, began with a major battle over who would direct the film. Warner Bros. approached Arthur Penn, Stanley Kubrick, and Mike Nichols. They all turned the project down. Nichols declined because he didn't think a 12-year-old girl could be found who would be capable of playing the part as well as handling the likely psychological stress it would cause.

When Mark Rydell was hired to direct, William Peter Blatty, author of the novel and screenplay, and one of the film's producers, vehemently objected, insisting on hiring William Friedkin, because he wanted his film to have the same energy as Friedkin's previous film, *The French Connection*. After a long standoff with the studio over Rydell, Blatty eventually got his way.

Warner Bros. decided they wanted name stars for the three leading roles.

Three A-List actresses were first considered for the role of Chris MacNeil. First, Friedkin approached Audrey Hepburn, who said she was willing to take the role, but only if the movie could be shot in Rome, since she had moved to Italy with her husband; that would have raised the costs of the movie considerably. Friedkin offered the role to Anne Bancroft, also willing, but asked if production could be delayed nine months as she had just gotten pregnant. Again, Friedkin declined her request as he could not wait that long, nor did he think the material was something she would want to be working on while tending to a newborn. Next on the list, Jane Fonda, turned it down, calling it a "piece of capitalist rip-off bullshit."

Shirley MacLaine turned down the role to make the similar, but less successful, *The Possession of Joel Delaney*. Geraldine Page and Barbra Streisand also reportedly turned down the role.

Debbie Reynolds and her daughter, Carrie Fisher, were in discussion to play Chris and Regan MacNeil, but nothing came of it.

For the male leads, Warner Bros. wanted Marlon Brando for Father Merrin. Friedkin immediately vetoed this, stating it would become a Brando movie, instead of the film he wanted to make. Jack Nicholson auditioned for the part, but Friedkin thought he was too unholy to ever play a priest.

Finally, after many name stars were considered, Blatty and Friedkin ultimately decided to use less well-known actors. Max von Sydow and Stacy Keach were cast in the roles of Father Merrin and Father Karras, respectively.

Weeks later, while in New York, Friedkin saw Jason Miller's performance in the play, *That Championship Season*. A discussion among the men ensued about the lapsed Catholicism presented in the play. Friedkin knew this subject was important as background for the film; Friedkin gave Miller a copy of the script since Miller had not read the book.

While still looking for an actress to play Chris, Ellen Burstyn, fresh off great reviews for *The King of Marvin Gardens*, phoned Friedkin and emphatically stated that she was "destined" to play Chris. Ted Ashley, the head of Warner Bros., vigorously opposed casting her. However, after no other alternatives acceptable to Friedkin emerged, Ashley finally relented, and Burstyn was cast in the part.

Friedkin was surprised when Miller called him back after reading the novel. He told Friedkin, "that guy is me," referring to Father Karras. Miller explained that he had had a Catholic education and had studied to be a Jesuit priest himself for three years until experiencing a crisis of faith, just as Karras. Friedkin thanked him for his interest, but told him that Stacy Keach had already been signed. Miller, who had done some stage acting but had never been in a movie, asked to at least be given a screen test.

Friedkin agreed to the screen test. After viewing the footage, Friedkin realized Miller's "dark good looks, haunted eyes, quiet intensity, and low, compassionate voice" qualities were exactly what the part needed, and had the studio buy out Keach's contract.

Anissa Jones, who played Buffy on the television show, *Family Affair,* audi-tioned for Regan, the last role to be cast in the film. Jones was rejected as being too well-known. Denise Nickerson, Violet in *Willy Wonka & the Chocolate Factory,* was considered, but the material troubled her parents. Friedkin interviewed young actresses as old as sixteen, but who looked young enough to play Regan. He wanted to talk to Jamie Lee Curtis, but her mother, Janet Leigh, refused. Friedkin was extremely frustrated, when Elinore Blair came in, unannounced, to the director's New York office with her daughter Linda; her agency had not sent Linda for the part, so her mother to take a chance and just walk in.

Both mother and daughter impressed Friedkin since Elinore was not a typical stage mother, and Linda's credits were primarily in modeling. "Smart, but not precocious. Cute but not beautiful. A normal, happy twelve-year-old girl," Friedkin later recalled saying to himself.

Having demonstrated the personal qualities Friedkin was looking for, he wanted to see whether Linda could handle the material. He asked if she knew what *The Exorcist* was about; she told him it was about a little girl who gets possessed by the devil and does a whole bunch of bad things.

Friedkin then asked her what sort of bad things she meant? Blair said, "She pushes a man out of her bedroom window, and she hits her mother across the face, and she masturbates with a crucifix." Friedkin then asked Linda if she knew what masturbation meant. "It's like jerking off, isn't it?" Friedkin saw that Elinore was smiling. "Have you ever done that?" she asked her daughter. "Sure; haven't you?" Linda responded. After doing a screen test with Ellen Burstyn, Linda Blair was cast as Regan.

BLAZING SADDLES (1974)

Sheriff Bart: Are we awake?
Waco Kid: We're not sure... Are we... black?
Sheriff Bart: Yes, we are.
Waco Kid: Then we're awake. But we're very puzzled.

Plot

A corrupt political boss in an attempt to ruin a western town, appoints a black sheriff who promptly becomes his most formidable adversary.

CASTING

Who Starred in the Role of Sheriff Bart?
Cleavon Little

Turned Down the Role of Sheriff Bart
Richard Pryor • James Earl Jones

Who Starred in the Role of "The Waco Kid"?
Gene Wilder

Turned Down the Role of "The Waco Kid"
John Wayne • Gig Young

WHO Trivia

Richard Pryor was Brooks' original choice to play Sheriff Bart. However, Warner Bros., citing Pryor's history of drug arrests, made him uninsurable, and refused to approve financing with Pryor as the star. Cleavon Little was cast in the role, and Pryor remained as a writer.

Gig Young was originally cast as "The Waco Kid," but collapsed during his first scene from alcohol withdrawal syndrome, and Gene Wilder was flown in to replace him.

Mel Brooks had numerous conflicts with Warner Bros. executives over the content of the film. Especially the frequent use of the N-word.

Years later, Brooks said, "If a remake of *Blazing Saddles* was done today, they would be forced to leave out the N-word, and then, you've got no movie." Brook also said, "I received many letters of complaint... but most of them were from white people."

DEATH WISH (1974)

Frank Ochoa: We want you to get out of New York... Permanently.
Paul Kersey: Inspector... (*smiles*) By sundown?

Plot
A New York City architect becomes a one-man vigilante squad after his wife is murdered and his daughter sexually assaulted during a home invasion.

CASTING

Who Starred as Paul Kersey?
Charles Bronson

Turned Down the Role of Paul Kersey
Steve McQueen • Clint Eastwood • Burt Lancaster
Frank Sinatra • George C. Scott • Jack Lemmon

WHO Trivia
The role of Paul Kersey was originally intended for Steve McQueen, who turned it down. Clint Eastwood also turned down the role, and suggested that Gregory Peck would be right for the part.

After Frank Sinatra, Burt Lancaster, and George C. Scott all turned down the lead role, director Sidney Lumet settled on Jack Lemmon to play Kersey, and Henry Fonda to play Detective Ochoa. For some reason, Lumet chose to direct *Serpico* instead, and both Lemmon and Fonda dropped out.

United Artists hired Michael Winner as the director based on his track record of gritty, violent action films. Winner had just finished *The Stone Killer* with Charles Bronson the year before, and both wanted to make another film together.

Winner told Bronson, "The best script I've got is, *Death Wish*. It's about a man whose wife is killed, his daughter is raped, and he goes out and shoots muggers." "I'd like to do that," Bronson said. "The film?" asked Winner. Bronson replied, "No... shoot muggers."

THE GREAT GATSBY (1974)

Nick Carraway: They say you killed a man.
   Jay Gatsby: Only one?

Plot

A Midwesterner becomes fascinated with his nouveau riche neighbor who obsesses over his lost love.

CASTING

Who Starred as Jay Gatsby?
Robert Redford

Turned Down the Role of Jay Gatsby
Steve McQueen • Warren Beatty
Jack Nicholson • Marlon Brando

Who Starred as Daisy Buchanan?
Mia Farrow

Turned Down the Role of Daisy Buchanan
Liza Minnelli • Natalie Wood

WHO Trivia

The rights to the novel were purchased in 1971 by studio head Robert Evans, so his wife Ali MacGraw could play the role of Daisy Buchanan. Since a shooting script wasn't ready yet, MacGraw agreed to star in *The Getaway*. During production, MacGraw fell in love with her co-star Steve McQueen. MacGraw divorced Evans and married McQueen. Ironically, McQueen was once offered the role of Jay Gatsby, but turned it down.

With the film back on the production schedule, Evans offered the role of Daisy to Liza Minnelli who turned it down. Subsequently, he offered it to Natalie Wood under the condition that she do a screen test because she had made only one movie in the previous seven years. She balked.

Before Robert Redford was cast as Jay Gatsby, Jack Nicholson, Warren Beatty, and Marlon Brando turned down the role. Brando turned it down because the studio would not submit to his salary demands.

Truman Capote was the original screenwriter. After Capote was fired, a young screenwriter named Robert Towne turned down a chance to do a rewrite and finish the screenplay, saying, "I didn't want to be the unknown Hollywood screenwriter who screwed up a literary classic." Instead, he wrote *Chinatown*.

JAWS (1975)

Chief Brody: Slow ahead. I can go slow ahead. Come on down here and chum some of this shit.
(Shark suddenly appears; Brody recoils in shock)
You're gonna need a bigger boat.

Plot
A police chief, a marine biologist, and a grizzled shark hunter set out to kill a great white shark menacing the seaside community of Amity Island.

CASTING

Who Starred as Chief Brody?
Roy Scheider

Turned Down the Role of Chief Brody
Robert Duvall

Who Starred as Quint?
Robert Shaw

Turned Down the Role of Quint
Lee Marvin • Sterling Hayden

Who Starred as Matt Hooper?
Richard Dreyfuss

Turned Down the Role of Matt Hooper
Jon Voight • Kevin Kline • Richard Dreyfuss

WHO Trivia
Originally, Steven Spielberg was not the director of Jaws. The first director, Dick Richards, during a meeting with the producers Richard D. Zanuck and David Brown, referred to the shark as a whale, which set them off, and resulted in Richards being fired. They then hired Spielberg.

Though Spielberg complied with a request from the producers to cast known actors, he wanted to avoid hiring any big stars. He thought that "somewhat anonymous" performers would help the audience "believe this was happening to regular people," whereas "stars bring a lot of memories along with them. Those memories can sometimes corrupt the story." Spielberg added that in his plans, "the superstar was gonna be the shark."

The role of Chief Brody was offered to Robert Duvall. Duvall turned it down, telling Spielberg he was only interested in portraying Quint. However, Spielberg turned Duvall down, telling him he was too young to play Quint.

Charlton Heston expressed a desire for the role, but Spielberg felt that Heston would bring a screen persona too grand for the part of a police chief of a modest community. It might imply to the audience that the shark had virtually no chance. Heston became very angry, and never forgave Spielberg, refusing to ever work with him.

Roy Scheider became interested in the project after overhearing Spielberg at a party talk with a screenwriter about having the shark jump up onto a boat. Spielberg was initially apprehensive about hiring Scheider, fearing he would portray a "tough guy," similar to his role in *The French Connection*.

Nine days before the start of production, neither Quint nor Hooper had been cast. Lee Marvin was Spielberg's first choice for the role of Quint, but Marvin turned him down. He then turned to Sterling Hayden, but he had problems with the IRS, and a deal could not be struck. So, Robert Shaw was cast on the recommendation of the film's producers, Zanuck and Brown. Shaw was reluctant to take the role since he did not like the book, but at the urging of his wife, decided to accept.

For the role of Matt Hooper, Spielberg initially wanted Jon Voight, who was not available. He then offered the part to Kevin Kline who turned it down. Spielberg then considered Timothy Bottoms and Jeff Bridges.

Spielberg's friend, George Lucas, suggested Richard Dreyfuss, whom he had directed in *American Graffiti*. The actor initially passed, but changed his decision after he attended a screening of *The Apprenticeship of Duddy Kravitz*. Dreyfuss was so disappointed in his performance, and fearing that no one would want to hire him once the film was released, he immediately called Spielberg and accepted the role in *Jaws*.

An interesting story about the film is that when composer John Williams played the score for Spielberg, he laughed and said, "That's funny, John, what do you really have in mind for the theme?" Spielberg later stated that without William's score, the movie would only have been half as successful. And according to Williams, "The film jumpstarted my career."

A STAR IS BORN (1976)

Esther Hoffman: *(to John Norman)* You can trash your life, but you're not going to trash mine.

Plot

A young singer meets and falls in love with a rock & roll star, only to find her career ascending while his goes into decline.

CASTING

Who Starred as John Norman Howard?
Kris Kristofferson

Turned Down the Role of John Norman Howard
Elvis Presley • Neil Diamond
James Taylor • Kenny Loggins

WHO Trivia

This version of the classic Judy Garland film was initially conceived as a vehicle for Carly Simon and James Taylor, but Taylor had had enough of movies after his "torturous" debut in *Two-Lane Blacktop* in 1971.

After producer Jon Peters came on board, he brought the project to his "partner" Barbra Streisand, but she initially turned it down. In time, he was able to persuade her to take another look, and she decided to do it.

Streisand really wanted Elvis Presley for the role of John Norman Howard. Presley was interested, thinking it would revive his film career, but his manager, Colonel Tom Parker, insisted Elvis have top billing, and asked for a substantial sum of money for the role. Parker also did not want to have Elvis portrayed as having a show business career in decline because this was far from the truth; Elvis played to packed auditoriums wherever he toured. This effectively ended Elvis's involvement.

Neil Diamond, who knew Streisand from their days at Erasmus Hall High School in Brooklyn, was also offered the role, but had to decline due to his extensive concert commitments. Kenny Loggins was offered the role, but also had to turn it down due to touring commitments.

Finally, Kris Kristofferson got the part of John Norman Howard.

NETWORK (1976)

Howard Beale: Things have got to change. But first, you've gotta get mad!...You've got to say, I'm mad as hell, and I'm not going to take this anymore! Then we'll figure out what to do about the depression and the inflation and the oil crisis. But first, get up out of your chairs, open the window, stick your head out, and yell, and say it: 'I'm as mad as hell, and I'm not going to take this anymore!'

Plot

A television network cynically exploits a deranged but enlightened former anchor's ravings and revelations about the news media for its own profit.

CASTING

Who Starred as Howard Beale?
Peter Finch

Turned Down the Role of Howard Beale
Henry Fonda • Jimmy Stewart • George C. Scott
Gene Hackman • William Holden

Who Starred as Diana Christensen?
Faye Dunaway

Turned Down the Role of Diana Christensen
Candice Bergen • Ellen Burstyn • Natalie Wood
Jane Fonda • Kay Lenz • Diane Keaton
Marsha Mason • Jill Clayburgh

WHO Trivia

Director Sidney Lumet wanted Henry Fonda, with whom he had worked several times, to play the role of Howard Beale. Fonda declined, finding the role too "hysterical" for his taste. James Stewart also turned down the role as he found the script unsuitable, objecting to the strong language.

In his notes, screenwriter Paddy Chayefsky jotted down his ideas about casting. For Howard Beale, he envisioned a number of A-List legends, and went so far as to write to Paul Newman, telling him that, "You and a very small handful of other actors are the only ones I can think of with the range for this part."

George C. Scott, Glenn Ford, and William Holden reportedly turned down the opportunity to play Beale.

Holden instead ended up playing Max Schumacher. For that role, Chayefsky had initially wanted Walter Matthau, or coincidentally, Gene Hackman.

Nancy Allen was the original choice for Diana Christensen, but was forced to turn down the role because she was already committed to *Carrie*. Kay Lenz was offered the role, but had to turn it down due to her commitment to the television mini-series, *Rich Man, Poor Man*.

Chayefsky thought Candice Bergen, Ellen Burstyn, and Natalie Wood would all be good in the role, while the studio suggested Jane Fonda, Diane Keaton, Marsha Mason and Jill Clayburgh.

Lumet wanted to cast Vanessa Redgrave in the film, but Chayefsky didn't want her. Lumet argued that he thought she was the greatest actress in the world. Chayefsky, a proud Jew and supporter of Israel, objected on the basis of her support of the PLO. Lumet, himself a Jew, said, "Paddy, that's blacklisting!" Chayefsky replied, "Not when a Jew does it to a Gentile."

Lumet and Chayefsky finally agreed to offer the role of Diana to Jane Fonda, but she turned it down. Faye Dunaway was then cast.

Peter Finch, who won the Oscar for Best Actor, died before the Academy Awards were voted on. He was the only performer to receive a posthumous award, until Heath Ledger won for the Joker in *The Dark Night*.

Peter Finch and Faye Dunaway, who won the Best Actor and Best Actress Oscars, have no scenes or dialog together in the film.

Interesting to note that Beatrice Straight, who played Louise Schumacher, is only on the screen for five minutes and two seconds, making it the briefest performance to win an Academy Award. She won for Best Supporting Actress.

ROCKY (1976)

Rocky: I just want to say hi to my girlfriend, OK? Yo, Adrian!... It's me, Rocky.

Plot
A rags-to-riches American dream story about a dull-witted but good-hearted "collection agent" for a Philadelphia loan shark, with a penchant for boxing who gets a shot at the world heavyweight title.

CASTING

Who Starred as Adrian?
Talia Shire

Turned Down the Role of Adrian
Carrie Snodgress • Bette Midler

Who Starred as Mickey?
Burgess Meredith

Turned Down the Role of Mickey
Lee Strasberg

WHO Trivia
After producers Irwin Winkler and Robert Chartoff became interested in the script, they offered Sylvester Stallone an unprecedented $350,000 for the rights. Stallone was basically broke, but refused to sell unless they agreed to allow him to star in the film. They agreed, on the condition that Stallone continue to work as a writer without a fee, and to work as an actor for scale.

After Winkler and Chartoff purchased the film, they took it to United Artists, who envisioned a large enough budget to sign Robert Redford, Ryan O'Neal, or Burt Reynolds. When Winkler and Chartoff told United Artists that Stallone had to play Rocky, United Artists then offered a budget of up to $1 million, and had Chartoff and Winkler sign agreements they would be personally liable if the film went over budget.

After Bette Midler turned down the role of Adrian, Carrie Snodgress was offered the part, but a money dispute forced her out. Talia Shire, who admired Stallone's journey, pursued the role, eager to get out of the shadow of her big brother, Francis Ford Coppola. Lee Strasberg was initially offered the role of Rocky's trainer, Mickey, but with the reduced budget, Winkler and Chartoff couldn't afford him. Burgess Meredith was cast instead.

TAXI DRIVER (1976)

Travis: You talkin' to me? You talkin' to me? You talkin' to me? Well, then who the hell else are you talking?... You talking to me? Well, I'm the only one here. Who the fuck do you think you're talking to?

Plot
A mentally unstable Vietnam war veteran works as a nighttime taxi driver in New York City. The decadence and sleaze around him feeds his urge to violently lash out.

CASTING

Who Starred as Travis Bickle?
Robert De Niro

Turned Down the Role of Travis Bickle
Al Pacino • Jack Nicholson • Burt Reynolds

Who Starred as Iris?
Jodie Foster

Turned Down the Role of Iris
Melanie Griffith • Mariel Hemingway • Carrie Fisher
Linda Blair • Geena Davis • Tatum O' Neal

Who Starred as Betsy?
Cybill Shepherd

Turned Down the Role of Betsy
Meryl Streep • Sigourney Weaver
Liza Minnelli • Barbara Hershey

WHO Trivia
While director Martin Scorsese and screenwriter Paul Schrader made one of the most iconic films in cinema history, the casting and directing issues could have been a movie unto itself. Initially, when Tony Bill was considering directing the film, the script was sent to Al Pacino, but he declined the role. Producer Julia Phillips thought the reason might have been that he didn't want to work with Tony Bill. Then director Brian de Palma came on board for a few weeks.

When Martin Scorsese became available, and offered to bring Robert De Niro along to play Travis Bickle, producer Julia Phillips let Brian de Palma go, giving him a gross point as a parting gift to assuage her guilt.

Not long after Robert De Niro signed a contract for the film in the amount of $35,000, he won the Oscar for his role in *The Godfather: Part II,* which made him a very much in-demand actor. The film's producers were terrified he would ask for a deserved pay hike. Since Columbia was very uncomfortable with the project, and looking for excuses to pull the plug on it, De Niro graciously honored his original deal, so the film would get made.

The casting of Iris, eventually played by Jodie Foster, then 12 years old, was very competitive with over two hundred actresses interested.

When Brian de Palma was the director, he supposedly offered the role to Melanie Griffith, but her mother, actress Tippi Hedren, made her turn it down.

Martin Scorsese first offered the role of Iris to Mariel Hemingway, but her family made her turn it down. Carrie Fisher turned down the part, uncomfortable with the role, as did Linda Blair. Model Geena Davis was offered the role, but decided to keep modeling instead.

Tatum O'Neal was offered the part, but turned it down because she thought the role was too small after winning an Oscar. Instead, she took the role of Amanda Wuerlitzer in *The Bad News Bears.* Ironically, Jodie Foster was originally offered the role of Amanda Wuerlitzer, but wanted to play Iris instead.

Other casting stories attached to the film include the fact that screenwriter Paul Schrader actually wrote the part of Travis Bickle with Jeff Bridges in mind. In his autobiography, Burt Reynolds says he regrettably turned down the role and that John Travolta, to boost his fame as a teen idol, auditioned for the part.

The role of presidential candidate Charles Palantine, played by Leonard Harris, was turned down by Rock Hudson, due to Hudson's commitment to his television show, *McMillan and Wife.*

Mia Farrow wanted the role of Betsy, but Scorsese turned her down.

Finally, the scene voted the 10th most memorable in Wikipedia history, in which Travis Bickle is talking to himself in the mirror, was completely ad-libbed by De Niro. He said he was inspired by Bruce Springsteen's banter with his audience at a mid-1970s gig. The script just said, "Travis looks in the mirror."

CLOSE ENCOUNTERS OF THE THIRD KIND (1977)

Roy Neary: I know this sounds crazy, but ever since yesterday on the road, I've been seeing this shape. Shaving cream, pillows... Dammit! I know this. I know what this is! This means something. This is important.

Plot

An electric lineman's quiet and ordinary life turns upside down after a close encounter with a UFO.

CASTING

Who Starred as Roy Neary?
Richard Dreyfuss

Turned Down the Role of Roy Neary
Steve McQueen • Al Pacino
Gene Hackman • Jack Nicholson

WHO Trivia

Richard Dreyfuss had become quite interested in the film while on the set of *Jaws,* and bugged Spielberg about casting him. When the actually casting began, he threw his hat into the ring and was relentless.

Steve McQueen was actually Spielberg's first choice, and although McQueen was impressed with the script, he felt he was not right for the role as he was unable to cry on cue. After McQueen turned him down, Spielberg decided to give the role to Dreyfuss. Universal did not want to meet Dreyfuss' price of $450,000 plus gross points so they offered the film to Al Pacino, who turned it down.

Jack Nicholson turned it down, thinking that any actor would be overwhelmed by the special effects, and then Gene Hackman turned it down, due to personal issues. Universal suggested James Caan, but he wanted $1 million plus 10% of the gross, so they decided to go back to Richard Dreyfuss and cut a deal.

Melinda Dillon was cast largely on the suggestion of director Hal Ashby, who sent Spielberg a couple of film reels containing Dillon's acting in *Bound for Glory.* Spielberg hired her immediately. While watching a television commercial, Spielberg discovered Teri Garr, who was given the role of Ronnie Neary.

STAR WARS (1977)

Ben Obi-Wan Kenobi: Remember, the Force will be with you always.

Plot
Luke Skywalker joins forces with a Jedi Knight, a cocky pilot, a Wookiee and two droids to save the galaxy from the Empire and Darth Vader.

CASTING

Who Starred as Han Solo?
Harrison Ford

Turned Down the Role of Han Solo
James Caan • Jack Nicholson
Robert De Niro • Burt Reynolds

Who Starred as Princess Leia?
Carrie Fisher

Turned Down the Role of Princess Leia
Jodie Foster

Who Starred as Ben Obi-Wan Kenobi?
Alec Guinness

Turned Down the Role of Ben Obi-Wan Kenobi?
Toshiro Mifune

WHO Trivia
Writer/Director George Lucas favored casting young actors who lacked long experience, and had pared his choices down to Mark Hamill and William Katt for the leading role of Luke Skywalker. While reading for the character, Hamill found the dialogue to be extremely odd because of its universe-embedded concepts. He chose to simply read it sincerely, and was rewarded when Lucas selected him instead of Katt, who subsequently was cast in *Carrie*.

Lucas initially rejected Harrison Ford for the Han Solo role because he "wanted new faces," and Ford had previously worked on *American Graffiti*. After James Caan, Jack Nicholson, Robert De Niro and Burt Reynolds turned down the part, Lucas asked Ford to assist in the auditions by reading lines with a long list of other actors. It was during these auditions that Lucas realized Ford was the best actor for the part.

Jodie Foster turned down the role of Princess Leia because she was working on two films at the time. Lucas then auditioned Amy Irving, Cindy Williams, Karen Allen and Carrie Fisher, with Fisher winning the role.

THE GOODBYE GIRL (1977)

Elliot: I happen to have a lease in my pocket. Are you gonna honor it or what?

Paula: I have a daughter in my bedroom. That tops the lease in your pocket.

Plot
After being dumped by her live-in boyfriend, an unemployed dancer and her 10- year-old daughter are reluctantly forced to live with a struggling off-Broadway actor who has sublet their apartment from the ex-boyfriend.

CASTING

Who Starred as Elliot Garfield?
Richard Dreyfuss

Turned Down the Role of Elliot Garfield
Robert De Niro • Jack Nicholson
James Caan • Tony Lo Bianco

WHO Trivia
Written by Neil Simon for his wife Marsha Mason, the film began as a screenplay called *Bogart Slept Here*, and was to star Robert De Niro and Mason. The esteemed Mike Nichols was hired as the director. It was also the first film for De Niro after *Taxi Driver*.

After filming began on *Bogart Slept Here,* it became apparent that De Niro wasn't right for the role. Simon recalled, "...it was clear that any of the humor I had written was going to get lost. It's not that De Niro isn't funny, but his humor comes mostly from his nuances, a bemused expression on his face or the way he would look at a character, smile and then look up at the ceiling."

Nichols insisted on recasting De Niro. Soon after, Nichols left the project. Other actors brought in to read for the role were Jack Nicholson, James Caan and Tony Lo Bianco, but none seemed to work for Simon. Richard Dreyfuss then came in to read with Mason in character as Paula McFadden. At the end of the read-through, Simon said, "It doesn't work, but they do."

Simon rewrote the screenplay, specifically to fit Dreyfuss who was a far cry from Robert De Niro.

ANIMAL HOUSE (1978)

Bluto: My advice to you is to start drinking heavily.

Plot
A misfit group of fraternity boys take on the system at their college.

CASTING

Who Starred as Otter?
Tim Matheson

Turned Down the Role of Otter
Chevy Chase

Who Starred as Boon?
Peter Riegert

Turned Down the Role of Boon
Bill Murray

Who Starred as D-Day?
Bruce McGill

Turned Down the Role of D-Day
Dan Aykroyd

WHO Trivia
Director John Landis' initial cast included Chevy Chase as Otter, Bill Murray as Boon, Dan Aykroyd as D-Day, and John Belushi as Bluto, but only Belushi wanted to do it.

Chevy Chase was a star from *Saturday Night Live*, which had recently become a cultural phenomenon. His name would have added credibility to the project, but he turned down the film to do *Foul Play* with Goldie Hawn. Landis, who wanted to cast unknown dramatic actors instead of famous comedians, takes credit for subtly discouraging Chase.

To cover himself, Landis met with Meat Loaf in case Belushi did not want to play Bluto. After he committed to the film, Landis worked with Belushi on his character, who hardly had any dialogue. They decided that Bluto was a cross between Harpo Marx and the Cookie Monster. Belushi developed his ability to communicate without talking because his grandmother spoke little English.

Belushi also worked on *Saturday Night Live* and was still committed to the show. He spent Monday through Wednesday making the movie, and then flew back to New York to do *Saturday Night Live* on Thursday through Saturday.

The character of D-Day was based on Dan Aykroyd, who was a serious motorcycle aficionado. Aykroyd turned down the part because he was committed to *Saturday Night Live*.

John Landis met with Jack Webb to play Dean Wormer and Kim Novak to play his wife. Webb ultimately backed out due to concerns over his clean-cut image, and was replaced by John Vernon.

Universal Pictures, the studio financing the film, considered Belushi a supporting actor, and wanted another star for the cast. Landis, who had been a crew member on *Kelly's Heroes*, and had become friends with actor Donald Sutherland, sometimes babysitting his son, Kiefer, asked Sutherland to be in the film and play Professor Dave Jennings.

For two days of work, Sutherland declined the initial offer of $20,000 plus points tied to the profits. Universal then offered him his day rate of $25,000 or 2% of the film's gross. Sutherland took the guaranteed day rate fee, assuming the film would not be successful. That decision cost Sutherland what he estimates as $14 million.

After the film came out and was a hit, Landis gave Sutherland the credit he was due, "It was Donald Sutherland who essentially got the film made."

COMING HOME (1978)

Luke Martin: I have killed for my country, or whatever, and I don't feel
good about it. 'Cause there's not enough reason, man,
to feel a person die in your hands, or to see your best
buddy get blown away.

Plot

A woman whose husband is fighting in Vietnam falls in love with another
man who suffered a paralyzing combat injury there.

CASTING

Who Starred as Luke Martin?
Jon Voight

Turned Down the Role of Luke Martin
Al Pacino • Jack Nicholson • Sylvester Stallone

WHO Trivia

In 1972, Jane Fonda wanted to make a film about Vietnam. She hired Nancy
Dowd to write a script about the consequences of the war as seen through
the eyes of a military wife. The project dragged on for six years until it was
reshaped by a circle of talent led by Fonda. United by their opposition to
the Vietnam War and by their concern for the veterans returning to America
and adapting to life back home. The film finally went into pre-production
in 1977.

While cast from the beginning as Sally Hyde, Jane Fonda knew a box office
star was needed for the male lead to offset the grim nature of the story.

Jack Nicholson, Al Pacino, and Sylvester Stallone all declined the part.

Jon Voight had been considered for the role of the husband, but after
becoming involved with the film, he campaigned to play the role of the
paraplegic veteran. Voight had participated in the anti-war movement and
was a friend of Fonda's, who was instrumental in helping him land the role,
even though he had fallen from popularity since *Midnight Cowboy*.

Bruce Dern, long stereotyped in sadistic roles, was chosen as the husband,
and was nominated for an Academy Award for Best Supporting Actor.
Jane Fonda and Jon Voight won the Oscar for Best Actress and Best Actor
respectively.

PRETTY BABY (1978)

Bellocq: Her father's unknown, and her mother deserted the child.
Priest: And she was caucasian, or other?
Violet: She was a whore, Father.

Plot
A 12-year-old girl lives as a prostitute in New Orleans in 1917.

CASTING

Who Starred as Violet?
Brooke Shields

Turned Down the Role of Violet
Jodie Foster • Melanie Griffith
Kristy McNichol • Tatum O'Neal

Who Starred as Bellocq?
Keith Carradine

Turned Down the Role of Bellocq
Erik Estrada • Sylvester Stallone • John Travolta
Robert Redford • Christopher Reeve • Joe Pesci

Who Starred as Hattie?
Susan Sarandon

Turned Down the Role of Hattie
Goldie Hawn

WHO Trivia
Kristy McNichol turned down the leading role of Violet because of commitments to her television show, *Family*. Jodie Foster, after Taxi Driver, turned it down because she didn't want to be typecast, Melanie Griffith didn't want to play a child prostitute, and Tatum O'Neal's father, Ryan O'Neal, made her turn down the role.

Robert Redford, Clint Eastwood and Jeff Bridges all turned down the role of Bellocq. Erik Estrada wanted the role but had to turn it down due to scheduling conflicts with his television show, *Chips*. Christopher Reeve turned it down to prepare for his role in *Superman,* Sylvester Stallone turned it down because he was filming *F.I.S.T.* John Travolta turned it down because he was committed to *Grease*.

After Farrah Fawcett turned down the role of Hattie, Goldie Hawn turned it down to do *Foul Play* with Chevy Chase instead.

SUPERMAN (1978)

(Superman flies up, grabbing the falling Lois Lane)
Superman: Easy, miss. I've got you.
Lois Lane: You... you've got me?... Who's got you?

Plot

An alien orphan is sent from his dying planet to Earth where he grows up to become Superman.

CASTING

Who Starred as Superman?
Christopher Reeve

Turned Down the Role of Superman
Robert Redford • Burt Reynolds
James Caan • Paul Newman

Who Starred as Lex Luthor?
Gene Hackman

Turned Down the Role of Lex Luthor
Paul Newman • Dustin Hoffman

WHO Trivia

Producer Ilya Salkind first conceived the idea for a Superman film in late 1973. In November 1974, after a difficult process with DC Comics, the film rights were purchased by Ilya, his father Alexander Salkind, and Pierre Spengler.

When the film was finally on the production schedule, and before Richard Donner was hired to direct, it was initially decided to sign an A-list actor for the role of Superman. Robert Redford was offered a large sum, but Redford actually thought he was too famous. Burt Reynolds also turned down the role. James Caan turned down the role saying, "I just couldn't wear that suit."

Paul Newman was offered his choice of roles as Superman, Jor-El or Lex Luthor for $4 million; he turned down all three roles. Dustin Hoffman, considered for Superman at one time, also turned down the role of Lex Luthor. It was Lynn Stalmaster who convinced Richard Donner and Ilya Salkind to let Christopher Reeve do a screen test. Reeve stunned them and was cast as Superman, receiving a mere $250,000 for the part.

ALIEN (1979)

Dallas: All right! Ripley, when I give an order, I expect to be obeyed!
Ripley: Even if it's against the law?!
Dallas: YOU'RE GODDAMN RIGHT!!
Parker: Well, now that she has a point, you know, who the hell knows what that thing is!

Plot
A mining ship, investigating a suspected SOS, lands on a distant planet where the crew discovers a strange creature.

CASTING

Who Starred as Ripley?
Sigourney Weaver

Turned Down the Role of Ripley
Jill Clayburgh

Who Starred as Captain Dallas?
Tom Skerritt

Turned Down the Role of Captain Dallas
Harrison Ford

Who Starred as Kane?
John Hurt

Turned Down the Role of Kane
Jon Finch

WHO Trivia
After Jill Clayburgh turned down the role of Ripley, director Ridley Scott decided to cast Veronica Cartwright in the role. After some thought, he changed his mind and cast her as Lambert.

Scott then narrowed his choices down to Sigourney Weaver or Meryl Streep. Ultimately, Scott offered the job to Weaver because Streep was mourning the death of her partner John Cazale, and felt she would be distracted.

Jon Finch was originally cast as Kane, but he became seriously ill from diabetes on the first day of shooting and had to pull out. Scott then called on John Hurt, whom he had wanted for the role, but Hurt had a commitment for another film. However, the film role he had been committed to was cancelled, so he was able to accept.

APOCALYPSE NOW (1979)

Colonel Kurtz:	Did they say why, Willard, why they want to terminate my command?
Capt. Willard:	I was sent on a classified mission, sir.
Colonel Kurtz:	It's no longer classified, is it? Did they tell you?
Capt. Willard:	They told me that you had gone totally insane, and that your methods were unsound.
Colonel Kurtz:	Are my methods unsound?
Capt. Willard:	I don't see any method at all, sir.
Colonel Kurtz:	I expected someone like you. What did you expect? Are you an assassin?
Capt. Willard:	I'm a soldier.
Colonel Kurtz:	You're neither. You're an errand boy, sent by grocery clerks, to collect a bill.

Plot

An Army officer is tasked to assassinate a renegade Special Forces colonel who has set himself up as a "god" to a band of guerrillas in the jungles of Viet Nam.

CASTING

Who Starred as Captain Willard?
Martin Sheen

Turned Down the Role of Captain Willard
Harvey Keitel • Steve McQueen • Al Pacino
Clint Eastwood • Jack Nicholson • Nick Nolte
Robert Redford • James Caan

Who Starred as Lt. Colonel Kilgore?
Robert Duvall

Turned Down the Role of Lt. Colonel Kilgore
Steve McQueen

WHO Trivia

Director/Producer Francis Ford Coppola's first move after *Apocalypse Now* went into pre-production in early 1976 was to persuade Marlon Brando to play the role of Colonel Kurtz.

Steve McQueen was Coppola's first choice to play Captain Willard. McQueen initially verbally agreed when Coppola agreed to his salary of $3 million.

Shortly afterwards, McQueen, after thinking about the fact the work required several months of location shooting in the Philippine jungle, told Coppola he'd rather play the Lt. Colonel Kilgore role instead, which would require less location work, but wanted the same salary. Coppola, essentially self-financing the movie, could not afford it, and said no.

Robert Duvall, who eventually played Lt. Colonel Kilgore, gave an iconic performance even though his time on the screen was just eleven minutes.

After McQueen was out, Al Pacino was offered the role. He too did not want to be away for that long, and was afraid of falling ill in the jungle as he had done during the shooting of *The Godfather Part II*.

In a 2015 interview, Clint Eastwood revealed that Coppola offered him the role of Captain Willard, but much like McQueen and Pacino, didn't want to be away from America for that long. Eastwood also revealed that McQueen tried to convince him to play Willard.

Still needing someone to play Captain Willard, Coppola had been impressed by Martin Sheen's screen test for Michael in *The Godfather,* and he became his top choice. However, Sheen had already accepted another project, so based on his work in Martin Scorsese's *Mean Streets*, Harvey Keitel was cast in the role.

A few days after principal photography began, Coppola was unhappy with Keitel's take on Willard. After viewing early footage, the director took a plane back to Los Angeles, and replaced Keitel with Martin Sheen.

James Caan was the first choice to play Colonel Lucas, but Caan wanted too much money for what was considered a minor part. Harrison Ford was eventually cast instead.

The film took its toll on Martin Sheen, who had a heart attack during the filming. It is rumored that Francis Ford Coppola, not only lost 100 pounds during the filming, but threatened suicide several times.

KRAMER VS. KRAMER (1979)

Billy Kramer: Will she pick me up after school?
 Ted Kramer: Probably. And if she doesn't I will.
Billy Kramer: What if you forget?
 Ted Kramer: I won't forget.
Billy Kramer: What if you get run over by a truck and get killed?
 Ted Kramer: Then Mommy will pick you up.

Plot

A man's wife suddenly up and leaves him, allowing for a lost bond to be rediscovered between him and his son: A heated custody battle ensues over the son, deepening the wounds left by the separation.

CASTING

Who Starred as Ted Kramer?
Dustin Hoffman

Turned Down the Role of Ted Kramer
Al Pacino • Jon Voight • James Caan

Who Starred as Joanna Kramer?
Meryl Streep

Turned Down the Role of Joanna Kramer
Jane Fonda • Goldie Hawn • Kate Jackson

WHO Trivia

Before Dustin Hoffman was cast as Ted Kramer, Al Pacino, Jon Voight and James Caan had all turned down the role. Caan thought the character just wasn't that interesting.

After Jane Fonda and Goldie Hawn turned down the role of Joanna Kramer, Kate Jackson accepted the role. Jackson was forced to walk away because of the shooting schedule conflicts for her television show, *Charlie's Angels*. Finally, director Robert Benton decided to give the role to Meryl Streep, who was cast already as Ted's one-night stand, a role eventually played by JoBeth Williams.

Dustin Hoffman was in favor of Streep playing Joanna Kramer. He suggested to Benton and the producer Stanley Jaffe that the recent loss of her fiancé, John Cazale, only months earlier, gave Streep that emotional edge and "still-fresh pain" to draw on for the performance.

Bonus Movies

Airport (1970)
After Shirley Booth turned down a chance to return to the big screen in the role of Ada Quonsett, Claudette Colbert also turned down the role, allowing Helen Hayes to accept it and win her second Oscar.

Love Story (1970)
After the role of Oliver was turned down by Beau Bridges, Michael York and Jon Voight, Ryan O'Neal was offered the part on the recommendation of Erich Segal, who had worked with the actor on *The Games*; O'Neal was paid $25,000.

Klute (1971)
Barbra Streisand was offered the role of call girl Bree Daniels, but turned it down. Subsequently, Jane Fonda was cast, and won an Oscar for Best Actress. In her autobiography, Fonda wrote about trying to convince the director to replace her with Faye Dunaway.

The Last Picture Show (1971)
Ben Johnson won an Academy Award for Best Supporting Actor for the role of "Sam the Lion." James Stewart, offered the role first, turned it down.

Shaft (1971)
In novelist Ernest Tidyman's original story, Shaft was white, but director Gordon Parks decided to cast Richard Roundtree, an African-American, as the eponymous hero. The entire dynamic of the film, its later success, and the future of blaxploitation films were all greatly impacted by Parks' decision. According to Parks, "This film was created less to impact black consciousness and more to simply to show a 'fun film,' which people could attend on Saturday night and see a black guy winning."

The Getaway (1972)
Peter Bogdanovich, was originally hired as the director and wanted to cast his girlfriend, Cybill Shepherd in the role of Carol, Doc McCoy's wife.

After Bogdanovich was fired, Sam Peckinpah was hired. He wanted to cast Stella Stevens with whom he had worked on *The Ballad of Cable Hogue*.

Producer David Foster suggested Ali MacGraw, a much in-demand actress after the success of *Love Story*. She was married to Robert Evans.

Evans wanted her to avoid being typecast in preppy roles. He set up a meeting for her with Foster, McQueen, and Peckinpah.

According to Foster, she was scared of McQueen and Peckinpah because they had reputations as wild, two-fisted, beer guzzlers. McQueen and MacGraw experienced a strong instant attraction, and began an affair during filming. This eventually led to her leaving Evans and becoming McQueen's second wife.

Jeremiah Johnson (1972)
The role of Jeremiah Johnson was originally intended for Lee Marvin, and then given to Clint Eastwood. However, director Sam Peckinpah and Eastwood did not get along. Peckinpah resigned, and Eastwood left the project to make *Dirty Harry*. Warner Bros. then stepped in and set up the John Milius screenplay for Robert Redford.

Harry and Tonto (1974)
James Cagney and Danny Kaye turned down director Paul Mazursky's offer of the Oscar-winning role of the elderly man evicted from his apartment who goes on the road with his beloved cat. A somewhat controversial Academy Award for Best Actor was given to Art Carney who played the elderly man

Lenny (1974)
Neil Diamond turned down the role of Lenny Bruce. Director Bob Fosse wanted Cliff Gorman to star, but studios would not bankroll the film with Gorman in the starring role. Fosse eventually cast Dustin Hoffman in the role of Lenny Bruce. Many thought Hoffman should have won an Oscar.

One Flew Over the Cuckoo's Nest (1975)
Kirk Douglas who, originated the role of Randle McMurphy in the Broadway stage version, purchased the film rights, and tried for a decade to bring it to the big screen. Eventually, he gave the rights to his son Michael Douglas who succeeded in getting the film made. The elder Douglas, by then nearly 60, was considered too old for the McMurphy role.

Director Milos Foreman had a meeting with director Hal Ashby who suggested Jack Nicholson for the role of McMurphy. Production was delayed for about six months because of Nicholson's schedule.

While Milos Foreman was screening *Thieves Like Us* to see if Shelley Duvall was right for the role of Candy, he became interested in Louise Fletcher, who had a supporting role in *Thieves*, for the role of Nurse Ratched in *Cuckoo's Nest* .

Over the next year, the role of Nurse Ratched was offered to Lily Tomlin, Angela Lansbury, Geraldine Page, and Anne Bancroft; all of whom turned it down. Finally, Milos Foreman decided to cast Fletcher in the role that won her an Oscar for Best Actress.

Carrie (1976)

Melanie Griffith was one of many young actresses who auditioned for the lead role of Carrie White. Jack Fisk, the film's Art Director and Sissy Spacek's husband, persuaded her to audition for the title role.

Director Brian De Palma's first choice for the role of Carrie was Betsy Slade, who received good notices for her role in the film *Our Time*. Determined to land the leading role, Sissy Spacek backed out of a television commercial she was scheduled to film to make her audition. She rubbed Vaseline into her hair, left her face unwashed, and arrived for her screen test clad in a sailor dress which her mother had made for her in the seventh grade; she was given the part.

Julia (1977)

Faye Dunaway turned down the lead role in *Julia,* a role made indelible by Vanessa Redgrave who won the Oscar for Best Supporting Actress.

Smokey and the Bandit (1977)

Director Hal Needham originally planned the film as a low-budget B movie with a production cost of $1 million. Jerry Reed was offered the role of Bandit. Then Needham's best friend Burt Reynolds read the script, and agreed to star in the film. Reed happily stepped aside and took the role of Bandit's sidekick.

Jackie Gleason, who played Sheriff Buford T. Justice, was given free rein to ad-lib dialogue and make suggestions. It was his idea to have Junior alongside him throughout. Sally Field only accepted the part after her agent advised her that she needed a big movie role on her resumé. Universal initially resisted, claiming Field was not attractive enough.

Heaven Can Wait (1978)

As the film's producer, Warren Beatty lobbied very hard for Cary Grant to accept the role of Mr. Jordan. Beatty went so far as to have Grant's ex-wife, Dyan Cannon, who starred as Julia Farnsworth, urge him to take the role. Although Grant was tempted to take the role, he ultimately decided not to end his retirement, but still turned down the role.

Beatty then turned to Muhammed Ali to play the central character, but, because of Ali's continued commitment to boxing, Beatty changed the character from a boxer to an American football player and played it himself.

The Deer Hunter (1978)

When Roy Scheider dropped out two weeks before the start of filming due to "creative differences," producer Michael Deeley pursued Robert De Niro to take the lead role of Michael Vronsky. Deeley thought he needed De Niro's star power to sell a film with a barely known director, Michael Cimino, and a "gruesome-sounding storyline."

"I liked the script, and director Michael Cimino had done a lot of good prep," said De Niro. "I was impressed." De Niro prepared for the role by socializing with steelworkers in local bars and by visiting their homes. Michael Cimino introduced De Niro as his agent, surprising both of them that nobody recognized the actor. De Niro claimed that this was his most physically exhausting film. He said the scene where Mike visits Steven in the hospital for the first time was the most emotional scene he was ever asked to play.

All That Jazz (1979)

In his autobiography, Paul Newman says he turned down the lead role of the Bob Fosse-like choreographer, Joe Gideon. A number of actors were considered for the role including: Alan Alda, Gene Hackman, Robert Blake, Elliott Gould, and Alan Bates, although the latter was considered too British. Jack Lemmon was also considered, but was deemed too old, and Warren Beatty flirted with the idea for a moment. Finally, Richard Dreyfuss was cast, but during rehearsals he dropped out over creative differences, and Roy Scheider replaced him.

Being There (1979)

Director Hal Ashby wanted Elvis for the role of "Chance the Gardener," ultimately played by Peter Sellers. However, he couldn't get Elvis because his manager, Colonel Parker, turned it down.

Manhattan (1979)

Jodie Foster turned down the role of Tracy that went to Mariel Hemingway.

Norma Rae (1979)

Marsha Mason, Jane Fonda, Faye Dunaway, and Jill Clayburgh all turned down the opportunity to play Norma Rae. Sally Field was ultimately cast in the role that won her an Academy Award for Best Actress.

Emmeline Lestrange • Richard Lestrange • Bud Davis • Sissy • Julian Kaye
Michelle Stratton • Indiana Jones • Marion Ravenwood • Snake Plissken
Arthur • Linda Marolla • Zach Mayo • Paula Pokrifki • Gunnery Sgt. Foley
Brad Hamilton • Stacy Hamilton • Spicoli • Rambo • Colonel Trautman
Sheriff Teasle • Michael Dorsey/Dorothy Michaels • Julie • Rick Deckard
Rupert Pupkin • Jerry Langford • Alex Owens • Nick Hurley • Tony Montana
Elvira • Garrett Breedlove • Aurora Greenway • Emma Greenway-Horton
Axel Foley • Ren McCormack • Ariel • Peter Venkman • Allen Bauer
Madison • The Terminator • Kyle Reese • Sarah Connor • Claire Standish
Alison Reynolds • Andrew Clarke • John Bender • Marty McFly • Doc Brown

1980s

Shug • Sofia • Dorothy Vallens • Jeffrey Beaumont • Pete "Maverick" Mitchell
Charlie Blackwood • Dan Gallagher • Alex Forrest • Gordon Gekko • Bud Fox
Eliot Ness • Al Capone • Jimmy Malone • Sarah Tobias • Kathryn Murphy
Josh Baskin • Susan Lawrence • John McClane • Francis "Baby" Houseman
Johnny Castle • Raymond "Ray" Babbit • Charlie Babbit • Tess McGill
Katherine Parker • Jack Trainer • Cora • Batman/Bruce Wayne • The Joker
Harry Burns • Sally Albright • Frances Farmer • Diane Freeling • Ponyboy
Two-Bit • Cherry • Joel Goodson • Lana • Edna Spalding • Susan • Roberta
John Book • Rachel Lapp • Ferris Bueller • Cameron Frye • Pvt. Chris Taylor
Sgt. Elias Grodin • Ray Kinsella • "Moonlight" Graham • John Keating
Emmeline Lestrange • Richard Lestrange • Bud Davis • Sissy • Julian Kaye
Michelle Stratton • Indiana Jones • Marion Ravenwood • Snake Plissken
Arthur • Linda Marolla • Zach Mayo • Paula Pokrifki • Gunnery Sgt. Foley
Brad Hamilton • Stacy Hamilton • Spicoli • Rambo • Colonel Trautman
Sheriff Teasle • Michael Dorsey/Dorothy Michaels • Julie • Rick Deckard
Rupert Pupkin • Jerry Langford • Alex Owens • Nick Hurley • Tony Montana
Elvira • Garrett Breedlove • Aurora Greenway • Emma Greenway-Horton
Axel Foley • Ren McCormack • Ariel • Peter Venkman • Allen Bauer
Madison • The Terminator • Kyle Reese • Sarah Connor • Claire Standish
Alison Reynolds • Andrew Clarke • John Bender • Marty McFly • Doc Brown
Shug • Sofia • Dorothy Vallens • Jeffrey Beaumont • Pete "Maverick" Mitchell
Charlie Blackwood • Dan Gallagher • Alex Forrest • Gordon Gekko • Bud Fox
Eliot Ness • Al Capone • Jimmy Malone • Sarah Tobias • Kathryn Murphy
Josh Baskin • Susan Lawrence • John McClane • Francis "Baby" Houseman
Johnny Castle • Raymond "Ray" Babbit • Charlie Babbit • Tess McGill
Katherine Parker • Jack Trainer • Cora • Batman/Bruce Wayne • The Joker
Harry Burns • Sally Albright • Frances Farmer • Diane Freeling • Ponyboy
Two-Bit • Cherry • Joel Goodson • Lana • Edna Spalding • Susan • Roberta

High Concept Films Next Blockbuster Sequels

The decade introduced the notion of 'high-concept' films with plots that could be easily characterized in a few sentences making them easy to market and promote. However, predictions were grim for the industry overall. Production costs soared while ticket prices declined. The average ticket price in 1980 was about $3, and $4 by the end of the decade while the average film budget had climbed to over $18 million.

As film budgets rose due to expensive special effects and inflated salaries, corporations (many of them foreign) increasingly took control of the movies and many Hollywood properties. These included United Artists, Columbia Pictures, Twentieth Century Fox, and Paramount Pictures.

To keep budgets down, more films were being made outside the United States. With decisions being made by financiers rather than filmmakers, movies were made only if they could guarantee financial success.

Studios looked to directors like Steven Spielberg and George Lucas to create the next blockbuster, which they did with *The Empire Strikes Back, Raiders of the Lost Ark, Return of the Jedi,* and *E.T. The Extra-Terrestrial.* This led other producers to focus on films with sequel potential: *Ghostbusters, Romancing the Stone* and *Back to the Future* were examples.

Cable television and the proliferation of videocassettes allowed for a broader marketplace. The revenues from pre-sold theatrical features sometimes outpaced their box office profits.

In 1986, Ted Turner purchased the film library of MGM and United Artists, and proposed colorization of their black and white films. Ultimately, this led to many classics being colorized for television including: *It's a Wonderful Life, Casablanca, Yankee Doodle Dandy, King Kong,* and *Arsenic and Old Lace.*

Films of the early 80s were being geared toward pre-teen and teenage audiences that were becoming sizeable segments of theater attendance.

For example, Barry Levinson's debut film *Diner* was a bittersweet, rite-of-passage tale of six male buddies growing up in Baltimore in the late 50s.

Writer/Director/Producer John Hughes made a significant impact on the film industry with teen comedies populated by a diverse group of relatable characters, such as *Sixteen Candles, The Breakfast Club,* Pretty *in Pink* and *Ferris Bueller's Day Off.* A decade later he would make *Home Alone.*

Other films examined disenfranchised, alienated youth: Tim Hunter's disturbing *River's Edge* inspired by a true story of a teen murder; Rob Reiner's *Stand By Me* about four small-town boys looking for a dead body; *The Lost Boys* about teen vampires; *Heathers* dealt with teen suicide, murder, and school bombings; *Less Than Zero* looked at both the lucrative side of business and the downside of failure and excess drug use. *Bright Lights, Big City* focused on an aspiring writer whose life is destroyed by drugs and alcohol.

Sequels thrived in the 1980s. Eight James Bond films were released starting with *For Your Eyes Only* with Roger Moore as Agent 007, and ending with *License to Kill* starring Timothy Dalton as the intrepid Bond.

Extremely successful sequels followed *Stars Wars,* with *The Empire Strikes Back* and *Return of the Jedi*; and *Raiders of the Lost Ark* with *Indiana Jones and the Temple of Doom* and *Indiana Jones and the Last Crusade.*

Other successful films cashed in with sequels: *Dirty Harry* was followed by *Sudden Impact* and *The Dead Pool; Saturday Night Fever* with *Staying Alive;* and *The Hustler,* 25 years later, with *The Color of Money.*

However, a steady stream of mindless sequels was produced each year, often inferior to their originals. The onslaught of sequels was designed to defray the monetary risks of filmmaking, but they usually resulted in dwindling box office returns.

One of the major pluses of the decade was that women producers and directors began to emerge in the male-dominated film industry. Barbra Streisand, Penny Marshall, Amy Heckerling, Jane Campion, and Susan Seidelman were winning awards, recognition, and box-office success. This paved the way, albeit slowly, within the insular Hollywood film industry for women to have a larger role.

The Academy Awards

1980

Best Picture: ***Ordinary People***

Best Actor: Robert De Niro (*Raging Bull*)

Best Actress: Sissy Spacek (*Coal Miner's Daughter*)

Best Supporting Actor: Timothy Hutton (*Ordinary People*)

Best Supporting Actress: Mary Steenburgen (*Melvin and Howard*)

1981

Best Picture: ***Chariots of Fire***

Best Actor: Henry Fonda (*On Golden Pond*)

Best Actress: Katharine Hepburn (*On Golden Pond*)

Best Supporting Actor: John Gielgud (*Arthur*)

Best Supporting Actress: Maureen Stapleton (*Reds*)

1982

Best Picture: ***Gandhi***

Best Actor: Ben Kingsley (*Gandhi*)

Best Actress: Meryl Streep (*Sophie's Choice*)

Best Supporting Actor: Louis Gossett Jr. (*An Officer and a Gentleman*)

Best Supporting Actress: Jessica Lange (*Tootsie*)

1983

Best Picture: ***Terms of Endearment***

Best Actor: Robert Duvall (*Tender Mercies*)

Best Actress: Shirley MacLaine (*Terms of Endearment*)

Best Supporting Actor: Jack Nicholson (*Terms of Endearment*)

Best Supporting Actress: Linda Hunt (*The Year of Living Dangerously*)

1984

Best Picture: ***Amadeus***

Best Actor: F. Murray Abraham (*Amadeus*)

Best Actress: Sally Field (*Places in the Heart*)

Best Supporting Actor: Haing S. Ngor (*the Killing Fields*)

Best Supporting Actress: Peggy Ashcroft (*A Passage to India*)

1985

Best Picture: ***Out of Africa***
Best Actor: William Hurt (*Kiss of the Spider Woman*)
Best Actress: Geraldine Page (*The Trip to Bountiful*)
Best Supporting Actor: Don Ameche (*Cocoon*)
Best Supporting Actress: Anjelica Huston (*Prizzi's Honor*)

1986

Best Picture: ***Platoon***
Best Actor: Paul Newman (*The Color of Money*)
Best Actress: Marlee Matlin (*Children of a Lesser God*)
Best Supporting Actor: Michael Caine (*Hannah and Her Sisters*)
Best Supporting Actress: Dianne Wiest (*Hannah and Her Sisters*)

1987

Best Picture: ***The Last Emperor***
Best Actor: Michael Douglas (*Wall Street*)
Best Actress: Cher (*Moonstruck*)
Best Supporting Actor: Sean Connery (*The Untouchables*)
Best Supporting Actress: Olympia Dukakis (*Moonstruck*)

1988

Best Picture: ***Rain Man***
Best Actor: Dustin Hoffman (*Rain Man*)
Best Actress: Jodie Foster (*The Accused*)
Best Supporting Actor: Kevin Kline (*A Fish Called Wanda*)
Best Supporting Actress: Geena Davis (The Accidental Tourist)

1989

Best Picture: ***Driving Miss Daisy***
Best Actor: Daniel Day-Lewis (*My Left Foot*)
Best Actress: Jessica Tandy (*Driving Miss Daisy*)
Best Supporting Actor: Denzel Washington (*Glory*)
Best Supporting Actress: Brenda Fricker (*My Left Foot*)

Casting
Trivia Quiz

1. In **Escape From New York,** this actor turned down the role of Snake Plissken before Kurt Russell was cast:
   - a. Nick Nolte
   - b. Chuck Norris
   - c. Charles Bronson
   - d. All of the Above

2. Liza Minelli starred as Linda Marolla in **Arthur** after this actress turned down the role:
   - a. Tuesday Weld
   - b. Carrie Fisher
   - c. Debra Winger
   - d. All of the Above

3. In **Scarface,** Al Pacino was cast as drug cartel boss, Tony Montana, after this actor turned down the role:
   - a. Sean Penn
   - b. Robert DeNiro
   - c. Mel Gibson
   - d. Tommy Lee Jones

4. Arnold Schwarzenegger was cast as **The Terminator**, after this actor turned down the role:
   - a. O.J. Simpson
   - b. Sylvester Stallone
   - c. Mickey Rourke
   - d. Jean-Claude Van Damme

5. Bill Murray was cast as Peter Venkman in **Ghostbusters** after this actor turned down the role:
   - a. Chevy Chase
   - b. Richard Pryor
   - c. John Candy
   - d. Eddie Murphy

6. The role of Axel Foley in **Beverly Hills Cop** was accepted by this actor, who rewrote the film, but then quit:
   - a. Tom Cruise
   - b. Sean Penn
   - c. Sylvester Stallone
   - d. Al Pacino

7. In **The Breakfast Club**, Judd Nelson was cast as John Bender after this actor turned down the role:
   - a. John Cusack
   - b. Jim Carrey
   - c. Mickey Rourke
   - d. Nicolas Cage

8. Michael J. Fox was the first choice to play Marty McFly in the classic film, ***Back To The Future,*** but a TV role didn't allow it, so this actor played the role for 4 weeks before Fox replaced him:
    a. Sean Penn   c. Matthew Broderick
    b. Eric Stolz   d. Emilio Estevez

9. Oprah Winfrey was cast as Sofia in ***The Color Purple*** after this actress turned the role down:
    a. Jennifer Holliday   c. Tina Turner
    b. Diana Ross   d. Lola Falana

10. Tom Cruise became "Maverick" in ***Top Gun*** after this actor turned down the role:
    a. Nicolas Cage   c. Sean Penn
    b. Matthew Modine   d. All of the Above

11. Before Glenn Close was cast as Alex Forrest in ***Fatal Attraction***, after this actress turned down the role:
    a. Sally Field   c. Meryl Streep
    b. Debra Winger   d. All of the Above

12. Before Michael Douglas was cast in ***Wall Street*** in the role of Gordon Gekko, this actor turned it down:
    a. Warren Beatty   c. Don Johnson
    b. Mickey Rourke   d. Al Pacino

13. Kevin Costner was cast as Elliot Ness in ***The Untouchables*** after this actor turned down the role:
    a. Mickey Rourke   c. Michael Douglas
    b. Bruce Willis   d. Sylvester Stallone

14. Bruce Willis was cast as detective John McClane in ***Die Hard***, but only after this actor turned down the role:
    a. Arnold Schwarzenegger   c. Don Johnson
    b. Frank Sinatra   d. All of the Above

15. Before Tom Cruise was cast as Charlie Babbit in ***Rain Man***, this actor was offered the role, but turned it down:
    a. Steve Martin   c. Bill Murray
    b. Mickey Rourke   d. Randy Quaid

THE BLUE LAGOON (1980)

Richard: We don't wanna go swimming! We don't have our bathing costumes.

Paddy: To hell with your bathing costumes. You don't wear 'em when you take a bath, do you?

Emmeline: This isn't a bathtub! This is the ocean!

Plot

After a shipwreck, two young children stranded on a tropical island in the South Pacific have to deal with their emotional feelings and physical changes as they grow to maturity and fall in love.

CASTING

Who Starred as Emmeline?
Brooke Shields

Turned Down the Role of Emmeline
Carrie Fisher • Dana Plato • Charlene Tilton
Lori Loughlin • Jennifer Jason Leigh
Michelle Pfeiffer • Tatum O'Neal

Who Starred as Richard?
Christopher Atkins

Turned Down the Role of Richard
Matt Dillon • John Travolta

WHO Trivia

A number of young actresses turned down the lead role of Emmeline: Carrie Fisher, due to her commitment with *Star Wars: Episode V;* Dana Plato due to her commitment to her television show, *Diff'rent Strokes;* Charlene Tilton because of *Dallas;* Michelle Pfeiffer due to her discomfort with the role; and Jennifer Jason Leigh's father, Vic Morrow, made her turn it down. Lori Loughlin and Tatum O'Neal also turned the role down.

Matt Dillon, the original choice for Richard, turned down the role because he was uncomfortable with the nudity. On the final day of auditions, Sean Penn lost out to Christopher Atkins. With respect to the nudity in the film, Atkins did most of the nude scenes without a body double, while Brooke Shields did not do any nude scenes.

Ironically, John Travolta turned down the role of Richard while his future wife Kelly Preston auditioned for the role of Emmeline.

URBAN COWBOY (1980)

Sissy: You a real cowboy?

Bud: Well that depends on what you think a real cowboy is.

Sissy: I saw you here the other night, you had a beard right? You shouldn't have shaved it, I thought it looked good.

Bud: Damn, who asked you?

Sissy: No one.... Know how to two-step?

Bud: Yup.

Sissy: Wanna prove it?

Bud: Alright.

Plot

The love-hate relationship between a cowboy and a cowgirl.

CASTING

Who Starred as Bud Davis?
John Travolta

Turned Down the Role of Bud Davis
Christopher Reeve • Sam Shepard

Who Starred as Sissy?
Debra Winger

Turned Down the Role of Sissy
Sissy Spacek

WHO Trivia

First, Sam Shepard turned down the role of Bud Davis. Christopher Reeve couldn't accept due to scheduling conflicts. Eventually, Dennis Quaid was cast in the role until he was replaced with John Travolta, a more successful actor at the time, who had expressed interest in the role.

Michelle Pfeiffer was producer Robert Evans preferred choice, and Rene Russo auditioned for the role of Sissy, but both lost out to Sissy Spacek.

According to Debra Winger's book, she only got the part after Spacek had a falling out with Travolta when the film was delayed because he got bitten by a dog. Studio executives were against casting the unknown Winger in the lead, but director James Bridges threatened to quit the film unless she was cast.

AMERICAN GIGOLO (1980)

Michelle Stratton:	How many languages do you speak?
Julian Kaye:	Five or six.
Michelle Stratton:	Plus, the, uh, international language?
Julian Kaye:	That's right.

Plot

A high-priced male escort, who mostly caters to an older female clientele, becomes romantically involved with a prominent politician's wife while simultaneously becoming the prime suspect in a murder case.

CASTING

Who Starred as Julian Kaye?
Richard Gere

Turned Down the Role of Julian Kaye
Christopher Reeve • John Travolta

Who Starred as Michelle Stratton?
Lauren Hutton

Turned Down the Role of Michelle Stratton
Julie Christie • Meryl Streep • Jessica Lange
Debra Winger • Mary Steenburgen

WHO Trivia

Christopher Reeve reportedly turned down the role of Julian Kaye despite being offered a fee of $1 million by Barry Diller, the head of Paramount Pictures. Writer/Director Paul Schrader didn't want to cast Reeve, and called his agent asking him to persuade Reeve not to even read the script. Reeve did read it, but didn't like the tone of the movie or the character.

One story that floated around Hollywood was that after Reeve turned down the role, Richard Gere was cast. When Gere changed his mind, John Travolta was cast, and briefly acted in it before getting cold feet; Travolta was replaced by Gere, who had decided he now wanted to do the film.

The casting story continued with the role of the politician's wife. Julie Christie was initially cast to play the role, but she backed out when Travolta replaced Gere. After Travolta dropped out and Gere was hired, Christie was not offered the role again.

Another rumored scenario is that Christie's departure was precipitated by Gere's replacement of Travolta.

Writer/Director Paul Schrader was said to have threatened Travolta with a lawsuit if Richard Gere didn't take the role, knowing full well that Travolta had his eye on another Paramount production, *Urban Cowboy*.

Gere said he was drawn to the role because of its gay subtext. "I read it and thought, 'This is a character I don't know very well. I don't own a suit. He speaks languages; I don't speak any languages. There's kind of a gay thing that's flirting throughout the film. I didn't know the gay community at all.' I wanted to immerse myself in all of that. I literally had two weeks, so I just dove in."

Gere's brief nude scenes marked the first time a major Hollywood actor was frontally nude in a film. According to Gere, the nudity was not in the original script. "It was just in the natural process of making the movie. I certainly felt vulnerable, but I think it's different for men than women."

Paul Schrader offered the role of Michelle to Meryl Streep, but she declined because she did not like the tone of the film. Schrader then considered casting Kay Lenz, Kim Basinger, Amy Irving, and Annie Potts.

Finally, Schrader narrowed down the choice to either Kim Basinger or Lauren Hutton, and decided he wanted Lauren Hutton for the role. The studio, however, wanted a bigger name, rejecting both Basinger and Hutton, and chose to go with Jessica Lange.

In the end however, Lange turned the role down because it was "too dark." Hutton was then cast.

Interesting to note, this was not the only role Travolta turned down which was then taken by Gere. The other roles were in the films: *Days of Heaven*, *An Officer and a Gentleman*, and *Chicago*.

RAIDERS OF THE LOST ARK (1981)

Marion: You're not the man I knew ten years ago.
Indiana Jones: It's not the years, honey; it's the mileage.

Plot
An archaeologist and adventurer is hired by the U.S. government to find the Ark of the Covenant before the Nazis do.

CASTING

Who Starred as Indiana Jones?
Harrison Ford

Turned Down the Role of Indiana Jones
Tom Selleck • Steve Martin • Bill Murray

Who Starred as Marion Ravenwood?
Karen Allen

Turned Down the Role of Marion Ravenwood
Debra Winger

WHO Trivia
Director Steven Spielberg suggested casting Harrison Ford as Indiana Jones. George Lucas, who created the story/character, objected stating he did not want Ford to become his "Bobby De Niro" or "that guy I put in all my movies," referring to Martin Scorsese who often worked with De Niro. Desiring a lesser-known actor, Lucas persuaded Spielberg to help him search for a new talent.

Television had an influence on casting. Tom Selleck was offered the role, but had to turn it down because of his commitment to his television series, *Magnum, P.I.*, while Bill Murray, preforming on *Saturday Night Live* had scheduling conflicts. Danny DeVito, set to play Sallah, had to drop out due to conflicts with *Taxi*.

It was rumored that Steve Martin was offered the role, but he chose to make the film, *Pennies from Heaven* instead.

In June, three weeks away from filming, Spielberg persuaded Lucas to cast Harrison Ford after producers Frank Marshall and Kathleen Kennedy were impressed by Ford's performance as Han Solo in *Star Wars*.

ESCAPE FROM NEW YORK (1981)

Bob Hauk: You go in, find the President, bring him out in 24 hours, and you're a free man.

Snake Plissken: 24 hours, huh?

Bob Hauk: I'm making you an offer.

Snake Plissken: Bullshit!

Bob Hauk: Straight just like I said.

Snake Plissken: I'll think about it.

Bob Hauk: No time. Give me an answer.

Snake Plissken: Get a new president!

Plot

Set in the near future in a crime-ridden United States that has converted Manhattan Island in NYC into a maximum-security prison, an ex-soldier is given 24 hours to find the President of the United States, who has been captured after the crash of Air Force One.

CASTING

Who Starred as Snake Plissken?
Kurt Russell

Turned Down the Role of Snake Plissken
Charles Bronson • Nick Nolte
Jeff Bridges • Chuck Norris

WHO Trivia

The film's financial backer wanted Charles Bronson to play Snake Plissken.

Director John Carpenter refused to cast Bronson on the grounds that Bronson was too old. Carpenter also worried that he could lose directorial control over the picture using such an experienced actor. As it turned out, Bronson refused the part; he also thought he was too old.

After Nick Nolte, Jeff Bridges, and Chuck Norris turned down the role, Tommy Lee Jones and Clint Eastwood were considered before Kurt Russell was cast in the iconic role.

John Carpenter's choice, Russell, wanted to overcome his "lightweight" screen image conveyed by his roles in several Disney comedies.

Russell was determined to get the part, and, to this day, says it was his favorite character to play. Interesting to note is that Snake Plissken's iconic eyepatch was suggested by Russell.

ARTHUR (1981)

Arthur: Have you ever been on a yacht?
Linda: No, is it wonderful?
Arthur: It doesn't suck.

Plot
An alcoholic NYC millionaire, on the brink of an arranged marriage to a wealthy heiress, falls for a common working-class girl from Queens.

CASTING

Who Starred as Arthur?
Dudley Moore

Turned Down the Role of Arthur
James Caan • Al Pacino • Robert Redford
John Travolta • John Belushi

Who Starred as Linda Marolla?
Liza Minnelli

Turned Down the Role of Linda Marolla
Debra Winger • Tuesday Weld • Carrie Fisher

WHO Trivia
Writer/Director Steve Gordon originally wrote the title character with an American actor in mind. After a number of A-List actors turned down the role, Gordon wanted to cast George Segal as Arthur. However, after the box office success of *10*, Dudley Moore was cast instead.

This was the second time that Moore replaced Segal, who was initially cast in the lead role in *10*, a film stolen by Bo Derek.

Debra Winger, Tuesday Weld, and Carrie Fisher turned down the role of Linda. Before Liza Minnelli was cast, a number of major actresses were considered: Mia Farrow, Farrah Fawcett, Goldie Hawn, Diane Keaton, Jessica Lange, Gilda Radner, Susan Sarandon, Bette Midler, and Meryl Streep.

John Gielgud won an Oscar for the role of Hobson. After turning it down twice he said, "They offered me so much money, I finally had to accept."

AN OFFICER AND A GENTLEMAN (1982)

Sergeant Foley: *(looking at Mayo's tattoo)* Hey, this is really wonderful work! Where'd you get this, Mayo?

Zack Mayo: Subic Bay, Philippines, sir.

Sergeant Foley: I thought I recognized the work. Be proud of them wings. They're the only one you're leaving here with... Mayo-NAISE.

Plot

An Aviator Officer Candidate with a damaged past comes into conflict with his Marine Corps Gunnery Sergeant.

CASTING

Who Starred as Zack Mayo?
Richard Gere

Turned Down the Role of Zack Mayo
John Denver • Jeff Bridges • John Travolta
Kurt Russell • Ken Wahl

Who Starred as Paula Pokrifki?
Debra Winger

Turned Down the Role of Paula Pokrifki
Sigourney Weaver • Anjelica Huston • Jennifer Jason Leigh

Who Starred as Gunnery Sergeant Foley?
Lou Gossett Jr.

Turned Down the Role of Gunnery Sergeant Foley
James Woods

WHO Trivia

Director Taylor Hackford's original choice for the lead role was Jeff Bridges, but Bridges had to turn it down due to a busy schedule.

Hackford then offered the role to singer and occasional actor John Denver, but he turned it down saying, "The script read like a 1950s movie." The part was then offered to John Travolta, who turned it down on the advice of his agent. Kurt Russell and Ken Wahl were both offered the role but turned it down.

Finally, Hackford offered the role to Richard Gere who was not that excited about the part but took the role anyway. In an interview with Barbara Walters, Gere said he did the movie strictly for the money. The film was his biggest box office hit until he made *Pretty Woman*.

Ironically, Richard Gere played the lead male role in three other films Travolta turned down, *American Gigolo, Days of Heaven,* and *Chicago*.

The role of Paula Pokrifki was originally given to Sigourney Weaver. After she dropped out, Anjelica Huston was cast. She also changed her mind. Subsequently, Jennifer Jason Leigh was cast. History repeated itself, and she dropped out to do the comedy film, *Fast Times at Ridgemont High*. Hackford replaced Leigh with Debra Winger.

Rebecca De Mornay, Meg Ryan, and Geena Davis all auditioned for the role, but Hackford did not offer them the part. However, he did almost give it to Kim Basinger.

The role of Gunnery Sergeant Foley was originally written as a short, white Southerner; the role was based on screenwriter Douglas Day Stewart's own drill instructor in the navy. After Robert Woods turned down the role, Hackford gave it to Lou Gossett Jr.

Hackford purposely kept Gossett in living quarters that were separate from other actors during production, so that Gossett could intimidate them more during his scenes as drill instructor.

Gossett Jr. was the first African-American to win the Academy Award for Best Supporting Actor.

In spite of the strong on-screen chemistry between Gere and Winger, the actors didn't get along during filming. She called him a "brick wall" while he admitted there was "tension" between them.

Thirty years later, Gere was complimentary towards Winger when he said that she was much more open to the camera than he was, and appreciated the fact that she presented him with an award at the Rome Film Festival.

FAST TIMES AT RIDGEMONT HIGH (1982)

Brad: Why don't you get a job, Spicoli?
Spicoli: What for?
Brad: You need money.
Spicoli: All I need are some tasty waves, a cool buzz, and I'm fine.

Plot
A group of California teenagers who enjoy malls, sex and rock & roll.

CASTING

Who Starred as Brad Hamilton?
Judge Reinhold

Turned Down the Role of Brad Hamilton
Matthew Broderick

Who Starred as Stacy Hamilton?
Jennifer Jason Leigh

Turned Down the Role of Stacy Hamilton
Brooke Shields • Ellen Barkin • Jodie Foster

WHO Trivia
The film's casting included a number of future stars.

Matthew Broderick turned down the role of Brad Hamilton when his father became terminally ill, as did Ralph Macchio when the producers wouldn't meet his asking price. Tom Hanks auditioned for the role of Brad, but wasn't cast.

Jodie Foster was offered the role of Stacy, played by Jennifer Jason Leigh, but turned it down due to her commitment to attend Yale University. Diane Lane auditioned for the role, but director Amy Heckerling didn't think she was right for it. Justine Bateman turned down the role of Linda, played by Phoebe Cates, to do the TV series, *Family Ties*. Melanie Griffith and Tatum O'Neal were considered for the role.

Christopher Reeve, *Superman*, was considered for the role of Spicoli, played by Sean Penn. Nicolas Cage made his feature film debut, portraying an unnamed co-worker of Brad's at All-American Burger, as Nicolas Coppola.

The film also marked the early appearances by several actors who later became stars, including Forest Whitaker, Eric Stoltz, and Anthony Edwards.

FIRST BLOOD (1982)

Rambo: I could have killed 'em all, I could kill you. In town you're the law, out here it's me. Don't push it. Don't push it or I'll give you a war you won't believe. Let it go... Let it go.

Plot

A troubled Vietnam War veteran fights back after he is pushed to the limit by a hostile small-town town sheriff, forcing him to flee into the mountains and wage an escalating one-man war against his pursuers.

CASTING

Who Starred as Rambo?
Sylvester Stallone

Turned Down the Role of Rambo
Al Pacino • James Garner

Who Starred as Colonel Trautman?
Richard Crenna

Turned Down the Role of Colonel Trautman
Lee Marvin • Kirk Douglas • Rock Hudson

Who Starred as Sheriff Teasle?
Brian Dennehy

Turned Down the Role of Sheriff Teasle
Gene Hackman • Robert Duvall

WHO Trivia

In 1974, Sydney Pollack considered doing the movie with Steve McQueen as Rambo and Burt Lancaster as Sheriff Teasle, but the studio considered McQueen too old to play a Vietnam veteran from 1975. Ultimately, Pollack changed his mind.

In 1975, Martin Bregman became attached, and developed the project as a vehicle for Al Pacino. Pacino wanted to make Rambo more of a madman, and when that request was refused, he turned the role down.

The role of Rambo was also offered to James Garner, but he turned it down. As a veteran of the Korean War and with two Purple Hearts, Garner did not want to play a man coming home from war who starts fighting cops.

In 1976, after Bregman walked away, producer Ted Kotcheff was approached, but he was too busy at the time and initially turned it down.

In 1977, producer William Sackheim got involved and wrote a new version of the script. He wanted John Badham to direct, and John Travolta to star as Rambo, George C. Scott as Trautman, and Charles Durning as the Sheriff. Sackheim spent eight months on the project, but could not get it financed.

Eventually, producer Carter DeHaven optioned the book for $25,000, and attached John Frankenheimer to direct. They considered Powers Boothe, Nick Nolte, and Michael Douglas for Rambo before casting Brad Davis, who was wrapping up *Midnight Express*. Cinema Group signed on to finance and Filmways to distribute the film. However, Filmways, was taken over by Orion, and the movie went back into limbo.

Ted Kotcheff only returned to the project after producers Mario Kassar and Andrew G. Vajna offered to finance one of his other projects. Kotcheff immediately offered the role of John Rambo to Sylvester Stallone; the actor accepted after reading the script over the weekend.

Various scripts adapted from David Morrell's book had been pitched to studios in the years since its publication. However it was when Stallone decided to become involved with the project that it was finally brought into production.

Stallone's star power after the success of the *Rocky* films enabled him to rewrite the script, making the character of John Rambo more sympathetic. Stallone also decided to let Rambo survive by turning himself in instead of keeping the book's ending in which Rambo dies.

For the role of Sheriff Teasle, Kotcheff approached Gene Hackman and Robert Duvall, but both turned the role down; Brian Dennehy was then cast.

After Lee Marvin turned down the part of Colonel Trautman, Kirk Douglas was hired. Just before shooting began, Douglas quit over a script dispute. Douglas wanted the film to end as the book did with Rambo and Teasle fatally wounding each other, Trautman finishing off Rambo with a kill shot, and then sitting with the dying Teasle for the sheriff's final moment.

Rock Hudson was approached, but was soon to undergo heart surgery, and had to pass up the chance to work with Stallone. Richard Crenna was quickly hired as a replacement; the role of Trautman became the veteran character actor's most famous role; his performance received much critical praise.

TOOTSIE (1982)

Jeff: I'm just afraid that you're going to burn in hell for all this.
Michael: I don't believe in hell. I believe in unemployment, but
not hell.

Plot
An unemployed actor with a reputation for being difficult, disguises himself
as a woman to get a role in a soap opera.

CASTING

Who Starred as Michael Dorsey/Dorothy Michaels?
Dustin Hoffman

Turned Down the Role of Michael/Dorothy
Peter Sellers • Michael Caine

Who Starred as Julie Nichols?
Jessica Lange

Turned Down the Role of Julie Nichols
Cher

WHO Trivia
In the 1970s, fashion company executive Charles Evans decided to get into
movie making and optioned a very successful play, *Would I Lie to You?*

Nine years later, after getting little traction with the play as it was, Evans,
director Dick Richards, and screenwriter Bob Kaufman co-wrote a screenplay
based on the play. A few months into the writing process, Richards showed
it to Dustin Hoffman, his partner in a company, which bought and developed properties for films. Hoffman was interested, but wanted complete
creative control. Evans agreed to remove himself from screenwriting tasks,
and became a producer on the film, which was renamed *Tootsie*.

Before Hoffman officially got involved, his role was offered to Peter Sellers
and Michael Caine, but both turned it down.

The film remained in development another year until Sydney Pollack signed
on to the film as both director and producer. The idea of having Sydney
Pollack play Hoffman's agent, George Fields, was Hoffman's. Originally, the
role was written for, and to be played by, Dabney Coleman. Pollack initially
resisted the idea, but Hoffman eventually convinced him play the role.
Pollack still wanted to keep Coleman on board, and cast him as the sexist,
arrogant, soap opera director Ron Carlisle.

BLADE RUNNER (1982)

Deckard: Replicants are like any other machine. They're either a benefit or a hazard. If they're a benefit, it's not my problem.

Plot

A cop, aka a "blade runner," must pursue and terminate four replicants who
stole a ship in space and have returned to earth to find their creator.

CASTING

Who Starred as Rick Deckard?
Harrison Ford

Turned Down the Role of Rick Deckard
Dustin Hoffman • Martin Sheen

WHO Trivia

Casting proved troublesome, particularly for the lead role of Rick Deckard.
Screenwriter Hampton Fancher envisioned Robert Mitchum as Deckard, and
wrote the character's dialogue with Mitchum in mind. Phillip K. Dick, the
author of the novel on which the film was based, speculated about Gregory
Peck as Deckard. Director Ridley Scott and the film's producers spent months
discussing the role with Dustin Hoffman who couldn't understand why they
wanted him to play such a "macho character." Hoffman was interested, but
wanted to create an entirely different character; he finally turned it down.

After Hoffman was out, a long list of actors was considered including: Sean
Connery, Arnold Schwarzenegger, Nick Nolte, Gene Hackman, Tommy Lee
Jones, Paul Newman, Raul Julia, and Christopher Walken.

Martin Sheen turned down the role claiming he was still too exhausted after
filming *Apocalypse Now*. In the end, Harrison Ford, who was looking for a
role with more depth, was ultimately chosen.

One role that was not difficult to cast was Rutger Hauer as Roy Batty, the
violent yet thoughtful leader of the replicants. Without having met Hauer,
Scott cast him based on Hauer's performances in three Paul Verhoeven
movies, *Soldier of Orange*, *Katie Tippel*, and *Turkish Delight*. Hauer's
portrayal of Batty was regarded by Philip K. Dick as "the perfect Batty –
cold, Aryan, flawless."

In one of her first film roles, Daryl Hannah was cast as Pris, a role intended
for singer Debbie Harry.

THE KING OF COMEDY (1982)

Langford: You realize what you're saying.

Pupkin: Come on, Jerry. This isn't a spur of the moment thing. Give me a little credit, will you. Sit down. Now, you're going to call your office and tell them this: that unless a man who identifies himself as the King is allowed on the show tonight as the first guest, they'll never see you alive again.

Plot

A passionate yet unsuccessful comic, obsessed with becoming a star, resorts to stalking and then kidnapping his idol, a late-night talk show host.

CASTING

Who Starred as Jerry Langford?
Jerry Lewis

Turned Down the Role of Jerry Langford
Johnny Carson

Who Starred as Marsha?
Sandra Bernhard

Turned Down the Role of Marsha
Meryl Streep

WHO Trivia

When Bob Fosse considered directing the film, he suggested controversial comedian Andy Kaufman as Rupert Pupkin and Sammy Davis Jr. as talk show host, Jerry Langford. Ultimately, Fosse passed on the film in favor of directing *Star 80* instead.

Director Martin Scorsese then came on board, bringing Robert De Niro along to play Rupert Pupkin. Scorsese's choice for Jerry Langford was late night television star Johnny Carson. Carson refused the role, saying, "You know that one take is enough for me." A number of other actors were considered including: Frank Sinatra, Dean Martin, Joey Bishop and Orson Welles, before a decision was made to select Jerry Lewis.

After Meryl Streep turned down the role of Marsha, Scorsese decided to cast Sandra Bernhard, a comic with no formal acting experience. He told her to improvise most of her lines, wanting her to be as natural as possible.

FLASHDANCE (1983)

Nick: When you give up your dream, you die.

Plot
A Pittsburgh woman with two jobs, as a welder and exotic dancer, dreams about getting into ballet school.

CASTING

Who Starred as Alex Owens?
Jennifer Beals

Turned Down the Role of Alex Owens
Holly Hunter • Debra Winger • Andie MacDowell

Who Starred as Nick Hurley?
Michael Nouri

Turned Down the Role of Nick Hurley
Gene Simmons • Al Pacino
Burt Reynolds • John Travolta

WHO Trivia
In the early stages of casting, Holly Hunter tuned down the role of Alex Owns because she didn't like the script. Debra Winger turned the part down to star in *Terms of Endearment*. Andie MacDowell also turned it down.

Director Adrian Lyne then auditioned a number of actresses: Michelle Pfeiffer, Jamie Lee Curtis, Mariel Hemingway, Jennifer Jason Leigh, Bridget Fonda, Melanie Griffith, Kathy Najimy, Demi Moore, Leslie Wing, and Jennifer Beals. The three finalists for the role of Alex were Moore, Wing, and Beals.

There are two different stories regarding how Beals was eventually selected. One story is that then-Paramount president Michael Eisner asked the women secretaries at the studio for their choice to play Alex after the women viewed the screen tests. The other story is that the film's screenwriter, Joe Eszterhas, claims Eisner asked "two hundred of the most macho men on the Paramount lot, the following question... I want to know which of these three young women you'd most want to f---?" Which story, if either, is true is one of those legendary Hollywood-casting mysteries.

The role of Nick Hurley was offered to KISS lead man Gene Simmons, who turned it down because it would conflict with his "demon" image. Al Pacino, Burt Reynolds and John Travolta all turned down the role. Kevin Costner, a struggling actor at the time, came very close to getting the part.

SCARFACE (1983)

Montana: Okay. You little cockroaches... come on. You wanna play games? Okay, I'll play with you. You wanna play rough? Okay!... Say hello to my little friend!

Plot

In 1980 Miami, a determined Cuban immigrant takes over a drug cartel and succumbs to greed at the highest level.

CASTING

Who Starred as Tony Montana?
Al Pacino

Turned Down the Role of Tony Montana
Robert De Niro

Who Starred as Elvira?
Michelle Pfeiffer

Turned Down the Role of Elvira
Brooke Shields

WHO Trivia

After Robert De Niro turned down the role of Tony Montana, Al Pacino took the role. He immediately began working with experts in knife combat, trainers, and boxer Roberto Duran to attain the body type that he wanted for the role.

During the audition process, casting director Alixe Gordin saw Steven Bauer on the set of a movie he was doing, and instantly noted Bauer was right for the role of Manny; both director Brian De Palma and producer Martin Bregman agreed. Bauer was the only actual Cuban in the principal cast. Bauer and a dialect coach helped Pacino learn aspects of the Cuban Spanish language and pronunciations. Pacino learned the word, "yeyo" as slang for cocaine, and ad-libbed the word during the chainsaw scene. De Palma liked it enough to keep using it throughout the film.

Michelle Pfeiffer was an unknown actress at the time. Both De Palma and Pacino had argued against her being cast as Elvira, but Bregman fought for her. Pacino wanted Glenn Close, but Bregman didn't think she was sexy enough.According to one source, Brooke Shields was offered the role of Elvira after a private interview with Al Pacino. However, her mother, Teri Shields, made her turn down the role.

TERMS OF ENDEARMENT (1983)

Aurora: Do you have any reaction at all to my telling you I love you?
Garrett: I was just inches from a clean getaway.

Plot
The story of an intense relationship between a mother and daughter.

CASTING

Who Starred as Garrett Breedlove?
Jack Nicholson

Turned Down the Role of Garrett Breedlove
Burt Reynolds • Paul Newman
Harrison Ford • James Garner

Who Starred as Emma Greenway-Horton?
Debra Winger

Turned Down the Role of Emma Greenway-Horton
Sissy Spacek • Jodie Foster

WHO Trivia
The character of Garrett Breedlove did not appear in Larry McMurtry's novel. Director/Writer/Producer James L. Brooks added the character of Breedlove specifically for Burt Reynolds.

Reynolds loved the script but had to turn it down because he was already committed to star in *Stroker Ace*. "There are no awards in Hollywood for being an idiot," Reynolds said of the decision.

After Paul Newman, Harrison Ford, and James Garner turned down the role, Jack Nicholson was cast, winning won an Oscar the Best Supporting Actor.

The role of Emma was written with Sissy Spacek in mind, but she turned it down, as did Jodie Foster due to her commitment to attend Yale.

A number of actresses were considered for the role of Aurora Greenway, including Louise Fletcher, but Brooks settled on Shirley MacLaine because "she was the only one who saw it as a comedy." MacLaine won the Academy Award for Best Actress.

James Brooks did consider real life mother and daughter, Janet Leigh and Jamie Lee Curtis, for the roles of Aurora and Emma respectively.

BEVERLY HILLS COP (1984)

Axel: This is the cleanest and nicest police car I've ever been in in my life. This thing's nicer than my apartment.

Plot
A freewheeling Detroit cop pursuing a murder investigation finds himself dealing with the very different culture of Beverly Hills.

CASTING

Who Starred as Axel Foley?
Eddie Murphy

Turned Down the Role of Axel Foley
Mickey Rourke • Sylvester Stallone

WHO Trivia
The role of Axel Foley was first offered to Mickey Rourke, fresh off his success in *Diner*. Rourke signed a $400,000 holding contract to do the film. When revisions and other preparations took longer than expected, Rourke left the project to do another film.

Sylvester Stallone was then offered the role. He came on board, and gave the script a dramatic rewrite, making it into a straight action film, and renaming the lead character, Axel Cobretti. However, Stallone's ideas were "too expensive" for Paramount Pictures to produce, and Stallone ultimately pulled out two weeks before filming was to start.

Two days later, the film's producers, Don Simpson and Jerry Bruckheimer, convinced Eddie Murphy to replace Stallone in the film, prompting more rewrites.

Director Martin Brest, who was a last ditch thought to direct the film after being fired off of *Wargames*, encouraged Murphy and the cast to improvise when they felt like it. This resulted in Murphy, John Ashton and Judge Reinhold improvising most of the comic lines. Subsequently, there were hundreds of ruined takes because actors broke into laughter during shooting.

Other actors who were considered for the role of Axel Foley included: Richard Pryor, Al Pacino, James Caan, Jeff Bridges, Billy Crystal, Bruce Willis, Richard Gere, Michael Keaton, Kurt Russell, and Robin Williams.

FOOTLOOSE (1984)

Ren: What's this I see? I thought this was a party! Let's dance!!

Plot

A big city teenager moves to a small town where rock music and dancing have been banned.

CASTING

Who Starred as Ren McCormack?
Kevin Bacon

Turned Down the Role of Ren McCormack
Jon Bon Jovi • Tom Cruise
Christopher Atkins • Rob Lowe

Who Starred as Ariel?
Lori Singer

Turned Down the Role of Ariel
Daryl Hannah • Elizabeth McGovern

WHO Trivia

At one time, Tom Cruise and Rob Lowe were both slated to play the lead role. The casting director was impressed with Cruise because of the famous underwear dance sequence in *Risky Business,* but Cruise was unavailable for the part because he was filming *All the Right Moves.* Lowe auditioned three times; he had dancing ability and the "neutral teen" look that the director wanted. However, an injury prevented Lowe from taking the role. Jon Bon Jovi was then offered the role, but turned it down because his band was just taking off.

At the same time, Kevin Bacon was asked to do a screen test for *Footloose*, he was offered the main role for the movie *Christine.* Bacon chose to take the gamble on the screen test. Director Herbert Ross, after watching his earlier movie *Diner*, persuaded the producers to go with Bacon.

Before Lori Singer was cast as Ariel, Reverend Moore's independent daughter, Elizabeth McGovern turned down the role to be in *Once Upon a Time in America.* Daryl Hannah turned down the role in order to play Madison in *Splash.*

Jamie Lee Curtis, Melanie Griffith, Meg Tilly, Phoebe Cates, Lori Loughlin, Brooke Shields, Bridget Fonda, Jodie Foster, Diane Lane, and Madonna were all considered for the role of Ariel.

GHOSTBUSTERS (1984)

Dr. Peter Venkman: We came, we saw, we kicked its ass!

Plot
Three unemployed parapsychology professors set up a ghost capture and removal business.

CASTING

Who Starred as Peter Venkman?
Bill Murray

Turned Down the Role of Peter Venkman
Chevy Chase • Steve Guttenberg • Michael Keaton

Who Starred as Winston Zeddemore?
Ernie Hudson

Turned Down the Role of Winston Zeddemore
Eddie Murphy

WHO Trivia
Writers Dan Aykroyd and Harold Ramis wrote the role of Peter Venkman for their friend John Belushi. After Belushi died, Aykroyd considered rewriting the script for Richard Pryor, but that never came to anything.

Chevy Chase turned down the role, as did Steve Guttenberg, who chose instead to star in *Police Academy*. Tom Hanks and Robin Williams were both considered before the role was awarded to Bill Murray.

Eddie Murphy was offered the role of Winston Zeddemore, but he turned it down and made *Beverly Hills Cop* instead. If Murphy had taken the role, the character would have been a bigger part of the film.

The role of Louis Tully was written for John Candy, but creative differences caused him to turn down the role. Rick Moranis loved the script, and signed on to play the part. Tully was conceived as a conservative man in a business suit, but Moranis portrayed Louis as a geek instead.

Sigourney Weaver and Julia Roberts auditioned for the Dana Barrett role, which eventually went to Sigourney Weaver. After Sandra Bernhard turned down the role of secretary Janine Melnitz, the role went to Annie Potts.

SPLASH (1984)

Madison: You said whatever my secret was, you'd understand.
Allen: Yeah... but...
Madison: You thought at least I was a human being.

Plot

A New York City produce supplier falls in love with a mermaid who saved him from drowning as a child in Cape Cod 20 years before.

CASTING

Who Starred as Allen Bauer?
Tom Hanks

Turned Down the Role of Allen Bauer
Chevy Chase • Bill Murray • Dudley Moore
John Travolta • David Morse • Michael Keaton

Who Starred as Madison?
Daryl Hannah

Turned Down the Role of Madison
Jamie Lee Curtis • Anjelica Huston
Tanya Roberts • Jodie Foster • Brooke Shields
Julia Louis-Dreyfus • Melanie Griffith
Genie Francis • Tatum O'Neal • Michelle Pfeiffer
Sharon Stone • Kathleen Turner

WHO Trivia

An issue at the time of production was the competition between *Splash* and another announced, but unnamed, mermaid film from Warner Bros. that had lined up Warren Beatty as its star. Director Ron Howard promised the studio that *Splash* would be filmed more quickly and cheaply than the other film; the other film eventually fell through.

Casting was a bit insane for Ron Howard after six A-list actors turned down the lead role of Allen Bauer. At the same time, a dozen actresses turned down the role of Madison, including: Jodie Foster, who chose to play the role of Franny Berry in *The Hotel New Hampshire*; and Brooke Shields, who turned down the role so she could go to Princeton to study French Literature. The others simply didn't want to play a mermaid.

Ron Howard decided to go with unknown actors, and gave the lead role of Allen Bauer to Tom Hanks, who originally read for the role of Freddie, subsequently played by John Candy.

THE TERMINATOR (1984)

Terminator: I'm a friend of Sarah Connor. I was told she was here. Could I see her please?
Desk Sergeant: No, you can't see her. She's making a statement.
Terminator: Where is she?
Desk Sergeant: Look, it may take a while. Want to wait? There's a bench over there.
Terminator: (looks around, then looks back at him) I'll be back.

Plot

A human-looking, apparently unstoppable cyborg, is sent from the machine-dominated future to assassinate the eventual mother of the human resistance leader.

CASTING

Who Starred as The Terminator?
Arnold Schwarzenegger

Turned Down the Role of The Terminator
Sylvester Stallone • Mel Gibson

WHO Trivia

Writer/Director James Cameron and Orion Pictures wanted a "box office" star for the role of Kyle Reese. The star needed to be popular in the United States as well as have some foreign appeal.

Orion co-founder Mike Medavoy knew Arnold Schwarzenegger, and sent his agent the script for *The Terminator*. Cameron was dubious about casting Schwarzenegger as Reese, feeling he would need someone even bigger to play the Terminator.

After Sylvester Stallone and Mel Gibson turned down the Terminator role, the studio suggested O. J. Simpson, but Cameron did not feel that Simpson would be believable as a killer.

Cameron agreed to meet with Schwarzenegger, and actually devised a plan to avoid casting him; he would pick a fight with Schwarzenegger and later find him unfit for the role. Upon meeting him however, Cameron was entertained by Schwarzenegger who talked about how the villain should be played.

Cameron immediately began sketching Schwarzenegger's face on a notepad.

After the meeting, Cameron called Medavoy saying Schwarzenegger shouldn't play Reese, but that "he'd make a hell of a Terminator."

Schwarzenegger was not nearly as excited about the film as Cameron. During an interview on the set of *Conan the Destroyer*, Schwarzenegger was asked about a pair of shoes he had, which belonged to the wardrobe for *The Terminator*. He responded, "Oh some shit movie I'm doing, take a couple weeks."

Schwarzenegger recounted in his memoir, *Total Recall*, that he was initially hesitant, but thought playing a robot in a contemporary film would be challenging, and that the film was low profile enough that it would not damage his career if it were unsuccessful.

Schwarzenegger also wrote that "It took him awhile to figure out Cameron was the real deal." In preparation for the role, Schwarzenegger spent three months training with weapons to be able to use them and feel comfortable around them.

Schwarzenegger speaks only 18 lines and fewer than 100 words in the film. Cameron said, "Somehow, even his accent worked... It had a strange synthesized quality, like they hadn't gotten the voice thing quite worked out."

For the lead role of Kyle Reese, various suggestions were made including rock musician Sting. Cameron chose Michael Biehn, who was originally skeptical about the part, thinking the film was silly. After meeting with Cameron, Biehn stated that his feelings about the project changed.

Producer Gale Anne Hurd, who later married Cameron, showed interest in the project in its early stages. Cameron sold her the rights for $1.00 with the promise that she would produce the film if Cameron got to direct it.

Cameron's final two choices for the role of Sarah Connor came down to Jennifer Jason Leigh and Linda Hamilton. Hamilton won the role based on her performance in *Children of the Corn*.

THE BREAKFAST CLUB (1985)

Brian: Dear Mr. Vernon, we accept the fact that we had to sacrifice a whole Saturday in detention for whatever it was we did wrong. But we think you're crazy to make us write an essay telling you who we think we are, because you see us as you want to see us: In the simplest terms, in the most convenient definitions. But what we found out is that each one of us is a brain...

Andrew: and an athlete...

Allison: and a basket case...

Claire: and a princess...

John: and a criminal.

Brian: Does that answer your question? Sincerely yours, The Breakfast Club.

Plot

Five high school students from completely different backgrounds meet in Saturday detention.

CASTING

Who Starred as John Bender?
Judd Nelson

Turned Down the Role of John Bender
Nicolas Cage

WHO Trivia

Writer/Director John Hughes wanted Molly Ringwald to play the character of Allison Reynolds, ultimately played by Ally Sheedy, but she wanted to play Claire Standish. In time, she convinced Hughes and the studio to let her play the role of Claire. Robin Wright, Jodie Foster, and Laura Dern were considered for the role of Claire, while Jodie Foster was considered for the role of Allison.

Emilio Estevez originally auditioned to play the role of John Bender, as did young comedian, Jim Carrey. However when Hughes was unable to find someone to play Andrew Clark, Estevez was recast in that role.

Nicolas Cage was then offered the role of Bender, but turned it down when Hughes wouldn't meet Cage's asking price. Hughes then narrowed down the casting choices to John Cusack and Judd Nelson, originally casting Cusack, but then deciding to replace him with Nelson before shooting began. Hughes made this change because he thought Cusack did not look threatening enough.

BACK TO THE FUTURE (1985)

Marty: Hey, Doc, we better back up. We don't have enough road to get up to 88.

Doc: Roads? Where we're going, we don't need roads.

Plot

A 17-year-old high school student is sent 30 years into the past in a time traveling DeLorean, where he accidentally interferes with his parents' courtship and must make them fall in love... or else he will never be born.

CASTING

Who Starred as Doc Brown?
Christopher Lloyd

Turned Down the Role of Doc Brown
John Lithgow

WHO Trivia

Michael J. Fox was writer/director Robert Zemeckis' first choice to play the role of Marty McFly, but he was unavailable due to scheduling conflicts with his work on the television show, *Family Ties*. Because Meredith Baxter was on maternity leave, Fox assumed a bigger workload. Gary David Goldberg, the show's producer, simply couldn't afford to let Fox go.

Zemeckis' solution was to cast Eric Stoltz as McFly. However, four weeks into filming, he determined Stoltz wasn't right for the part and Stoltz agreed.

Although Zemeckis and Spielberg realized re-shooting the film would add another $3 million to the budget, they decided to recast.

Following the pregnancy, Baxter returned to *Family Ties,* and Fox's schedule opened up. Subsequently after a meeting between Goldberg. Zemeckis, and the *Back to the Future* shooting crew, a deal was made that stipulated Fox's priority would be *Family Ties*, making the bulk of the film's shooting between 6pm and 6am. Fox would only have five hours of sleep to accommodate both filming schedules.

Melora Hardin was originally cast in the role of Marty's girlfriend Jennifer, but she was let go after Stoltz was dismissed, with the explanation that the actress was simply too tall to be playing opposite Fox. Hardin was dismissed before she had a chance to shoot a single scene. She was replaced by Claudia Wells.

THE COLOR PURPLE (1985)

Celie: He beat me when you ain't here.
Shug: Who do? Albert?
Celie: Mister.
Shug: Why he do that?
Celie: He beat me for not being you.

Plot

The problems faced by African-American women during the early 1900s, including poverty, racism, and sexual abuse, are shown through the eyes of a young African-American girl.

CASTING

Who Starred as Shug?
Margaret Avery

Turned Down the Role of Shug
Chaka Khan • Patti LaBelle • Tina Turner
Diana Ross • Lola Falana

Who Starred as Sofia?
Oprah Winfrey

Turned Down the Role of Sofia
Nell Carter • Jennifer Holliday

WHO Trivia

This was the first feature film for both Whoopi Goldberg and Oprah Winfrey.

Director Steven Spielberg was seriously considering Alfre Woodard for the role of Celie Johnson, but gave it to Whoopi Goldberg after she auditioned for Spielberg and two of his friends, Michael Jackson and Quincy Jones. Goldberg's audition included a comedy bit about a stoned E.T. getting arrested for possession. Spielberg immediately offered Goldberg the role.

Chaka Khan turned down the role of Shug because she was afraid of acting at that time in her life. Patti LaBelle turned down the Oscar-nominated role, ultimately played by Margaret Avery, because she was not interested in doing a same-sex kiss. Tina Turner, Diana Ross, and Lola Falana also turned down the role of Shug

Jennifer Holliday, who turned down the role of Sofia, starred as Effie in the Broadway musical, *Dreamgirls*.

BLUE VELVET (1986)

Raymond: He's a pussy, Frank!
   Frank: Yeah, but he's our pussy. (Looks at Dorothy) Ain't that right, tits?

Plot
An innocent young man discovers a dark underworld exists beneath the surface of his seemingly quiet hometown.

CASTING

Who Starred as Dorothy Vallens?
Isabella Rossellini

Turned Down the Role of Dorothy Vallens
Debbie Harry • Debra Winger

Who Starred as Jeffrey Beaumont?
Kyle MacLachlan

Turned Down the Role of Jeffrey Beaumont
Val Kilmer

WHO Trivia
Writer/Director David Lynch originally wrote the role of Dorothy for singer Debbie Harry, but she turned it down, sick of playing "the weirdo" after playing such a character in *Videodrome*. Debra Winger then turned it down because of the erotic nature of the film.

After considering a number of established actresses for the part, Lynch decided to cast Isabella Rossellini in her first role. In the early 1980s, Rossellini had some notoriety from her Lancome ads and for being the daughter of legendary actress Ingrid Bergman and director Roberto Rossellini.

The role of Jeffrey was turned down by Val Kilmer, who described the version of the script he read as "pornography." He did say he would've done the version that finally made it to the screen.

Harry Dean Stanton and Steve Berkoff turned down the role of Frank, played by Dennis Hopper, the role that resurrected Hopper's career.

TOP GUN (1986)

Maverick: I feel the need…
Maverick & Goose: …the need for speed!

Plot

As students at the United States Navy's elite fighter weapons school compete to be best in the class, one daring young pilot learns a few things from a female civilian instructor that are not taught in the classroom.

CASTING

Who Starred as Lt. Pete "Maverick" Mitchell?
Tom Cruise

Turned Down the Role of Lt. Pete "Maverick" Mitchell
Matthew Modine • Patrick Swayze
John Cusack • Matthew Broderick • Sean Penn
Emilio Estevez • Nicolas Cage
Michael J. Fox • Scott Baio • Tom Hanks

Who Starred as Charlie Blackwood?
Kelly McGillis

Turned Down the Role of Charlie Blackwood
Tatum O'Neal • Jodie Foster • Daryl Hannah
Diane Lane • Sarah Jessica Parker • Linda Hamilton

WHO Trivia

Producer Jerry Bruckheimer claims he always wanted Tom Cruise for the role of "Maverick" and that Cruise kept turning it down. A number of future A-List actors also turned down the role including: Matthew Broderick, Sean Penn, Patrick Swayze, Emilio Estevez, Nicolas Cage, John Cusack, Michael J. Fox, Scott Baio, Tom Hanks, and Matthew Modine. Modine turned the role down because he felt the film's pro-military stance went against his politics.

In addition to the ten actors who turned down the role of "Maverick," the following were considered: Charlie Sheen, Robert Downey Jr., Kevin Bacon, Rob Lowe, Jim Carrey, and Eric Stoltz.

In addition to the six actresses who turned down the role of Charlie, the following were considered: Brooke Shields, Debra Winger, and Julianne Phillips. Ultimately, an unknown actress, Kelly McGillis, was cast.

FATAL ATTRACTION (1987)

Alex Forrest: You're here with a strange girl being a naughty boy.
Dan Gallagher: I don't think having dinner with anybody's a crime.

Plot

A married man's one-night stand comes back to haunt him when that lover begins to stalk him and his family.

CASTING

Who Starred as Dan Gallagher?
Michael Douglas

Turned Down the Role of Dan Gallagher
Christopher Reeve • Bruce Willis

Who Starred as Alex Forrest?
Glenn Close

Turned Down the Role of Alex Forrest
Sally Field • Elizabeth Shue • Isabella Rossellini
Isabelle Adjani • Barbara Hershey • Debra Winger
Amy Irving • Linda Hamilton • Kelly McGillis
Christine Ebersole • Annie Potts • Meryl Streep
Miranda Richardson • Mary Steenburgen

WHO Trivia

Sally Field was considered for the role of Alex Forrest, but immediately turned it down because she feared that her fans would not accept her as an antagonist. Elizbeth Shue had to turn down the role because she was signed to the movie, *Adventures in Babysitting*. Isabella Rossellini turned down the part because she didn't want to be typecast as a "femme fatale." French actress Isabelle Adjani had scheduling conflicts. Ten other well-regarded actresses turned down the role for a variety of reasons.

Glenn Close wanted the role. Producers Sherry Lansing and Stanley Jaffe had serious doubts. They didn't think she could be sexual enough.

Close was persistent. After meeting with Jaffe in New York, she was asked to fly out to Los Angeles to read with Michael Douglas. For the audition, Close let her naturally frizzy hair "go wild," and selected a slimming black dress she thought made her look "fabulous." This impressed Sherry Lansing. She thought Close "came in looking completely different... and into the part."

THE UNTOUCHABLES (1987)

Ness: I want to get Capone. I don't know how to get him.
Malone: You want to get Capone?... Here's how you get him... He pulls a knife, you pull a gun... He sends one of yours to the hospital, you send one of his to the morgue!... That's the Chicago way and that's how you get Capone!

Plot

During the era of Prohibition, Federal Agent Eliot Ness sets out to stop ruthless Chicago gangster Al Capone.

CASTING

Who Starred as Eliot Ness?
Kevin Costner

Turned Down the Role of Eliot Ness
Mickey Rourke • Don Johnson • Jack Nicholson

Who Starred as Al Capone?
Robert De Niro

Turned Down the Role of Al Capone
Marlon Brando

WHO Trivia

During the early casting, Marlon Brando turned down $5 million to play the role of Al Capone for two weeks work. Later, director Brian De Palma met with Bob Hoskins to discuss Hoskins playing the role of Capone in case Robert De Niro, De Palma's first choice for the part, turned it down. When De Niro took the part, De Palma mailed Hoskins a check for $20,000 with a "Thank You" note. This prompted Hoskins to call De Palma and ask him if there were any more movies he didn't want him to be in.

After Mickey Rourke turned down the role of Eliot Ness, De Palma offered it to Don Johnson, who was currently the star of *Miami Vice*, but he also turned it down. Following the success of *Witness,* Paramount Pictures wanted Harrison Ford to play Ness, but De Palma decided on the lesser known Kevin Costner.

De Palma talked to Gene Hackman about playing Jimmy Malone, ultimately played by Sean Connery. The role won Connery his only Academy Award for Best Supporting Actor. De Palma first noticed Andy Garcia in the action film, *8 Million Ways to Die.* De Palma pictured him playing a villain, in this case, Frank Nitti. Garcia insisted on reading for George Stone, and got the part.

WALL STREET (1987)

Gordon Gekko: Lunch? Aw, you gotta be kidding... Lunch is for
wimps.

Plot
A young stockbroker desperate to succeed becomes involved with his hero,
a wealthy, unscrupulous corporate raider.

CASTING

Who Starred as Gordon Gekko?
Michael Douglas

Turned Down the Role of Gordon Gekko
Richard Gere • Warren Beatty
Jack Nicholson • James Woods

WHO Trivia
Originally, 20th Century Fox wanted Warren Beatty to play Gordon Gekko,
but Beatty was not interested. Writer/Director Oliver Stone wanted Richard
Gere, but he passed on the role. Jack Nicholson turned down the role due
to a commitment to *The Witches of Eastwick*. James Woods turned down the
role to do the film, *Cop*.

The word was that Michael Douglas was looking for something dark and
edgy. Stone remembers being warned by everyone in Hollywood that
Douglas was a producer more than an actor. Nevertheless, Stone said he
saw "that villain quality" in Douglas, and offered him the role.

Douglas remembers that when he first read the screenplay, "I thought it was
a great part. It was a long script, and there were some incredibly long and
intense monologues to open with. I'd never seen a screenplay where there
were two or three pages of single-spaced type for a monologue. I thought,
Whoa! I mean, it was unbelievable."

Stone did meet with Tom Cruise, who really wanted the role of Bud Fox,
but Stone had already committed the role to Charlie Sheen. Stone liked the
"stiffness" of Sheen's acting style and used it to convey Bud's naiveté.

Stone gave Charlie Sheen the choice of Jack Lemmon or Martin Sheen to
play his father in the film, and Sheen chose his father. Stone cast Daryl
Hannah as Fox's materialistic girlfriend Darien, but felt she was never happy
with the role, and did not know why she accepted it.

THE ACCUSED (1988)

Sarah Tobias: What are our chances?
Kathryn Murphy: 50-50 at the most. Good night.
Sarah Tobias: Good night.

Plot

After a woman suffers a brutal rape in a bar one night, a prosecutor assists her in bringing the perpetrators to justice, including the spectators who encouraged and cheered on the attack.

CASTING

Who Starred as Sarah Tobias?
Jodie Foster

Turned Down the Role of Sarah Tobias
Jennifer Grey • Joan Cusack • Jennifer Beals
Ally Sheedy • Kim Basinger
Justine Bateman • Tatum O'Neal • Kelly Preston
Demi Moore • Meg Tilly

Who Starred as Kathryn Murphy?
Kelly McGillis

Turned Down the Role of Kathryn Murphy
Jane Fonda • Ellen Barkin • Geena Davis • Meryl Streep
Carrie Fisher • Kathleen Turner • Sigourney Weaver

WHO Trivia

The casting process of the film was extremely difficult. The studio was looking for a bankable actress who could sell the film. Numerous actresses were offered the part of Sarah Tobias, but all of them rejected the film due to its gruesome and controversial themes.

Jane Fonda was initially attached to play the role of Asst. District Attorney Kathryn Murphy, but left the project as she found the script exploitative and poorly written. The producers then turned to Kelly McGillis, who had just come off *Top Gun*. McGillis was initially offered the part of Sarah, but declined, acknowledging that she had survived a violent sexual assault at knifepoint by two men in 1982, and instead fought for the part of Kathryn Murphy.

Foster, who had recently graduated from Yale and hadn't made any successful films during her time at school, wasn't the first choice for the producers. Following numerous auditions, as well as rejection from various established actresses, she was finally cast in the part of Sarah Tobias.

BIG (1988)

Billy: So, you got a job, where you play with all these toys?
Josh: Yup!
Billy: And they're gonna pay you for that?
Josh: Yup!
Billy: SUCKERS!

Plot

A boy wishes to be "big" at a magic wish machine and wakes up the next morning to find himself in an adult body.

CASTING

Who Starred as Josh Baskin?
Tom Hanks

Turned Down the Role of Josh Baskin
Robert De Niro • Dennis Quaid • Steve Guttenberg
Albert Brooks • Bill Murray

Who Starred as Susan Lawrence?
Elizabeth Perkins

Turned Down the Role of Susan Lawrence
Debra Winger

WHO Trivia

When director Penny Marshall first got the script, nobody was interested in doing the movie. Steve Guttenberg turned it down, busy doing *3 Men and a Baby*. Dennis Quaid chose *Everybody's All American* over *Big*, while Bill Murray elected to make *Scrooged* instead. Albert Brooks just simply declined.

Then Robert De Niro announced he wanted the part of Josh, and suddenly the script was a hot item. From the onset, Penny Marshall's first choice was always Tom Hanks, who was interested but unavailable due to other commitments. When 20th Century Fox would not meet De Niro's $6 million quote, he walked away, and the project looked like it was never going to get made.

A few months later, Tom Hanks became available, and the studio put the film into production.

The role of Susan Lawrence was offered to Debra Winger, but she turned it down because she was pregnant. She recommended Elizabeth Perkins.

DIE HARD (1988)

McClane: "Yippee-ki-yay, motherfucker!"

Plot
An rule-breaking NYPD detective tries to save his estranged wife and fellow workers taken hostage by German terrorists during her company Christmas party at the Nakatomi Plaza in Los Angeles.

CASTING

Who Starred as Det. John McClane?
Bruce Willis

Turned Down the Role of Det. John McClane
Arnold Schwarzeneggger • Richard Gere • Clint Eastwood
Burt Reynolds • Sylvester Stallone • Harrison Ford
Don Johnson • Nick Nolte • Frank Sinatra

WHO Trivia
Die Hard is based on *Nothing Lasts Forever,* a sequel to *The Detective,* which was adapted in 1968 into a film starring Frank Sinatra. When a movie based on the sequel went into production, 20th Century Fox was contractually obligated to offer Sinatra the lead role. Then in his early 70s, Sinatra turned it down.

At the time, Bruce Willis, known for his role as detective David Addison on the television series *Moonlighting,* had to initially turn down the role due to his contractual commitments. However, after Cybil Shepherd, his co-star on the show, became pregnant, *Moonlighting* was shut down for 11 weeks, which provided sufficient time for Willis to work on *Die Hard.*

Bruce Willis was paid $5 million to star in the film, a figure virtually unheard of at the time for an actor who had starred in only one moderately successful film, and normally only paid to major stars. Fox justified the cost, stating the film was reliant on its lead actor. Other sources within the studio later admitted that Fox was desperate for a star for *Die Hard*, especially after nine A-list actors turned down the role. The film was intended to be Fox's summer blockbuster.

Die Hard was Alan Rickman's first feature film role. Rickman was cast in the role of Hans Gruber after producer Joel Silver saw his performance in the Broadway run of *Les Liaisons Dangereuses.*

DIRTY DANCING (1988)

Johnny Castle: Nobody puts Baby in the corner.

Plot
In 1963, a teenage girl crosses over into womanhood, both physically and emotionally, through a relationship with a dance instructor during a family summer vacation in the Catskills.

CASTING

Who Starred as Francis "Baby" Houseman?
Jennifer Grey

Turned Down the Role of Frances "Baby" Houseman
Mindy Cohn • Heather Graham • Robin Wright Penn

Who Starred as Johnny Castle?
Patrick Swayze

Turned Down the Role of Johnny Castle
Val Kilmer • Jeff Fahey

WHO Trivia
The first choice to play Frances "Baby" Houseman was Mindy Cohn, but she was unavailable due to her television show, *The Facts of Life*.

Director Emile Ardolino was adamant they choose dancers who could also act. He did not want to use the "stand-in" method which had been used with *Flashdance*.

After Mindy Cohn, Heather Graham, and Robin Wright Penn turned down the role of "Baby," screenwriter Eleanor Bergstein suggested Jennifer Grey, daughter of the Oscar-winning actor and dancer, Joel Grey.

After casting Grey, producer Linda Gottlieb sought a male lead, initially considering Billy Zane, but he didn't have the dancing skills. After Jeff Fahey and Val Kilmer passed, the next choice was Patrick Swayze, who was a seasoned dancer, given his experience with the Joffrey Ballet.

Jennifer Grey was initially not happy about the choice, as she and Swayze had difficulty getting along during the filming of *Red Dawn*, but after they sat down and talked, she changed her mind. When they did their dancing screen test, the chemistry between them was obvious.

RAIN MAN (1988)

Raymond: K-Mart.
   Charlie: You know what I think, Ray? I think this autism is a bunch of shit! Because you can't tell me that you're not in there somewhere!
Raymond: Boxer shorts. K-Mart.

Plot
A selfish yuppie, desperately in need of money, discovers his father has left all of his estate to an autistic savant brother, decides to travel cross-country with him to get what he thinks he deserves.

CASTING

Who Starred as Raymond "Ray" Babbitt?
Dustin Hoffman

Turned Down the Role of Raymond "Ray" Babbitt
Jack Nicholson • Robert De Niro • Mel Gibson

Who Starred as Charlie Babbitt?
Tom Cruise

Turned Down the Role of Charlie Babbitt?
Mickey Rourke

WHO Trivia
Dustin Hoffman was originally hired to play Charlie Babbitt, but after seeing a savant named Leslie Lemke, who was blind, mentally handicapped, and had cerebral palsy play full concertos on a piano by ear, he decided to play the part of Raymond instead. In hindsight, it was a great decision since Hoffman went on to win the Academy Award for Best Actor.

Raymond was also supposed to be mentally handicapped, but Hoffman insisted it be changed to an autistic savant, which led to director Martin Brest quitting the project. Barry Levinson, who initially turned down the film to make *Good Morning Vietnam,* replaced Brest.

After taking on the role of Raymond, Hoffman wanted Bill Murray to play his brother Charlie. Levinson had a different idea. He offered the role, ultimately played by Tom Cruise, to Mickey Rourke, who turned it down because of scheduling conflicts.

The script was originally written for brothers Dennis and Randy Quaid.

WORKING GIRL (1988)

Jack Trainer: Oh, I didn't know that they let bad girls into these things.

Tess McGill: Do I look like I don't belong here?

Jack Trainer: No. No, I'm sure that you're a real ace in whatever it is that you do... do.

Tess McGill: Damn straight.

Jack Trainer: But how you look...

Tess McGill: I have a head for business and a bod for sin... Is there anything wrong with that?

Plot

A spunky Wall Street secretary, whose business idea is stolen by her boss, seizes an opportunity to steal it back when her boss is injured by pretending she has her boss' job.

CASTING

Who Starred as Tess McGill?
Melanie Griffith

Turned Down the Role of Tess McGill
Jodie Foster　•　Nicolette Sheridan

WHO Trivia

Jodie Foster turned down the role of Tess McGill in order to play Sarah Tobias in *The Accused*. Nicolette Sheridan also turned down the role as she was too busy working on the hit television show, *Knots Landing*.

Actresses who auditioned for the role of Tess McGill included: Michelle Pfeiffer, Jennifer Jason Leigh, Sarah Jessica Parker, Tia Carrere, Christine Ebersole, Alexandra Paul, Mary Stuart Masterson, and Lorraine Bracco. Bracco later said that not getting the role was a heartbreaking blow to her career.

Isabella Rossellini was considered, but her Italian accent didn't work for the American character. After graduating from Princeton, Brooke Shields really wanted the role to launch her career as an adult actress, but she didn't get it.

Before Sigourney Weaver was cast as Katharine Parker, actresses Meryl Streep, Kathleen Turner, Geena Davis, Shelley Long, and Cher were all considered.

Alec Baldwin was initially cast as Jack Trainer before Harrison Ford ultimately got the part. Baldwin was recast to play Tess' boyfriend. The role of Cyn, played by Joan Cusack, was intended for Whoopi Goldberg.

BATMAN (1989)

Nick: Don't kill me! Don't kill me, man! Don't kill me, man!!
Batman: I'm not gonna kill you. I want you to do me a favor. I want you to tell all your friends about me.
Nick: What are you?!
Batman: I'm Batman.

Plot
Batman, the caped crusader, fights his arch-nemesis, the Joker.

CASTING

Who Starred as Batman/Bruce Wayne?
Michael Keaton

Turned Down the Role of Batman/Bruce Wayne
Mel Gibson • Pierce Brosnan

WHO Trivia
Similar to the *Superman* casting, a who's who of Hollywood stars were considered for the role of Batman, including Mel Gibson, Pierce Brosnan, Kevin Costner, Charlie Sheen, Tom Selleck, Bill Murray, and Harrison Ford. Director Tim Burton was pressured to cast a "box office" action star.

The two leading candidates were Mel Gibson, who was committed to filming *Lethal Weapon 2*, and Pierce Brosnan, who had no interest in the part.

Producer Jon Peters suggested Michael Keaton, arguing he had the right "edgy, tormented quality" after having seen Keaton in *Clean and Sober*. Burton had also directed Keaton in *Beetlejuice,* and ultimately agreed, but Keaton's casting caused a controversy among comic book fans.

On the other hand, the idea of Jack Nicholson as the Joker was well received, but he hesitated so long the role was offered to Robin Williams, who accepted. When Nicholson finally accepted the role, Williams was released, but resented being used as bait. Williams refused to play the Riddler in *Batman Forever,* or work for Warner Bros. until he received an apology.

Sean Young was originally cast as Vicki Vale, but was injured in an accident prior to commencement of filming; she was replaced by Kim Basinger.

The famous line, "I'm Batman," came from Michael Keaton on the day the line was to be filmed. The original line in the script was, "I am the night."

WHEN HARRY MET SALLY... (1989)

Harry: You don't think that I could tell the difference?
Sally: No.
Harry: Get outta here.
(Sally begins to fake an orgasm)
Are you OK?
(Sally continues, attracting the attention of nearly every customer in the cafe. Afterwards, she returns to eating her dessert)
Woman Customer: *(to Waiter)* I'll have what she's having.

Plot
Two very good friends are confronted with the problem, "Can a man and a woman be friends, without sex getting in the way?"

CASTING

Who Starred as Harry Burns?
Billy Crystal

Turned Down the Role of Harry Burns
Tom Hanks • Albert Brooks

Who Starred as Sally Albright?
Meg Ryan

Turned Down the Role of Sally Albright
Susan Dey • Molly Ringwald

WHO Trivia
Albert Brooks turned down the role of Harry Burns; Tom Hanks turned it down because he thought it was "too lightweight." Before Billy Crystal was cast, director Rob Reiner considered Michael Keaton, Bill Murray, Jeff Bridges and Harrison Ford.

Reiner initially envisioned Susan Dey, best known for her role on the television show, *The Partridge Family,* for the role of Sally, but Dey turned it down. Reiner then offered the role to Molly Ringwald, who also turned it down because her schedule was too busy. Knowing the role was available, Meg Ryan lobbied hard for the part.

In the infamous orgasm scene, the original script called for Harry and Sally to talk about a woman faking an orgasm until Ryan suggested Sally actually fake an orgasm at the table. The final line was suggested to Ephron by Billy Crystal.

Bonus Movies

The Postman Always Rings Twice (1981)
In this remake, the steamy role of the frustrated backwater wife, Cora, was played by Jessica Lange. Theresa Russell claimed "boyfriend troubles," thus preventing her from taking the role. Meryl Streep also turned down the role.

Frances (1982)
Victoria Principal turned down the leading role of Frances Farmer due to scheduling conflicts with her television show, *Dallas*. Sissy Spacek and Tuesday Weld were considered before Jessica Lange was cast.

Around 1966, Natalie Wood was attached to star in a biopic of Frances Farmer, but the project stalled.

Poltergeist (1982)
Shirley MacLaine was originally cast as the mother, Diane Freeling, but left the project to star in *Terms of Endearment*. After Barbra Streisand, Lily Tomlin, Susan Sarandon, and Joanna Cassidy all turned down the role, JoBeth Williams was finally cast.

The Outsiders (1983)
Val Kilmer, due to a previous commitment, turned down the role of Ponyboy, which was played by C. Thomas Howell. Nicolas Cage auditioned for the role of Dally, ultimately played by Matt Dillon, but didn't get it, and was offered the role of Two-Bit, but turned it down. Two-Bit was played by Emilio Estevez. After Brooke Shields turned down the role of Cherry to do another movie, Diane Lane was cast.

Risky Business (1983)
Before Tom Cruise was cast in the role of Joel Goodson, John Cusack, Matthew Broderick, Michael J. Fox, Tom Hanks, Timothy Hutton were all considered for the part.

Kim Basinger, who didn't like the script, turned down the role of Lana, ultimately played by Rebecca De Mornay. Tom Cruise, who got the script while filming *The Outsiders*, wanted Diane Lane to audition for the part, but her father said, "No daughter of mine is going to play a hooker."

Places in the Heart (1984)

Jessica Lange turned down the role of Edna Spalding, the role that won Sally Field her second Academy Award for Best Actress.

Sally Field's heartfelt Oscar acceptance speech became infamous: "This means so much more to me this time, I don't know why. I think the first time I hardly felt it because it was all too new. I haven't had an orthodox career. And I've wanted more than anything to have your respect. The first time I didn't feel it. But this time I feel it. And I can't deny the fact that you like me...You really like me! Thank you."

Desperately Seeking Susan (1985)

Ellen Barkin was the first choice for the part of Susan, but turned it down, as did Kelly McGillis. After Susan Dey and Jennifer Jason Leigh were considered for the part, Madonna was cast.

Brooke Shields was offered the role of Roberta, played by Rosanna Arquette, but declined due to her attendance at Princeton.

Witness (1985)

Jack Nicholson was offered the role of John Book. While he liked the script, there wasn't a director he liked attached at that point, so he passed on it. Producer Edward Feldman considered Kevin Costner, Sylvester Stallone, Richard Gere, and Clint Eastwood before Harrison Ford won the role that generated his one and only Oscar nomination.

Ferris Bueller's Day Off (1986)

Writer/Director John Hughes had Matthew Broderick in mind when he wrote the screenplay, saying Broderick was the only actor he could think of who could pull off Ferris. Paramount Pictures wanted Hughes to consider casting Johnny Depp, Jim Carrey, John Cusack, Robert Downey Jr., Michael J. Fox, Tom Cruise, or Rob Lowe. Eventually, Hughes convinced the studio that Matthew Broderick was whom the role needed.

Even though Anthony Michael Hall had great success working with Hughes in *The Breakfast Club,* he turned down the role of Cameron Frye to avoid being typecast. After Emilio Estevez also turned it down, Alan Ruck, who really wanted the part, had his agent reach out to Hughes. Hughes, remembering Alan Ruck's audition to play Bender in *The Breakfast Club,* decided to offer him the role.

Platoon (1986)

After Keanu Reeves turned down the part of Pvt. Chris Taylor, it went to Charlie Sheen. The part of Sgt. Elias Grodin went to Willem Dafoe after Mickey Rourke turned it down.

Predator (1987)

Jean-Claude Van Damme was originally cast as the Predator with the intent that the action star would use his martial arts skills to make the Predator an agile, ninja-like hunter. When compared to Schwarzenegger, known for his bodybuilding regimens, it became apparent a more physically imposing man was needed to make the creature appear more threatening. Van Damme was removed from the film and replaced by the much larger Kevin Peter Hall.

Field of Dreams (1989)

Tom Hanks turned down the role of Ray Kinsella, played by Kevin Costner. Director Phil Alden Robinson wanted James Stewart to play the key role of "Moonlight" Graham, but ultimately cast Burt Lancaster, in what turned out to be his last screen role.

Dead Poets Society (1989)

Mel Gibson was offered the lead role of John Keating when Jeff Kanew was attached as director, but Gibson wanted too much money. Liam Neeson was actually cast as John Keating, but dropped out after Jeff Kanew left the project to direct *Troop Beverly Hills*.

When Peter Weir came on as the director, Mickey Rourke was offered the lead role, but he turned it down when Weir refused to make changes to the script that Rourke wanted. The role eventually went to Robin Williams.

The Fabulous Baker Boys (1989)

Madonna and Debra Winger turned down the role of Susie Diamond before Michelle Pfeiffer was cast. Chevy Chase and Bill Murray both turned down roles in the film.

Sherman McCoy • Peter Fallow • Sam Wheat • Molly Jensen • Oda Mae Brown
Jack Ryan • Captain Ramius • Paul Sheldon • Annie Wilkes • Vivian Ward
Edward Lewis • Clarice Starling • Dr. Hannibal Lecter • Jack Crawford
Thelma • Louise • J.D. • Det. Hal Slocumb • Dottie Hinson • Jimmy Dugan
Kit Keller • Walter Harvey • Catherine Tramell • Nick Curren • Diana Murphy
David Murphy • John Gage • Frank Horrigan • Lilly Raines • Mitch Leary
Dr. Alan Grant • Dr. Ellie Sattler • Ian Malcolm • Lloyd Christmas • Harry
Forrest Gump • Jenny • Bubba Blue • Lestat • The Interviewer • Louis
Vincent Vega • Jules • Mia Wallace • Butch Coolidge • Marsellus Wallace
Andy Dufresne • "Red" Redding • Jack Traven • Annie Porter • Mike Lowrey

1990s

Marcus Burnett • Det. David Miles • Det. William Somerset • John Doe
Woody • Buzz Lightyear • Jerry Maguire • Dorothy Bird • Rod Tidwell
Melvin Udall • Carol Connelly • Simon Bishop • Dirk Diggler • Jack Horner
Amber Waves • Buck Swope • Rollergirl • Agent K • Agent J • Edgar the Bug
Jack Dawson • Rose • Cal Hockney • Viola de Lesseps • William Shakespeare
Lester Burnham • Carolyn Burnham • Jane Burnham • Angela Hayes • Neo
Trinity • Morpheus • John Kimble • Peter Pan • Captain Hook • Jim Garrison
Johnny Utah • Bodhi • Tom Wingo • Dr. Susan Lowenstein • Frank Farmer
Rachel Marron • Vinny Gambini • Mona Lisa Vito • Mr. Blonde • Phil Connors
Mitch McDeer • Abby McDeer • Richard Kimble • Sam Gerard • Dr. Nichols
Andrew Beckett • Joe Miller • Annie Reed • Helen Trasker • William Wallace
Francesca Johnson • Chili Palmer • Martin Ware • Harry Zimm • Karen Flores
Det. David Kujan • Keyser Soze • Almasy • Caravaggio • Katherine • Evita
Aaron Stampler • Sidney Prescott • Gail Weathers • Dewey • Lynn Bracken
Will Hunting • Mary • Ted Stroehmann • Pat Healy • Tyler Durden • Narrator
Sherman McCoy • Peter Fallow • Sam Wheat • Molly Jensen • Oda Mae Brown
Jack Ryan • Captain Ramius • Paul Sheldon • Annie Wilkes • Vivian Ward
Edward Lewis • Clarice Starling • Dr. Hannibal Lecter • Jack Crawford
Thelma • Louise • J.D. • Det. Hal Slocumb • Dottie Hinson • Jimmy Dugan
Kit Keller • Walter Harvey • Catherine Tramell • Nick Curren • Diana Murphy
David Murphy • John Gage • Frank Horrigan • Lilly Raines • Mitch Leary
Dr. Alan Grant • Dr. Ellie Sattler • Ian Malcolm • Lloyd Christmas • Harry
Forrest Gump • Jenny • Bubba Blue • Lestat • The Interviewer • Louis
Vincent Vega • Jules • Mia Wallace • Butch Coolidge • Marsellus Wallace
Andy Dufresne • "Red" Redding • Jack Traven • Annie Porter • Mike Lowrey
Marcus Burnett • Det. David Miles • Det. William Somerset • John Doe
Woody • Buzz Lightyear • Jerry Maguire • Dorothy Bird • Rod Tidwell
Melvin Udall • Carol Connelly • Simon Bishop • Dirk Diggler • Jack Horner

Bigger Budgets
Special Effects
Mega-Stars

The 1990s saw a rise in film budgets, which averaged $53,000,000, as well as ticket prices which increased from slightly over $4.00 to $5.00 by the end of the decade. Multi-screen complexes added to the rising number of available screens from over 22,00 screens in 1990 to almost 36,000 screens by the end of the decade.

Extravagant demands sometimes reached epidemic proportions for many of the highest-paid stars including Arnold Schwarzenegger, Tom Cruise, Sylvester Stallone, Mel Gibson, Eddie Murphy, Kevin Costner, Harrison Ford, Robin Williams, Jim Carrey, Demi Moore and Julia Roberts. These stars often demanded script approval, directorial and other casting choices, restrictions on film scheduling, and their choice of the positioning of credits on all marketing and advertising of their films.

Although the same number of pictures was being produced every year as in the Golden Age of Hollywood (about 450-500) many of these films went directly to video or cable television with no theatrical release. Additionally, the time between a film's theatrical opening and availability for cable shortened. The creation of a public World Wide Web and the proliferation of home computers would have vast repercussions for the film industry.

Meanwhile, Hollywood was also attempting to deal with serious themes. *Philadelphia* was the first big-studio attempt to deal with AIDS; *Schindler's List* told the story of an opportunistic German businessman who ultimately saved over 1,000 Jews from death; Kevin Costner's *Dances with Wolves* retold the story of the Wild West from the viewpoint of Native Americans; while *Forrest Gump* examined the 60s and the Vietnam War era through the eyes of a slow-witted everyman. *Falling Down* with Michael Douglas revealed racial issues and social tensions, while *Dead Man Walking* confronted the issue of capital punishment.

African-American filmmakers were starting to make an impact with John Singleton's semi-autobiographical *Boyz N The Hood*, about gang violence in South Central L.A.; Spike Lee's *Jungle Fever* told a story of interracial romance; *Malcolm X* dealt with the controversial leader.

The decade also saw an increase of talented women filmmakers. Barbra Streisand directed the very personal *Yentl,* followed by *The Prince of Tides*; Penny Marshall directed the box office hit *Big* and *A League of Their Own*; Penelope Spheeris directed *Wayne's World*; Kathryn Bigelow made the hard-hitting *Point Break;* New Zealand director Jane Campion made *The Piano*; Nora Ephron created the romantic comedy *Sleepless in Seattle*, followed by the fantasy *Michael*; and Jodie Foster became both producer and director with *Little Man Tate.*

Action films, such as *Mission Impossible, The Fugitive, Face/Off, Speed, The Rock, Braveheart, Apollo 13,* and *Con Air* regained their place on the studio's production charts, as did romance and comedies with *Kindergarten Cop, Groundhog Day, Sister Act, Mrs. Doubtfire, City Slickers,* and *My Cousin Vinny.*

Sequels continued with Pierce Brosnan making three films as the next James Bond; Tom Clancy's best-selling Jack Ryan novels became a trilogy of films; and adaptations continued when John Grisham's best seller, *The Firm*, was made into a film.

Aside from Alan Parker's *Evita*, most of the best musicals were animated features; *Beauty and The Beast, Aladdin,* and *The Lion King.*

Making history with *Titanic*, writer/director James Cameron grossed almost $2 billion worldwide. Budgets rose dramatically from an average of $18 million in the 80s to $53 million by 1998, with many films costing over $100 million to produce.

The Academy Awards

1990
Best Picture: ***Dances with Wolves***
Best Actor: Jeremy Irons (*Reversal of Fortune*)
Best Actress: Kathy Bates (*Misery*)
Best Supporting Actor: Joe Pesci (*Goodfellas*)
Best Supporting Actress: Whoopi Goldberg (*Ghost*)

1991
Best Picture: ***The Silence of the Lambs***
Best Actor: Anthony Hopkins (*The Silence of the Lambs*)
Best Actress: Jodie Foster (*The Silence of the Lambs*)
Best Supporting Actor: Jack Palance (*City Slickers*)
Best Supporting Actress: Mercedes Ruehl (*The Fisher King*)

1992
Best Picture: ***Unforgiven***
Best Actor: Al Pacino (*Scent of a Woman*)
Best Actress: Emma Thompson (*Howards End*)
Best Supporting Actor: Gene Hackman (*Unforgiven*)
Best Supporting Actress: Marisa Tomei (*My Cousin Vinny*)

1993
Best Picture: ***Schindler's List***
Best Actor: Tom Hanks (*Philadelphia*)
Best Actress: Holly Hunter (*The Piano*)
Best Supporting Actor: Tommy Lee Jones (*The Fugitive*)
Best Supporting Actress: Anna Paquin (*The Piano*)

1994
Best Picture: ***Forrest Gump***
Best Actor: Tom Hanks (*Forrest Gump*)
Best Actress: Jessica Lange (*Blue Sky*)
Best Supporting Actor: Martin Landau (*Ed Wood*)
Best Supporting Actress: Dianne Wiest (*Bullets over Broadway*)

1995

Best Picture: ***Braveheart***
Best Actor: Nicolas Cage (*Leaving Las Vegas*)
Best Actress: Susan Sarandon (*Dead Man Walking*)
Best Supporting Actor: Kevin Spacey (*The Usual Suspects*)
Best Supporting Actress: Mira Sorvino (*Mighty Aphrodite*)

1996

Best Picture: ***The English Patient***
Best Actor: Geoffrey Rush (*Shine*)
Best Actress: Frances McDormand (*Fargo*)
Best Supporting Actor: Cuba Gooding Jr. (*Jerry Maguire*)
Best Supporting Actress: Juliette Binoche (*The English Patient*)

1997

Best Picture: ***Titanic***
Best Actor: Jack Nicholson (*As Good as it Gets*)
Best Actress: Helen Hunt (*As Good as it Gets*)
Best Supporting Actor: Robin Williams (*Good Will Hunting*)
Best Supporting Actress: Kim Basinger (*L.A. Confidential*)

1998

Best Picture: ***Shakespeare in Love***
Best Actor: Roberto Benigni (*Life is Beautiful*)
Best Actress: Gwyneth Paltrow (*Shakespeare in Love*)
Best Supporting Actor: James Coburn (*Affliction*)
Best Supporting Actress: Judi Dench (*Shakespeare in Love*)

1999

Best Picture: ***American Beauty***
Best Actor: Kevin Spacey (*American Beauty*)
Best Actress: Hilary Swank (*Boys Don't Cry*)
Best Supporting Actor: Michael Caine (*The Cider House Rules*)
Best Supporting Actress: Angelina Jolie (*Girl, Interrupted*)

Casting Trivia Quiz

1. Julia Roberts was cast as Vivian Ward in **Pretty Woman** after this actress turned the role down:
    a. Molly Ringwald
    b. Diane Lane
    c. Meg Ryan
    d. All of the Above

2. Dr. Hannibal Lecter was memorably played by Anthony Hopkins in **The Silence of the Lambs** after this actor turned down the role:
    a. Daniel Day-Lewis
    b. Sean Connery
    c. Gene Hackman
    d. All of the Above

3. The two leading characters in **Thelma and Louise** were played by Geena Davis and Susan Sarandon. The original actors for the roles were:
    a. Jodie Foster & Michelle Pfeiffer
    b. Meg Ryan & Cher
    c. Julia Roberts & Goldie Hawn
    d. Meg Tilly & Cher

4. Harrison Ford went on the run in **The Fugitive** after this actor turned down the role of Dr. Richard Kimble:
    a. Al Pacino
    b. Kevin Costner
    c. Alec Baldwin
    d. Charlie Sheen

5. Bill Murray relived the same day over and over until he gets it right in **Groundhog Day.** The role was first offered to:
    a. Tom Hanks
    b. Johnny Depp
    c. Chevy Chase
    d. Robin Williams

6. In **The Shawshank Redemption,** Andy Dufresne was played by Tim Robbins. The original choice for the role was:
    a. Tom Cruise
    b. Tom Hanks
    c. Kevin Costner
    d. All of the Above

7. Tom Hanks was ultimately cast as **Forrest Gump,** but this actor was the original choice to play the title role:
    a. Dustin Hoffman
    b. Bill Murray
    c. John Travolta
    d. Johnny Depp

8. Jim Carrey played Lloyd in **Dumb and Dumber**. That only happened because this actor turned down the role:
   - a. Steve Martin
   - b. Bill Murray
   - c. Dana Carvey
   - d. Jeff Daniels

9. Vincent Vega was played by John Travolta in Tarantino's **Pulp Fiction.** The role of Vega was first offered to:
   - a. Michael Madsen
   - b. Christian Slater
   - c. Brad Pitt
   - d. All of the Above

10. In **Se7en**, Brad Pitt's role as Detective Mills was first offered to:
    - a. Mel Gibson
    - b. Michael Douglas
    - c. Denzel Washington
    - d. Al Pacino

11. Before Tom Cruise was cast as sports agent **Jerry Maguire**, the role was turned down by:
    - a. Tom Hanks
    - b. Billy Crystal
    - c. Brad Pitt
    - d. Steve Guttenberg

12. Mark Wahlberg plays porn star Dirk Diggler in **Boogie Night.** This actor turned down the part:
    - a. Tom Cruise
    - b. Brad Pitt
    - c. Ben Affleck
    - d. Leonardo DiCaprio

13. Doomed lovers Jack and Rose met on the **Titanic**, but before Kate Winslet was cast as Rose, this actress turned down the part:
    - a. Meg Ryan
    - b. Gwyneth Paltrow
    - c. Ali McGraw
    - d. Cameron Diaz

14. Keanu Reeves made the role of Neo/Thomas A. Anderson his own in **The Matrix.** The role was first offered to:
    - a. Will Smith
    - b. Brad Pitt
    - c. Nicolas Cage
    - d. All of the Above

15. The role of Molly Jensen played by Demi Moore in **Ghost** was turned down by this actress:
    - a. Madonna
    - b. Mary Steenburgen
    - c. Kathleen Turner
    - d. All of the Above

THE BONFIRE OF THE VANITIES (1990)

Sherman McCoy: I suppose we could still go to the police. We could get a very talented lawyer...

Maria Ruskin: And put our heads right into the tiger's mouth?

Plot

A Wall Street hotshot sees his life unravel in the spotlight after his mistress runs over a young teen, attracting the interest of a down-and-out reporter.

CASTING

Who Starred as Sherman McCoy?
Tom Hanks

Turned Down the Role of Sherman McCoy
Christopher Reeve • Chevy Chase • Jon Voight

Who Starred as Peter Fallow?
Bruce Willis

Turned Down the Role of Peter Fallow
Christopher Reeve • Jack Nicholson • John Cleese

WHO Trivia

Mike Nichols, the original director, wanted Steve Martin for the role of Sherman McCoy, but the studio rejected the idea because they felt Martin was too old for the role. The writer, Tom Wolfe, wanted Chevy Chase, but Chase turned down the role.

After Nichols left the production, Brian De Palma came to direct. He offered Christopher Reeve was offered the role of Sherman McCoy or Peter Fallow, but Reeve turned down both roles. Jon Voight then turned down the role of Sherman before Tom Hanks was cast. After Jack Nicholson and John Cleese turned down the role of Peter, Warner Bros. forced De Palma to cast Bruce Willis who was coming off the success of *Die Hard*.

De Palma wanted Uma Thurman to play Maria Ruskin. However, Tom Hanks did not think she was right for the part, and after Michelle Pfeiffer turned down the role, Melanie Griffith was signed.

Walter Matthau turned down the role of Judge White when the producers would not meet his quote of $1 million. Alan Arkin was signed instead, but he was replaced when the studio decided to change the judge's ethnicity from Jewish to African-American, and hired Morgan Freeman.

GHOST (1990)

Oda Mae: I don't know you. I don't know Sam, but let me tell you what he did to me... He kept me up all night singing I'm Henry the Eighth I Am.

Molly: That's how he got me to go out with him.

Plot
After a young man is murdered, his spirit stays behind to warn his lover of impending danger with the help of a reluctant psychic.

CASTING

Who Starred as Sam Wheat?
Patrick Swayze

Turned Down the Role of Sam Wheat
Paul Hogan • Eddie Murphy • Bruce Willis

Who Starred as Molly Jensen?
Demi Moore

Turned Down the Role of Molly Jensen
Kim Basinger • Geena Davis
Mary Steenburgen • Kathleen Turner • Debra Winger
Madonna • Molly Ringwald

WHO Trivia
Initially, Paul Hogan, off the success of *Crocodile Dundee*, was offered the role of Sam Wheat; he turned it down. Bruce Willis also turned it down. The role was then offered to Eddie Murphy, but his agent turned it down. Alec Baldwin, Harrison Ford, Tom Cruise, Kevin Bacon, and Tom Hanks were all considered for the role before Patrick Swayze was cast.

Before Demi Moore was cast as Molly, Mary Steenburgen turned down the role because she thought the script was "silly," while Kathleen Turner turned it down fearing the movie would be a flop.

Rumor had it that after Jennifer Jason Leigh won the part of Molly Jensen in *Ghost,* and Demi Moore won the part of Susie Waggoner in *Miami Blues,* Demi Moore refused to star in *Miami Blues,* and they just switched parts.

Before Whoopi Goldberg was cast as psychic Oda Mae Brown, Patti LaBelle, Oprah Winfrey, and Tina Turner were being considered.

THE HUNT FOR RED OCTOBER (1990)

Captain Ramius: There's one thing you haven't yet asked me: why?
Jack Ryan: Well, I figured you would tell me when you felt ready.
Captain Ramius: Well, there are those who believe we should attack the United States first. Settle everything in one moment. Red October was built for that purpose.

Plot
The question, "Is he trying to defect or start a war, "is raised when one of the USSR's most senior submarine captains in their newest sub violates orders and heads for the United States.

CASTING

Who Starred as Jack Ryan?
Alec Baldwin

Turned Down the Role of Jack Ryan
Harrison Ford • Kevin Costner

Who Starred as Captain Ramius?
Sean Connery

Turned Down the Role of Captain Ramius
Klaus Maria Brandauer

WHO Trivia
Before Alec Baldwin was cast as Jack Ryan, Harrison Ford turned down the role to make *Presumed Innocent*. Kevin Costner also turned down the role to make *Dances with Wolves*.

Initially, Klaus Marie Brandauer was cast in the role Marko Ramius, the Soviet sub commander. Two weeks into filming, Brandauer quit for medical reasons. Brandauer suggested his friend, Sean Connery, to the producers.

The producers faxed a script to Connery. At first he declined because the script seemed implausible, portraying the Soviet Union as an ambitious naval power. As it turned out, Connery was missing the first page of the script, which set the story before Gorbachev came to power. This made the events of the book more plausible to Connery, who then accepted the role.

Most of the scenes with Caroline Ryan, Jack's wife, were deleted. Meryl Streep and Sally Field turned down the role before Gates McFadden was cast.

MISERY (1990)

Annie Wilkes: I thought you were good Paul... but you're not good.
You're just another lying ol' dirty birdy.

Plot
A famous novelist is saved from a car wreckage and then trapped by a maniacal fan who forces him to write a novel specifically for her.

CASTING

Who Starred as Paul Sheldon?
James Caan

Turned Down the Role of Paul Sheldon
William Hurt • Kevin Kline • Michael Douglas
Harrison Ford • Dustin Hoffman • Robert De Niro
Al Pacino • Richard Dreyfuss • Mel Gibson
Gene Hackman • Robert Redford • Warren Beatty

Who Starred as Annie Wilkes?
Kathy Bates

Turned Down the Role of Annie Wilkes
Debra Winger • Barbra Streisand
Anjelica Huston • Bette Midler

WHO Trivia
During a plane ride, producer Andrew Scheinman read Stephen King's novel *Misery*, and recommended it to his partner, Rob Reiner.

The part of Paul Sheldon was originally offered to a host of A-list actors, but they all turned it down. Warren Beatty was very interested in the role, although wanting to turn Paul into a less passive character, but eventually had to say no because post-production of *Dick Tracy* was extended.

Eventually, James Caan agreed to play the part. Caan said that he was attracted by the character of Sheldon; it was a role unlike any other role Caan had played. Caan commented that "being a totally reactionary character is really much tougher to play."

After a number of well-known actresses turned down the lead role of Annie Wilkes, screenwriter William Goldman suggested Kathy Bates, then unknown, should be cast.

PRETTY WOMAN (1990)

Edward: I want to find Beverly Hills. Can you give me directions?
  Vivian: Sure. For five bucks.
Edward: That's ridiculous.
  Vivian: Price just went up to ten.
Edward: You can't charge me for directions!
  Vivian: I can do anything I want to, baby; I ain't lost.

Plot
A man in a legal but hurtful business, who needs an escort for some social events, hires a beautiful prostitute... only to fall in love.

CASTING

Who Starred as Vivian Ward?
Julia Roberts

Turned Down the Role of Vivian Ward
Karen Allen • Molly Ringwald • Meg Ryan • Diane Lane
Daryl Hannah • Michelle Pfeiffer • Sandra Bullock
Valeria Golino • Jennifer Jason Leigh • Emily Lloyd

Who Starred as Edward Lewis?
Richard Gere

Turned Down the Role of Edward Lewis
Al Pacino • Burt Reynolds
Albert Brooks • Sylvester Stallone

WHO Trivia
Because of the dark nature of the original script, many well-known actresses turned down the role of Vivian: Meg Ryan and Molly Ringwald were both uncomfortable playing a sex worker; Michelle Pfeiffer didn't like the script's tone; Daryl Hannah thought the role "degrading to women." Diane Lane came close to playing Vivian, even doing costume fittings, but had to walk away due to scheduling conflicts. Finally, Julia Roberts, with only sleeper hit *Mystic Pizza* and the yet-to-be-released *Steel Magnolias* to her credit, won the role.

With Julia Roberts on board as Vivian, director Garry Marshall decided to change the tone of the film, making it a romantic comedy, which made Roberts very happy. The next step was casting the role of Edward Lewis. Marshall offered the role to Al Pacino, Burt Reynolds, Albert Brooks, Sylvester Stallone, and Richard Gere. They all turned it down. Marshall then had Gere meet with Roberts privately, and Roberts eventually persuaded him to take the role.

THE SILENCE OF THE LAMBS (1991)

Hannibal Lecter:　A census taker once tried to test me.... I ate his liver with some fava beans and a nice Chianti.

Plot

A young FBI trainee hunts a serial killer who skins and butchers his victims with the help of an imprisoned psychopath, with whom she plays a deadly psychological game of cat-and-mouse.

CASTING

Who Starred as Clarice Starling?
Jodie Foster

Turned Down the Role of Clarice Starling
Michelle Pfeiffer　•　Meg Ryan

Who Starred as Dr. Hannibal Lecter?
Anthony Hopkins

Turned Down the Role of Hannibal Lecter
Jeremy Irons　•　Sean Connery

WHO Trivia

Jodie Foster was interested in playing the role of Clarice Starling immediately after reading the novel. However, in spite of the fact that Foster had just won an Oscar for *The Accused,* Director Jonathan Demme was not convinced that she was right for the part.

Having just directed *Married to the Mob*, Demme's first choice for the role was Michelle Pfeiffer. She turned it down when Orion Pictures wasn't willing to pay her $2 million quote. Still not convinced about Foster, Demme offered the role to Meg Ryan who rejected it because of its gruesome themes. Eventually, Jodie Foster finally won the part; her passion towards the character convinced Demme that she was perfect for the role. Foster was rewarded with her second Academy Award for Best Actress.

For the role of Hannibal Lecter, Demme originally approached Sean Connery. After he turned it down, Anthony Hopkins was offered the role based on his performance in *The Elephant Man*. Hopkins went on to win the Academy Award for Best Actor.

Before Scott Glenn was cast as FBI agent Jack Crawford, Michael Keaton, Mickey Rourke, and Kenneth Branagh were considered for the part.

THELMA & LOUISE (1991)

(with a cliff in front of them and cops behind them)

Thelma: OK, then listen; let's not get caught.
Louise: What're you talkin' about?
Thelma: Let's keep goin'!
Louise: What d'you mean?
Thelma: Go.
Louise: You sure?
Thelma: Yeah.

Plot

Two best friends, an Arkansas waitress and a housewife, shoot a rapist and take off in a '66 Thunderbird.

CASTING

Who Starred as Thelma?
Geena Davis

Turned Down the Role of Thelma
Jodie Foster • Cher • Kelly McGillis • Kathleen Turner

Who Starred as Louise?
Susan Sarandon

Turned Down the Role of Louise
Michelle Pfeiffer

WHO Trivia

Written by *Nashville* creator Callie Khouri and directed by Ridley Scott, the film attracted A-list attention from the beginning.

Michelle Pfeiffer and Jodie Foster were cast originally, but had to back out when production was delayed. Kelly McGillis, Kathleen Turner, Cher, and Sissy Spacek were offered the role of Thelma, but they all turned it down.

Meryl Streep and Goldie Hawn were interested, and even went to the production company to pitch themselves as a pair. While Ridley Scott found Goldie Hawn "funny as hell," she was already a big star at the time, he thought she wasn't quite right for the part. Streep, meanwhile, was "wonderful" but ended up having a conflict with another project.

Screenwriter Khouri wanted Holly Hunter and Frances McDormand as Thelma and Louise, respectively, but that never materialized.

When the production was finally ready to begin, Michelle Pfeiffer had to turn down the role of Louise. Pfeiffer had a scheduling conflict with the Kennedy assassination drama, *Love Field*, for which Pfeiffer's performance resulted in an Oscar nomination.

Scott finally chose Geena Davis for Thelma. Since it was taking a long time to find someone for the role of Louise, the producers had Davis sign a contract stating that they could cast her in either role if need be.

Scott then decided to contact Susan Sarandon, one of the few actresses who didn't ask for the part. Sarandon was interested, but wanted to make sure she wasn't signing on to an angry women's "revenge fantasy." She had particular concern over the scene where Louise shoots a man who's trying to rape Thelma. "It's a huge thing to take another life," Sarandon told Scott. "I am not interested in doing a revenge film. I'm not interested in being Arnold Schwarzenegger or Charles Bronson. I'm interested in the fact that taking a life has consequences, that she has to pay for that."

Up-and-coming actors Johnny Depp, Tom Cruise, Sean Penn, Kevin Bacon, Christopher Atkins, and Scott Baio were all considered for the role of J.D., the good-looking drifter, before William Baldwin got the part. Baldwin then dropped out.

With production about to begin, Robert Downey Jr. was considered, but Scott deemed him too short compared to Davis. Scott then asked Davis to select from five choices whom she wanted to play the part of her young lover. Davis picked Brad Pitt. There is a story that George Clooney auditioned for the role of J.D. multiple times, but Scott just kept rejecting him.

The part of Detective Hal Slocumb, played by Harvey Keitel, almost went to Beau Bridges, and the role of Jimmy, Louise's boyfriend, was originally offered to Kris Kristofferson. After Kristofferson turned down the role, Michael Madsen was cast.

There was a great deal of behind-the-scenes debate about writer Khouri's decision to end the film with the women driving off a cliff. Several production companies turned the project down because of this scene. Eventually, MGM agreed to take the film, but continued to push for an alternate ending until the last days of filming.

A LEAGUE OF THEIR OWN (1992)

Jimmy: Evelyn, which team do you play for?
Evelyn: Well, I'm a Peach.
Jimmy: Well I was just wonderin', 'cause I couldn't figure out why, you throw home when we got a two-run lead! You let the tying run get to second, and we lost the lead because of you! You start using your head! That's the lump that's three feet above your ass!
(Evelyn starts to cry)
Are you crying? Are you crying? Are you crying?!... There's no crying!... There's no crying in baseball!

Plot

During World War II, two sisters join the first female professional baseball league, "All-American Girls Professional Baseball League," and struggle to help it succeed amidst their own growing rivalry

CASTING

Who Starred as Dottie Hinson?
Geena Davis

Turned Down the Role of Dottie Hinson
Brooke Shields • Debra Winger

WHO Trivia

During the initial development of the film, Jim Belushi was set to play the role of Jimmy Dugan, and Laura Dern was cast as Dottie Hinson, but the production of the film was delayed.

When director Penny Marshall was hired, she immediately cast Tom Hanks as Dugan, and Brooke Shields as Dottie. After the writer's strike in 1988, Shields backed out. Marshall replaced her with Debra Winger.

Moira Kelly was then signed on to play the role of Dottie's sister, Kit Keller, but she hurt her ankle filming, *The Cutting Edge*, and had to drop out. Lori Petty was then cast as Kit because of her resemblance to Winger.

Winger then dropped out due to a back injury. When Geena Davis replaced Winger, Marshall did not want to recast Lori Petty because she was the best ballplayer of the entire cast. Petty had her hair dyed to match Davis', which made them look more like sisters. Marshall cast her brother, Garry Marshall as Walter Harvey because she could not afford her first choice for the part, Christopher Walken.

BASIC INSTINCT (1992)

Nick: Beating that machine can't be easy.
Catherine: If I was guilty and I wanted to beat that machine, it wouldn't be hard. It wouldn't be hard at all. You took a lie detector test after you shot those two people, didn't you?
Nick: I passed.
Catherine: You see, we're both innocent, Nick.

Plot

A police detective investigating the brutal murder of a wealthy rock star becomes involved in a torrid and intense relationship with the prime suspect, an enigmatic writer and psychologist.

CASTING

Who Starred as Catherine Tramell?
Sharon Stone

Turned Down the Role of Catherine Tramell
Kim Basinger • Julia Roberts • Greta Scacchi • Meg Ryan
Michelle Pfeiffer • Isabelle Adjani • Demi Moore
Emma Thompson • Debra Winger • Kelly Lynch
Ellen Barkin • Mariel Hemingway • Kathleen Turner

WHO Trivia

Writer Joe Eszterhas wrote the role of Detective Nick Curren originally as a lesbian cop, with Kathleen Turner in mind to play her. After the gender was switched, the film's director, Paul Verhoeven, considered Peter Weller for the role, having worked with him on *RoboCop*.

Before Verhoevan cast Michael Douglas in the role of Nick Curren, he considered Patrick Swayze, Kevin Costner, Robert De Niro, Bruce Willis, and Mel Gibson for the role.

Relatively unknown at the time, Sharon Stone was only offered the role of Catherine Tramell, after Kim Basinger, Michelle Pfeiffer, Greta Scacchi, and ten other actresses turned down the role. Michael Douglas suggested Stone.

The infamous leg-uncrossing scene was not in the original script, but thought up by Verhoeven while the movie was being shot. It was based on a memory from his college years when a woman at a party had done the exact same thing to embarrass him.

INDECENT PROPOSAL (1993)

John: So, you're saying you can't buy love? That's a bit of a cliché don't you think?
Diana: It's absolutely true.
John: Is it? What do you think?
David: I agree with Diana.
John: You do? Well let's test the cliché. Suppose... I were to offer you one million dollars for one night with your wife.
David: I'd assume you're kidding.
John: Let's pretend I'm not. What would you say?
Diana: He'd tell you to go to hell.
John: *(looking at David)* I didn't hear him.

Plot
A married couple's relationship is put into turmoil by a billionaire's offer of a million dollars for her to spend one night with him.

CASTING

Who Starred as Diana Murphy?
Demi Moore

Turned Down the Role of Diana Murphy
Julia Roberts • Nicole Kidman • Debra Winger

Who Starred as David Murphy?
Woody Harrelson

Turned Down the Role of David Murphy
Kevin Bacon • Tom Cruise • John Cusack • Charlie Sheen

Who Starred as John Gage?
Robert Redford

Turned Down the Role of John Gage
Warren Beatty

WHO Trivia
The film was originally to be a vehicle for Tom Cruise and Nicole Kidman with Warren Beatty playing billionaire John Gage. They all passed, as did others, before Demi Moore, Woody Harrelson, and Robert Redford were cast.

Actress Halle Berry was very interested in the role of Diana. Because the studio was afraid of adding an unnecessary racial undertone to the already controversial plot, it refused to give Berry an opportunity to audition.

IN THE LINE OF FIRE (1993)

Leary: What's kept you in the game all these years?
Horrigan: Why don't we get together? We could talk about that.
Leary: Oh, I'd love to, but I think the less you know about me the better.
Horrigan: Oh, why?
Leary: Because I'm planning to kill the President.

Plot

Secret Service agent Frank Horrigan couldn't save JFK, but is determined not to let a clever assassin take out the current president.

CASTING

Who Starred as Frank Horrigan?
Clint Eastwood

Turned Down the Role of Frank Horrigan
Robert Redford • Sean Connery

Who Starred as Lilly Raines?
Rene Russo

Turned Down the Role of Lilly Raines
Glenn Close • Sharon Stone

Who Starred as Mitch Leary?
John Malkovich

Turned Down the Role of Mitch Leary
Robert De Niro • Jack Nicholson • Willem Dafoe

WHO Trivia

Originally, Dustin Hoffman was slated to play the role of Frank Horrigan, and Michael Apted was going to direct. When David Puttnam became the head of Columbia Pictures, he killed the project. Most thought it was due to his animosity towards Dustin Hoffman over *Ishtar,* a notorious flop.

Robert Redford soon became attached to the project, but he left the role; it was offered to Sean Connery, who turned it down. The part was then offered to Clint Eastwood, who initially turned it down thinking he was too old for the role. A conversation with Puttnam changed his mind.

Robert De Niro was set to play Mitch Leary, but had to turn it down due to scheduling conflicts with *A Bronx Tale.* Finally, after both Jack Nicholson and Willem Dafoe turned down the role, John Malkovich was cast.

JURASSIC PARK (1993)

John Hammond: All major theme parks have had delays. When they opened Disneyland in 1956, nothing worked.
Ian Malcolm: Yeah, but John, if the Pirates of the Caribbean breaks down, the pirates don't eat the tourists.

Plot

During a preview tour, a dinosaur theme park suffers a series of mishaps, strands everyone on the tour inside, and under attack by the resurrected predators.

CASTING

Who Starred as Dr. Alan Grant?
Sam Neill

Turned Down the Role of Dr. Alan Grant
Harrison Ford • William Hurt • Kurt Russell

WHO Trivia

William Hurt was initially offered the role of Alan Grant, but he turned it down without reading the script. Harrison Ford was offered the role, but turned it down thinking the part wasn't right for him. Kurt Russell also turned it down, because director Steven Spielberg would not agree to his salary demands.

Ultimately, Sam Neill was cast as Alan Grant four weeks before filming began. Neill said, "It all happened real quick. I hadn't read the book, knew nothing about it, hadn't heard anything about it, and in a matter of weeks I'm working with Spielberg."

Before casting Laura Dern as Dr. Ellie Sattler, Spielberg auditioned a number of A-list actresses for the role: Sandra Bullock, Julianne Moore, Helen Hunt, Elizabeth Hurley, Amanda Plummer, Juliette Binoche, Robin Wright Penn, Kristen Davis, and Kyra Sedgwick.

Before Richard Attenborough was cast as John Hammond, Sean Connery turned down the role.

Janet Hirshenson, the film's casting director, thought Jeff Goldblum would be the right choice to play Ian Malcolm. Jim Carrey auditioned, and according to Hirshenson, "was terrific, too, but I think we all loved the idea of Jeff."

DUMB AND DUMBER (1994)

Harry: So, you got fired again?
Lloyd: Yeah, they always freak out when you leave the scene of an accident, ya know.
Harry: Yeah, I lost my job too.
Lloyd: Man, you are one pathetic loser. No offense.
Harry: No, none taken.

Plot

Two well-meaning but incredibly stupid friends travel across the country to Aspen, Colorado to try to give back a briefcase left in an airport as part of a ransom payment.

CASTING

Who Starred as Lloyd Christmas?
Jim Carrey

Who Turned Down the Role of Lloyd Christmas
Steve Martin • Martin Short

WHO Trivia

The film was written by Peter and Bobby Farrelly, and directed by Peter Farrelly. They originally wanted Nicolas Cage and Gary Oldman to play the characters, Harry and Lloyd, but that idea quickly faded. After Steve Martin and Martin Short turned down the role of Lloyd, Jim Carrey was suggested.

The Farrelly brothers didn't know who Jim Carrey was. They were only told he was known as "The White Guy" in the television show, *In Living Color.* It was only after they were invited to watch the screening of Carrey's first major acting job in *Ace Ventura: Pet Detective,* that they realized they had struck gold.

Carrey was initially offered $700,000 to appear in *Dumb and Dumber.* However, the week the offer was made, *Ace Ventura: Pet Detective* opened at the top of the box office. Carrey's fee went to $7 million, almost half of the film's budget.

New Line Cinema originally did not want Jeff Daniels for the role of Harry. However, the Farrelly brothers and Carrey wanted Daniels for the part. Although New Line agreed to their demands, Daniels was offered the low salary of $50,000 in the hopes it would discourage him from signing on to the film. Despite his agent's fear that the role would kill his career, Daniels ultimately accepted.

FORREST GUMP (1994)

Forrest: My momma always said, Life was like a box of chocolates. You never know what you're gonna get.

Plot
A slow-witted but kind-hearted man's epic journey through life, meeting historical figures, influencing popular culture, and experiencing first-hand historical incidents while largely unaware of their significance.

CASTING

Who Starred as Forrest Gump?
Tom Hanks

Turned Down the Role of Forrest Gump
John Travolta • Chevy Chase

Who Starred as Jenny?
Robin Wright

Turned Down the Role of Jenny
Jodie Foster • Demi Moore • Nicole Kidman

Who Starred as Bubba Blue?
Mykelti Williamson

Turned Down the Role of Bubba Blue
David Alan Grier • Ice Cube • Dave Chappelle

WHO Trivia
John Travolta was the original choice to play the title role, and admits passing on the role was a mistake. Before Tom Hanks was cast, Chevy Chase turned down the role because he didn't think the script was good enough. Later, Chase claimed that Hanks tweaked the script to make it what it eventually became.

Tom Hanks signed on to the film an hour and a half after reading the script. Initially, Hanks wanted to ease Forrest's pronounced Southern accent, but was eventually persuaded by director Robert Zemeckis to portray the heavy accent stressed in the novel.

Dave Chappelle turned down the role of Bubba Blue because he believed the film would be unsuccessful; he later acknowledged that he regretted turning down the role. Ice Cube said he also didn't want to play the role because he didn't want to appear "stupid." Tupac Shakur auditioned for the role of Bubba, but was not offered the part.

INTERVIEW WITH THE VAMPIRE (1994)

Louis: Where are we?
Lestat: Where do you think, my idiot friend? We're in a nice, filthy cemetery. Does this make you happy? Is this fitting, proper enough?
Louis: We belong in hell.

Plot
A vampire tells his epic life story: love, betrayal, loneliness, and hunger.

CASTING

Who Starred as Lestat?
Tom Cruise

Turned Down the Role of Lestat
Johnny Depp

Who Starred as Louis?
Brad Pitt

Turned Down the Role of Louis
Val Kilmer

WHO Trivia
Originally, River Phoenix was cast for the role of The Interviewer, but he died four weeks before filming was due to begin. After considering Leonardo DiCaprio, Stephen Dorff, and Christian Slater as the replacement, Slater was cast. Slater donated his entire salary to Phoenix's favorite charity.

Daniel Day-Lewis was reportedly the first choice to play Lestat; he was actually cast and then dropped out.

The casting of Tom Cruise was initially criticized by Anne Rice, who said, "It is so bizarre; it's almost impossible to imagine how it's going to work." She even suggested Brad Pitt and Tom Cruise switch roles. When Rice finally saw the completed film, she said, "From the moment Tom appeared, he was Lestat for me," and "It was something I couldn't see in a crystal ball." Rice called Cruise to compliment him and to admit she was wrong.

Eleven-year-old actress Kirsten Dunst was spotted by talent scouts, and was the first girl tested for the role of Claudia. She beat out Christina Ricci and Dominique Swain for the role.

PULP FICTION (1994)

Vincent:	You know what they call a Quarter Pounder with Cheese in Paris?
Jules:	They don't call it a Quarter Pounder with Cheese?
Vincent:	Nah, man, they got the metric system..
Jules:	What do they call it?
Vincent:	They call it a "Royale with Cheese."
Jules:	"Royale with Cheese?"
Vincent:	That's right.
Jules:	What do they call a Big Mac?
Vincent:	A Big Mac's a Big Mac, but they call it "Le Big Mac."

Plot

The lives of two mob hit men, a boxer, a gangster's wife, and a pair of diner bandits intertwine in four tales of violence and redemption.

CASTING

Who Starred as Vincent Vega?
John Travolta

Turned Down the Role of Vincent Vega
Michael Madsen

Who Starred as Mia Wallace?
Uma Thurman

Turned Down the Role of Mia Wallace
Julia Louis-Dreyfus

Who Starred as Butch Coolidge?
Bruce Willis

Turned Down the Role of Butch Coolidge
Mickey Rourke

WHO Trivia

Miramax pushed for Sean Penn or William Hurt to play Vincent Vega, but writer/director Quentin Tarantino wrote the part for Michael Madsen, who had played the character Vic in *Reservoir Dogs* after Travolta had passed. This time, Madsen passed in order to play Virgil Earp in *Wyatt Earp*.

Harvey Weinstein, pushed for Daniel Day-Lewis, but Tarantino turned him down. Tarantino wanted John Travolta, whose career was at a low point, and thought he would work for a lot less; this pleased the studio.

Tarantino wrote the role of Jules Winnfield for Samuel L. Jackson, however, it almost went to Paul Calderon after a great audition. When Jackson heard this, he flew to L.A. and auditioned again to secure the role. Calderone ended up in the film in a small role, as Paul.

Julia Louis-Dreyfus turned down the role of Mia Wallace due to her commitment to the television show, *Seinfeld*. Miramax favored Holly Hunter or Meg Ryan, but Tarantino desperately wanted Uma Thurman, who originally turned down the role. To convince Thurman, Tarantino began reading the script to her on the phone until she agreed to play the part.

The role of Butch Coolidge was originally supposed to be an up-and-coming boxer. Matt Dillon had talks about the role, but never committed. Tarantino changed the role, and met with Mickey Rourke. Rourke turned it down in order to pursue his boxing career. Finally, Tarantino offered it to Bruce Willis, who had been disappointed at not being cast as Vincent Vega.

Another interesting casting decision for the film concerned casting Tim Roth as Ringo/"Pumpkin". The studio preferred Johnny Depp or Christian Slater, but Tarantino had his way in the end.

Early in development, Tarantino contemplated casting Tim Roth as Vincent and Gary Oldman as Jules, rewriting the characters as "two English guys." Samuel L. Jackson eventually played Jules, Vincent's partner.

For the part of Marsellus Wallace, played by Ving Rhames, a violent crime boss and employer of Jules and Vincent, Sid Haig was offered the part, but turned it down.

For the role of Jody, Lance's wife, Pam Grier and Ellen DeGeneres both read for the part that was eventually given to Rosanna Arquette. Lance was played by Eric Stoltz, although the studio pushed for Gary Oldman.

THE SHAWSHANK REDEMPTION (1994)

Red: His first night in Shawshank Prison, Andy Dufresne cost me two packs of cigarettes. He never made a sound.

Plot

Two imprisoned men bond over a number of years, finding solace and eventual redemption through acts of common decency.

CASTING

Who Starred as Andy Dufresne?
Tim Robbins

Turned Down the Role of Andy Dufresne
Gene Hackman • Robert Duvall • Tom Hanks
Kevin Costner • Tom Cruise • Jeff Bridges

WHO Trivia

Director Rob Reiner loved writer Frank Darabont's script so much that he offered him $2.5 million for the film rights.

Darabont seriously considered Reiner's offer, but ultimately decided that it was his chance to do something great by directing the movie himself; he even took a pay cut in order to direct the film.

Initially, Darabont wanted Gene Hackman or Robert Duvall for the role of Andy Dufresne, but they were unavailable. Darabont then offered the role to Tom Hanks, who was committed to *Forrest Gump*. Kevin Costner, who was signed to *Waterworld* and Tom Cruise, who did not want to work for an inexperienced director. They all turned down the role.

Before casting Tim Robbins, Darabont considered Nicolas Cage, Matthew Broderick, Jeff Bridges, Johnny Depp, and Charlie Sheen for the role. Morgan Freeman was cast as inmate "Red" Redding at the suggestion of producer Liz Glotzer, who ignored the novella's character description of a white Irishman, nicknamed "Red." Morgan Freeman's character alluded to this when queried by Andy on why he is called Red. He replied, "Maybe it's because I'm Irish."

Cast initially as young convict Tommy, Brad Pitt dropped out following his success in *Thelma & Louise*.

SPEED (1994)

Jack: Miss, can you handle this bus?
Annie: Oh sure. It's just like driving a really big Pinto.

Plot
A young police officer must prevent a bomb from exploding aboard a city bus by keeping its speed above 50 miles per hour.

CASTING

Who Starred as Jack?
Keanu Reeves

Turned Down the Role of Jack
Stephen Baldwin • William Baldwin • Tom Cruise
Johnny Depp • Richard Grieco • Jeff Bridges
Tom Hanks • Bruce Willis

Who Starred as Annie?
Sandra Bullock

Turned Down the Role of Annie
Kim Basinger • Halle Berry • Alyssa Milano

WHO Trivia
Reportedly, besides the eight actors listed above who turned down the role of Jack Traven, another dozen also turned down the role. Initially, Keanu Reeves declined the role because he felt the character was too much like the *Die Hard* character, John McClane.

Director Jan de Bont wanted Reeves after seeing him in *Point Break*. He felt that Reeves was "vulnerable on the screen, not threatening to men because he's not that bulky, and looked great to women."

After an un-credited re-write by Josh Whedon, Reeves changed his mind.

For the character of Annie Porter, writer Graham Yost initially wrote her as an African-American paramedic to justify how she would be able to handle driving a speeding bus through traffic. Halle Berry declined the role.

Later, Annie was changed to a driver's education teacher, making her more of a comic-relief sidekick to Jack; Ellen DeGeneres was considered for the role. Finally, Annie became both Jack's sidekick and his love interest.

After Kim Basinger and Alyssa Milano both turned down the role, and only weeks away from the start of production, Sandra Bullock was cast as Annie.

BAD BOYS (1995)

Mike Lowrey: Shut up, shut up, Marcus. Slow-ass driver. Drivin' like a bitch. Slow-ass.

Marcus Burnett: Why I gotta be all that? I'll take you and me off this fuckin' cliff if you keep fuckin' with me. Then it'll be, what, two bitches in the sea? Huh, is that it? Is that what you want?

Mike Lowrey: Shut up, Marcus.

Marcus Burnett: My wife knows I ain't no bitch... I'm a bad boy.

Plot

Two hip Miami detectives protect a witness to a murder, while investigating a case of $100 million of seized Mafia heroin stolen from the evidence storage room in their precinct.

CASTING

Who Starred as Mike Lowrey?
Will Smith

Who Turned Down the Role of Mike Lowrey
Arsenio Hall • Dana Carvey

Who Starred as Marcus Burnett?
Martin Lawrence

Turned Down the Role of Marcus Burnett
Jon Lovitz

WHO Trivia

In the film's early stages of development, the original title of *Bad Boys* was *Bulletproof Hearts*. Producers Don Simpson and Jerry Bruckheimer initially envisioned Dana Carvey and Jon Lovitz in the roles.

To celebrate their upcoming work, Simpson arranged a trip to Las Vegas for the actors and himself. Carvey was so horrified by the notoriously wild Simpson that he withdrew from the project. Lovitz followed causing Disney's rights to the film to expire. When Columbia Pictures acquired the rights, there was talk about Eddie Murphy and Wesley Snipes in the two lead roles, but nothing came of it.

When the project reappeared and went into pre-production, comedian Arsenio Hall was offered the lead role of Mike Lowrey, but he turned it down. Hall later said "not taking the role of Mike Lowrey was the worst mistake I ever made." Eventually, the role went to Will Smith.

SE7EN (1995)

Detective Mills: Who knows. So many freaks out there doin' their little evil deeds they don't wanna do... "The voices made me do it. My dog made me do it. Jodie Foster told me to do it."

Plot
Two cops, one new and one about to retire, are chasing a serial killer who is using the "seven deadly sins" as inspiration for his murders.

> ## CASTING
> **Who Starred as Detective David Mills?**
> Brad Pitt
>
> **Turned Down the Role of Detective David Mills**
> Denzel Washington • Sylvester Stallone
>
> **Who Starred as Detective William Somerset?**
> Morgan Freeman
>
> **Turned Down the Role of Detective William Somerset**
> Al Pacino • Robert Duvall • Gene Hackman

WHO Trivia
Denzel Washington and Sylvester Stallone both regretted turning down the role of Detective David Mills. Washington thought that the film was too "dark and evil." Kevin Costner and Nicolas Cage were briefly considered before Bard Pitt took the role.

During pre-production, Al Pacino was considered for the role of veteran Detective Somerset, but he declined due to scheduling conflicts with the film, *City Hall*. Robert Duvall turned down the role. Gene Hackman also turned it down because there were too many night shoots.

Director David Fincher's first choice to play Detective Mills' wife, Tracy, was Gwyneth Paltrow, but she was not interested. After Christina Applegate turned down the role, Fincher asked her then-boyfriend, Brad Pitt, to convince Paltrow to meet with him. She did and agreed to play the role.

Just two days before filming began, Kevin Spacey took the role of John Doe. Spacey asked Fincher if he should shave his head for the part and Fincher told him, "If you do it, I'll do it." The role of John Doe was turned down by Val Kilmer .

TOY STORY (1995)

Woody: *(screaming)* This is the part where we blow up!
  Buzz: Not today!
    (Buzz soars up carrying Woody)
Woody: Hey, Buzz! You're flying!
  Buzz: This isn't flying. This is falling with style!
Woody: *(laughing)* To infinity and beyond!

Plot

A cowboy toy doll is profoundly threatened and jealous when a new spaceman figure supplants him as the top toy in a boy's room.

CASTING

Who Starred as Woody?
Tom Hanks

Turned Down the Role of Woody
Steve Guttenberg

Who Starred as Buzz Lightyear?
Tim Allen

Turned Down the Role of Buzz Lightyear
Billy Crystal • Chevy Chase

WHO Trivia

Originally, Pixar wanted Jim Carrey to voice Buzz Lightyear and Paul Newman to voice Woody, but neither actor could do the role due to budget constraints.

Director John Lasseter wanted Tom Hanks to voice the character of Woody. Lasseter claimed Hanks "has the ability to take emotions and make them appealing." Not sure if he could sign Hanks, Lasseter offered the role to Steve Guttenberg, who turned it down. Lasseter then created some early test footage using Hank's voice from *Turner & Hooch* to convince Hanks to sign on. Hanks recorded his dialogue over a two-year period while on breaks from two films, *A League of Their Own* (1992), and *Sleepless in Seattle* (1993),

Tim Allen was attracted to the role of Buzz Lightyear because it was offered to Chevy Chase, his biggest career influence. Chase turned it down. Billy Crystal was then approached. He also turned it down; a mistake he admitted after the film was released. Tim Allen was then cast.

JERRY MAGUIRE (1996)

Jerry: Our little company had a good night tonight. A really big night. But it wasn't complete, it wasn't nearly close to being in the same vicinity as complete, because I couldn't share it with you. I couldn't hear your voice, or laugh about it with you. I missed my wife. We live in a cynical world, and we work in a business of tough competitors, I love you. You complete me. And I just...

Dorothy: Shut up. Just shut up. You had me at hello.

Plot

A sports agent, who has a moral epiphany and is fired for expressing it, decides to put his new philosophy to the test as an independent with the only athlete who stays with him.

CASTING

Who Starred as Jerry Maguire?
Tom Cruise

Turned Down the Role of Jerry Maguire
Tom Hanks   •   Edward Burns

Who Starred as Dorothy Boyd?
Renee Zellweger

Turned Down the Role of Dorothy Boyd
Jennifer Lopez   •   Mira Sorvino

WHO Trivia

Writer/Director Cameron Crowe originally wrote the part of Jerry Maguire for Tom Hanks. Crowe took so long to write the screenplay that by the time the film was ready to be made, Hanks was tied up directing *That Thing You Do*.

Edward Burns was Crowe's second choice to play Jerry. He was offered the role, but declined. He wanted to concentrate on two of his own films, the completed *The Brothers McMullen,* and in pre-production, *She's the One*.

Jennifer Lopez turned down the role of Dorothy at the behest of her agent, who felt it wasn't a good fit for her. Mira Sorvino turned it down when the producers wouldn't meet her quote.

Before Cuba Gooding Jr. won the role of Rod Tidwell, Damon Wayans, Mykelti Williamson, and Jamie Foxx were all considered for the role.

AS GOOD AS IT GETS (1997)

Carol: I'm not going to sleep with you. I will never sleep with you. Never, ever. Not ever.

Melvin: I'm sorry, but, um, we don't open for the no-sex oaths until nine a.m.

Carol: I'm not kidding.

Melvin: Okay. Anything else?

Plot

A misanthropic author, a waitress, and a gay artist form very unlikely friend-ship after the artist is in an accident.

CASTING

Who Starred as Carol Connelly?
Helen Hunt

Turned Down the Role of Carol Connelly
Holly Hunter • Melanie Griffith • Courtney Love

Who Starred as Simon Bishop?
Greg Kinnear

Turned Down the Role of Simon Bishop
John Cusack

WHO Trivia

Although he briefly considered Jim Carrey, director/writer James L. Brooks couldn't think of anyone better to play Melvin Udall besides Jack Nicholson. Later Brooks said, "Carrey would have made it a completely different movie."

Holly Hunter turned down the role of Carol because she objected to the age difference between her character and Jack Nicholson's. Melanie Griffith turned down the role because she was pregnant, and Courtney Love turned it down because she was in the middle of recording an album, in addition to thinking she was too young for the role. When Helen Hunt accepted the role, she was 34, although her character was written as a forty-year-old. Nicholson was 60.

John Cusack turned down the role of Simon Bishop due to writing, filming and producing conflicts with the film, *Grosse Pointe Blank.*

An earlier version of the script, called *Old Friends,* had Kevin Kline attached to play Melvin, and Mike Newell attached as the director.

BOOGIE NIGHTS (1997)

Jack Horner: *(to Dirk)* I got a feeling that behind those jeans is something wonderful just waiting to get out.

Plot
A young man's adventures in the California pornography industry in the late 1970s and early 1980s as he deals with the highs and lows of success.

CASTING

Who Starred as Dirk Diggler?
Mark Wahlberg

Turned Down the Role of Dirk Diggler
Leonardo DiCaprio • Joaquin Phoenix
Jason Lee • Vincent Gallo

Who Starred as Jack Horner?
Burt Reynolds

Turned Down the Role of Jack Horner
Warren Beatty • Sydney Pollack • Albert Brooks
Harvey Keitel • Bill Murray • Jack Nicholson

WHO Trivia
Writer/Director Paul Thomas Anderson originally wanted Leonardo DiCaprio to play the lead role of Dirk Diggler, but he had to turn it down having just signed on to star in *Titanic*. Joaquin Phoenix was then offered the role, but turned it down due to concerns about playing a porn star.

Burt Reynolds admitted to turning down his role as Jack Horner seven times before finally accepting the part. In an interview, Reynolds told Conan O'Brien that despite earning critical acclaim and his first and only Oscar nomination, he never watched the film, saying "It just wasn't my kind of film."

A number of other notable actors turned down parts in the controversial film. Samuel L. Jackson turned down the role of Buck Swope, which was played by Don Cheadle; Marisa Tomei turned down the role of Amber Waves that went to Julianne Moore; and Gwyneth Paltrow turned down the part of Rollergirl, because she didn't want to do nudity.

Paul Thomas Anderson considered Drew Barrymore and Tatum O'Neal for the role of Rollergirl before hiring Heather Graham.

MEN IN BLACK (1997)

Agent J: You do know Elvis is dead, right?
Agent K: No, Elvis is not dead, he just went home.

Plot

A NYPD street-smart cop is recruited to a secret government agency that monitors and polices alien activity on earth, unbeknownst to the public.

CASTING

Who Starred as Agent K?
Tommy Lee Jones

Turned Down the Role of Agent K
Clint Eastwood

Who Starred as Agent J?
Will Smith

Turned Down the Role of Agent J
Chris O'Donnell • David Schwimmer

Who Starred as Edgar?
Vincent D'Onofrio

Turned Down the Role of Edgar
John Turturro

WHO Trivia

After Clint Eastwood turned down the role of Agent K, Tommy Lee Jones said he'd take it. His acceptance of the role was based on his respect for producer Steven Spielberg's track record, and Spielberg promised to improve the script.

Chris O'Donnell turned down the role of Agent J thinking it was just another "new recruit" role and too similar to his performance as Dick Grayson in the films, *Batman Forever* and *Batman & Robin*. David Schwimmer, popular due to the television show *Friends,* was then offered the role, but he turned it down.

Initially, Will Smith turned the role down. It was his wife, Jada Pinkett Smith, who convinced him to take the part.

John Turturro was offered the role of Edgar, but turned it down due to other commitments. The role went to Vincent D'Onofrio.

TITANIC (1997)

Jack: I'm the King of the World!

Plot
The story of two fictional young lovers aboard the ill-fated RMS Titanic during her maiden voyage in 1912.

CASTING

Who Starred as Jack Dawson?
Leonardo DiCaprio

Turned Down the Role of Jack Dawson
Johnny Depp • Tom Cruise
Stephen Dorff • Billy Crudup

Who Starred as Rose Dewitt Bukater?
Kate Winslet

Turned Down the Role of Rose Dewitt Bukater
Gwyneth Paltrow • Winona Ryder • Claire Danes
Gabrielle Anwar • Reese Witherspoon

WHO Trivia
Writer/Director/Producer James Cameron's first choice to play Jack Dawson was River Phoenix. By the time the movie was ready to be made, Phoenix had died, so the role was offered to Johnny Depp, who turned it down.

Tom Cruise was next to turn down the role. His reason was that the studio would not meet his asking price. Cameron considered Jared Leto, but he refused to audition. Cameron then offered the role to Stephen Dorff and Billy Crudup. Both turned it down.

Co-producing studios, Paramount Pictures and 2oth Century Fox, both wanted Mathew McConaughey to play the role of Jack, but Cameron insisted on the unknown Leonardo DiCaprio.

When five up-and-coming young actresses turned down the role of Rose, the relatively unknown Kate Winslet began campaigning heavily for it. Winslet sent Cameron daily notes from England, which led Cameron to invite her to Hollywood to audition. As with DiCaprio, casting director Mali Finn originally brought Winslet to Cameron's attention.

The role of Cal Hockley, eventually played by Billy Zane, was turned down by Matthew McConaughey who wanted the role of Jack Dawson. Hugh Grant also turned down the role. He felt the film wasn't his kind of thing.

SHAKESPEARE IN LOVE (1998)

(after having sex)

Viola: I would not have thought it: There is something better than a play!

Shakespeare: There is.

Viola: Even your play.

Shakespeare: Hmm?

Viola: And that was only my first try.

Plot

A young William Shakespeare, out of ideas and short of cash, meets his ideal woman and is inspired to write one of his most famous plays.

CASTING

Who Starred as Viola de Lesseps?
Gwyneth Paltrow

Turned Down the Role of Viola de Lesseps
Julia Roberts • Nicole Kidman
Penelope Ann Miller • Kate Winslet

Who Starred as William Shakespeare?
Joseph Fiennes

Turned Down the Role of William Shakespeare
Daniel Day-Lewis • Ben Affleck • Russell Crowe

WHO Trivia

There is a story about the casting of Julia Roberts and Daniel Day-Lewis. Supposedly, six years before the film was made, Julia Roberts was cast as Viola; she flew to the UK to try to persuade Daniel Day-Lewis to take the part of Shakespeare, but he declined in favor of *In the Name of the Father*. This caused Roberts to drop out, and Universal Pictures to drop the project when no suitable alternatives could be found.

When Miramax Films took control of the project, besides Julia Roberts and the three actresses listed that turned down the role of Viola, the following were considered: Bridget Fonda, Winona Ryder, Michelle Pfeiffer, Helen Hunt, Ashley Judd, Meg Ryan, and Diane Lane.

Eventually Gwyneth Paltrow was cast. Producer Harvey Weinstein then asked Ben Affleck, Paltrow's boyfriend, to play William Shakespeare, but he declined. Affleck, still wanting to be near Paltrow, took the role of Edward Alleyn.

According to Russell Crowe, he was offered the lead role by Weinstein, but only if he would sign on for a package deal of four films.

AMERICAN BEAUTY (1999)

Carolyn: Well, I see you're smoking pot now. I think using psychotropic drugs is a very positive example to set for our daughter.

Lester: You're one to talk, you bloodless, money-grubbing freak.

Plot
A husband and father going through a mid-life crisis, and newfound quest for love, freedom, and self-liberation impacts his family and neighbors.

CASTING

Who Starred as Lester Burnham?
Kevin Spacey

Turned Down the Role of Lester Burnham
Chevy Chase • Tom Hanks

Who Starred as Angela Hayes?
Mena Suvari

Turned Down the Role of Angela Hayes
Kirsten Dunst • Sarah Michelle Gellar
Brittany Murphy • Katie Holmes

WHO Trivia
While a director was being sought, Chevy Chase turned down the lead role of Lester Burnham because he only wanted to do family films.

After Mike Nichols and Robert Zemeckis turned down offers to direct the film, Steven Spielberg, as co-founder of DreamWorks, recommended Sam Mendes, then a theater director, known for the Broadway hit, *Cabaret*. Mendes was hired.

From the beginning, Mendes had Kevin Spacey and Annette Bening in mind for the leads, but DreamWorks executives were unenthusiastic. The studio suggested several alternatives, including:Kevin Costner, John Travolta, and Bruce Willis to play Lester; Helen Hunt or Holly Hunter for Carolyn. Mendes did not want a big star "weighing the film down." Mendes was proven right when Spacey won the Best Actor Oscar, and the film won for Best Film.

Sarah Michelle Gellar turned down the role of Angela, played by Mena Suvari, due to her commitment to her television show, *Buffy the Vampire Slayer*.

Jessica Biel was originally cast as Jane Burnham, but had to drop out due to conflicts with her show, *7th Heaven*. The part finally went to Thora Birch.

THE MATRIX (1999)

Neo: What is the Matrix?

Trinity: The answer is out there, Neo, and it's looking for you, and it will find you if you want it to.

Plot

A computer hacker learns from mysterious rebels about the true nature of his reality and his role in the war against the controllers of it.

CASTING

Who Starred as Neo?
Keanu Reeves

Turned Down the Role of Neo
Will Smith • Nicolas Cage • Brad Pitt • Val Kilmer
Ewan McGregor • David Duchovny • Leonardo DiCaprio

Who Starred as Trinity?
Carrie-Anne Moss

Turned Down the Role of Trinity
Janet Jackson • Sandra Bullock • Gillian Anderson

WHO Trivia

Will Smith turned down the role of Neo to make *Wild Wild West*. Smith later stated he was "not mature enough as an actor" at that time, and that if given the role, he "would have messed it up." Nicolas Cage turned it down, as did Ewan McGregor who was still filming *Star Wars: Episode One*. David Duchovny and Gillian Anderson both turned down the lead roles to star in the sci-fi television show, *The X-Files*.

After Brad Pitt and Val Kilmer turned down the role, the Wachowskis', who wrote and directed the film, wanted Johnny Depp for the lead. Warner Bros. pushed for Keanu Reeves and won out.

Janet Jackson turned down the role of Trinity due to scheduling conflicts. Sandra Bullock turned down the role because she couldn't see herself alongside Will Smith, originally intended to play Neo. This was before Keanu Reeves, who Bullock worked with on *Speed* and *The Lake House*, was cast.

Russell Crowe turned down the role of Morpheus, eventually played by Laurence Fishburne.

Bonus Movies

Kindergarten Cop (1990)
Bill Murray and Jack Nicholson turned down the role of John Kimble, played by Arnold Schwarzenegger.

Hook (1991)
Originally Kelvin Kline was cast as Peter Pan, but backed out because of an over-extended commitment to film *Soapdish*. Robin Williams played the role. David Bowie was offered the role of Captain Hook, but turned it down. Ultimately, Dustin Hoffman played the role.

JFK (1991)
Originally, Kevin Costner, Harrison Ford, and Mel Gibson all turned down the role of Jim Garrison. However, Costner's agent, Michael Ovitz, was a big fan of the project, and helped writer/director Oliver Stone convince Costner to reconsider and take the role. Two months after finally signing in January 1991, Costner's film, *Dances with Wolves* won seven Academy Awards, greatly enhancing *JFK*'s bankability in the studio's eyes.

Point Break (1991)
After Matthew Broderick turned down the role of Johnny Utah, a number of actors including Johnny Depp, Val Kilmer, and Charlie Sheen were all considered for the part before Keanu Reeves was cast.

Prince of Tides (1991)
In pre-production, Barbra Streisand talked to Robert Redford about playing the role of Tom Wingo. Although the two wanted to work together again since they made *The Way We Were*, scheduling conflicts interfered. The role was then offered to Kevin Costner who turned it down. Ultimately, Nick Nolte was finally cast in the role and received an Academy Award nomination.

The Bodyguard (1992)
Originally, when the film was first proposed in 1977, Steve McQueen was going to play opposite Diana Ross, but the project stalled. Fourteen years later, when the film went into production, Kevin Costner was cast as Frank Farmer, and became one of the film's producers. After Patti LaBelle turned down the leading female role, Whitney Houston became interested. Pat Benatar, Joan Jett, Debbie Harry, and Janet Jackson were all considered. Costner fought for Houston, convinced she was the right person to play Rachel Marron.

My Cousin Vinny (1992)

Marisa Tomei won an Academy Award for Best Supporting Actress playing Mona Lisa Vito in *My Cousin Vinny*. Before winning the role, Lorraine Bracco and Geena Davis turned it down.

In his 2014 autobiography, *The Filthy Truth*, Andrew Dice Clay wrote that the film was originally developed as a starring vehicle for him at Fox. After the failure of *The Adventures of Ford Fairlane*, the studio severed ties with Clay.

While appearing on the *Don Le Batard* radio show, Jim Belushi said he regretted turning down the role of Vinny Gambini, played by Joe Pesci.

Reservoir Dogs (1992)

The role of Vic Vega (Mr. Blonde), played by Michael Madsen, was actually written for John Travolta, but he declined the low budget independent film. When Christopher Walken turned down the role, Tarantino cast Madsen. George Clooney also read for it.

Tarantino wrote a part in the film with James Woods in mind, and made numerous offers all of which Woods' agent shot down. Woods later met with Tarantino, and discovered Woods' agent never even told him about the offers. Woods fired his agent over this incident. It is widely assumed that Woods was meant to play Mr. Orange.

Samuel L. Jackson auditioned for Mr. Orange, but lost out to Tim Roth. However he left an impression with Tarantino who eventually wrote the part of Jules in *Pulp Fiction* specifically for Jackson.

The Firm (1993)

Jason Patric turned down the role of Mitch McDeere ultimately played by Tom Cruise. Robin Wright Penn and Glenn Close turned down the role of Abby McDeere before Jeanne Tripplehorn was cast.

The Fugitive (1993)

Alec Baldwin was originally cast in the role of Dr. Richard Kimble. After he dropped out, Nick Nolte, Kevin Costner, Michael Douglas and Andy Garcia were all considered before Harrison Ford was cast.

The character of Dr. Nichols was recast for Jeroen Krabbé after Richard Jordan, the original actor who landed the role, fell ill with a brain tumor and had to drop out. Jordon died three weeks after the film's release.

Groundhog Day (1993)

Prior to Bill Murray's casting, Tom Hanks and Michael Keaton turned down the lead role of weatherman Phil Connors. Writer Harold Ramis had known Murray since their days at *Second City*. To make the role more suited to

Murray's comedic talents, Ramis decided to make a major change in the second draft, changing Phil's attitude from having come to accept the nature of the time loop, to one that was more optimistic about being able to end the loop.

Philadelphia (1993)

Christopher Reeve was offered the part of Andrew Beckett, but declined, writing a letter to the producers that the role was too depressing. Daniel Day-Lewis, Andy Garcia, and Michael Keaton were all considered. Finally, the role was given to Tom Hanks, who won an Oscar for Best Actor.

Director Jonathan Demme considered both Robin Williams and Bill Murray in the role of Joe Miller feeling a comedic actor would be a good counter balance for Tom Hanks. Demme finally decided to cast Denzel Washington.

Sleepless in Seattle (1993)

The role of Annie Reed was originally offered to Julia Roberts, but she turned it down. It was then offered to Kim Basinger who turned it down because she thought the premise was ridiculous. Jodie Foster thought the movie was "silly" and would not be successful also turned it down. The role was also turned down by Michelle Pfeiffer and Jennifer Jason Leigh before Meg Ryan was cast.

True Lies (1994)

Writer/Director/Producer James Cameron considered Ellen DeGeneres and Isabella Rossellini for the role of Helen Tasker. Cameron thought DeGeneres was "too funny," and Isabella Rossellini was "too Italian." Cameron actually wanted Kyra Sedgwick for the role, but she turned him down. Also considered for the role: Helen Hunt, Lena Olin, Amanda Plummer, and Robin Wright Penn. Cameron finally gave it to Jamie Lee Curtis.

Braveheart (1995)

When MGM was going through new management in 1993, Alan Ladd Jr., a senior producer left the studio and took some of its top properties, including *Braveheart,* with him. Months later, Mel Gibson came across the script. Even though he liked it, he initially passed on it. However Gibson seemed to be preoccupied by the story, and decided to take on the project. Initially interested in directing only, he considered casting Brad Pitt in the role of William Wallace, but reluctantly agreed to play the role of Wallace himself.

The Bridges of Madison County (1995)

Lena Olin and Kathleen Turner both passed on the role of Francesca Johnson. Tiffani Thiessen was originally cast, but lost the part when Clint Eastwood came on board as the character Robert Kincaid and as the director. Eastwood cast Meryl Streep. He felt he needed to go with an older actress.

A number of other actresses were considered, including: Glenn Close, Geena Davis, Melanie Griffith, Catherine Deneuve, Anjelica Huston, Susan Sarandon, Cher, Jessica Lange, Emma Thompson, and Sonia Braga.

Get Shorty (1995)

DeVito was the first choice to play Chili Palmer, but took the part of Martin Weir instead because of scheduling problems. Dustin Hoffman, Michael Keaton, Al Pacino, Robert De Niro, and Bruce Willis were all considered for the part. John Travolta, who at first turned down the film, signed on after supposedly talking with Quentin Tarantino.

The Usual Suspects (1995)

After both Christopher Walken and Al Pacino turned down the role of Detective Dave Kujan, Chazz Palminteri was cast.

The English Patient (1996)

Daniel Day-Lewis turned down the role of Count Laszlo de Almasy before Ralph Fiennes was cast. Sean Connery had to turn down the role of Caravaggio, played by Willem Dafoe, because of scheduling conflicts. Before Kristin Scott Thomas was cast as Katharine, Demi Moore and Miranda Richardson were considered.

Evita (1996)

Gloria Estefan was the first person invited to play the role, but did not accept because of the political connotations of the character. It is also reported that Barbra Streisand turned the role down.

During development, Cher, Michelle Pfeiffer, Glenn Close, Jennifer Lopez, and Meryl Streep were all considered. There is a story that Madonna sent a four-page letter to Alan Parker, the film's director, saying she was the best person to portray Eva and would be fully committed to the role. Parker insisted if Madonna was to be his Eva, she must understand that the film was not a glorified Madonna video. Andrew Lloyd Webber was wary about her singing. Madonna underwent vocal training to learn how to use her voice in a way she had never used it, actually developing an upper register she didn't know she had.

Primal Fear (1996)
Before Edward Norton was cast in his first role as Aaron Stampler, Leonardo DiCaprio and Wil Wheaton turned it down.

Scream (1996)
Molly Ringwald, then 27, turned down the role of Sidney Prescott because she did not want to play a teen. Drew Barrymore also turned down the role, before accepting the role of Casey Becker. Neve Campbell was then cast as Sidney. David Arquette auditioned for the role of Billy, played by Skeet Ulrich, but liked the role of Dewey more, and was cast in it. After Janeane Garofalo declined the role of reporter Gale Weathers, Courtney Cox was signed to play it.

L.A. Confidential (1997)
Before Kim Basinger was cast as Lynn Bracken, the role that brought her into the spotlight, the following actresses turned it down: Melanie Griffith, Lorraine Bracco, Geena Davis, Jennifer Jason Leigh, and Kathleen Quinlan.

Good Will Hunting (1997)
After Ben Affleck and Matt Damon sold their first script, *Good Will Hunting*, they anticipated acting in the lead roles, but the studio wanted Brad Pitt and Leonardo DiCaprio. When an opportunity to get control of the project presented itself, Damon and Affleck got director Kevin Smith to walk it into Harvey Weinstein's office at Miramax. After Weinstein read the script, he agreed to let Damon and Affleck star in the film.

There's Something About Mary (1998)
Writers/Directors, Peter and Bobby Farrelly were set on Cameron Diaz as Mary from the beginning. They wanted to cast Ben Stiller, a relatively unknown actor, as Ted Stroehmann, but the studio was reluctant; they decided on another unknown actor, Owen Wilson instead. The studio was even more reluctant to cast Wilson, and finally agreed to allow the Farrelly brothers to cast Stiller.

   Bill Murray was considered for the role of private detective Pat Healy, but the brothers thought he was too old. They then considered Cuba Gooding Jr., Hank Azaria, and Vince Vaughn, before casting Matt Dillon.

Fight Club (1999)
Producer Ross Bell met with Russell Crowe to discuss his candidacy for the role of Tyler Durden. Producer Art Linson, who joined the project late, met with Brad Pitt regarding the same role, and cast Pitt instead of Crowe.

For the role of the unnamed "Narrator," the distributor, 20th Century Fox, desired a sexier marquee name such as Matt Damon to increase the film's commercial prospects; Fox also considered Sean Penn. Director David Fincher wanted Ed Norton based on his performance in *The People vs. Larry Flynt*.

Sarah Michelle Gellar was approached for the role of Marla Singer, but had to turn it down because of her contract with *Buffy the Vampire Slayer*.

David Fincher then considered Courtney Love and Winona Ryder, but the studio wanted a bigger name and insisted on casting Reese Witherspoon. Fincher felt she was too young, and wanted Helena Bonham Carter instead. Finally, Witherspoon turned down the role because she thought it was "too dark," and Bonham Carter was cast.

Patrick Bateman • Natalie • Dylan • Alex • Maximus • Commodus • Proximo
Wolverine • Storm • Rogue • Jane Grey • Bridget Jones • Leticia Musgrove
Buck Grotowski • Sonny Grotowski • Det. Alonzo Harris • Jake Hoyt
Jason Bourne • Marie • Roxie Hart • Velma Kelly • Billy Flynn • Mama Morton
Bill "The Butcher" Cutting • Amsterdam Vallon • Jenny Everdeane
Edward Sumner • Connie Sumner • Paul Martel • Vincent • Max Durocher
John Creasy • Rayburn • Maggie Fitzgerald • Frankie Dunn • "Scrap-Iron"
Batman/Bruce Wayne • Alfred • Ra's Al Ghul • James Bond • Vesper Lynd
Bill Costigan • Colin Sullivan • Frank Costello • Sean Dignam • Queenen
Giselle • Robert Phillip • Prince Edward • Llewelyn Moss • Anton Chigurh

2000s

Randy "The Ram" Robinson • Stephanie • Leigh Anne Touhy • Michael Oher
Phil Wenneck • Dr. Stu Price • Alan Garner • Jade • Wilson • Gabriel Martin
John Nash • Alicia Nash • Lara Croft • Elle Woods • Satine • Christian
Spider-Man/Peter Parker • Green Goblin/Norman Osborn • Marlin
Nemo • Regina George • Karen Smith • Cady Herron • Harry Lockhart
"Gay" Perry • Michael Clayton • Alison Scott • Benjamin Button • Bryan Mills
Hans Landa • Bridget von Hammersmark • Donny Donowitz • Archie Hicox
Patrick Bateman • Natalie • Dylan • Alex • Maximus • Commodus • Proximo
Wolverine • Storm • Rogue • Jane Grey • Bridget Jones • Leticia Musgrove
Buck Grotowski • Sonny Grotowski • Det. Alonzo Harris • Jake Hoyt
Jason Bourne • Marie • Roxie Hart • Velma Kelly • Billy Flynn • Mama Morton
Bill "The Butcher" Cutting • Amsterdam Vallon • Jenny Everdeane
Edward Sumner • Connie Sumner • Paul Martel • Vincent • Max Durocher
John Creasy • Rayburn • Maggie Fitzgerald • Frankie Dunn • "Scrap-Iron"
Batman/Bruce Wayne • Alfred • Ra's Al Ghul • James Bond • Vesper Lynd
Bill Costigan • Colin Sullivan • Frank Costello • Sean Dignam • Queenen
Giselle • Robert Phillip • Prince Edward • Llewelyn Moss • Anton Chigurh
Randy "The Ram" Robinson • Stephanie • Leigh Anne Touhy • Michael Oher
Phil Wenneck • Dr. Stu Price • Alan Garner • Jade • Wilson • Gabriel Martin
John Nash • Alicia Nash • Lara Croft • Elle Woods • Satine • Christian
Spider-Man/Peter Parker • Green Goblin/Norman Osborn • Marlin
Nemo • Regina George • Karen Smith • Cady Herron • Harry Lockhart
"Gay" Perry • Michael Clayton • Alison Scott • Benjamin Button • Bryan Mills
Hans Landa • Bridget von Hammersmark • Donny Donowitz • Archie Hicox
Patrick Bateman • Natalie • Dylan • Alex • Maximus • Commodus • Proximo
Wolverine • Storm • Rogue • Jane Grey • Bridget Jones • Leticia Musgrove
Buck Grotowski • Sonny Grotowski • Det. Alonzo Harris • Jake Hoyt
Jason Bourne • Marie • Roxie Hart • Velma Kelly • Billy Flynn • Mama Morton
Bill "The Butcher" Cutting • Amsterdam Vallon • Jenny Everdeane
Edward Sumner • Connie Sumner • Paul Martel • Vincent • Max Durocher
John Creasy • Rayburn • Maggie Fitzgerald • Frankie Dunn • "Scrap-Iron"
Batman/Bruce Wayne • Alfred • Ra's Al Ghul • James Bond • Vesper Lynd

The New Millennium

Before the new millennium even began, James Cameron's blockbuster *Avatar* became the highest grossing film in history surpassing his own film of two years earlier, *Titanic*. The new decade was also inundated with new media and social-networking sites: Netflix, Hulu, Amazon, YouTube, iTunes, smart phones, iPods, laptops and online movies. These media and social networking sites competed for audiences, and distracted people from going to theaters to watch movies.

Six global entertainment companies dominated Hollywood: Time Warner, Twentieth Century Fox, Viacom, Disney, Sony and NBC Universal. By 2005, every $100 million box office success came from one of these major studios.

Even after the horror of 9/11, moviegoers were mostly reluctant to attend films that dealt with the realities of an unpopular war, and most studios shied away from making war films for much of the decade. However, there were some exceptions: *Home of the Brave* told of four American soldiers ambushed on their last mission in Iraq, and subsequently suffered from PTSD upon their return home; *In the Valley of Elah* reflected the atrocities of war; *A Mighty Heart* told of the kidnapping-disappearance of journalist Daniel Pearl in Pakistan in 2002; *Rendition* revealed a falsely accused man, detained and tortured in a secret detention facility; and Kathryn Bigelow's award-winning *The Hurt Locker* conveyed the terror experienced by bomb experts in Iraq.

Foreign language films rarely dominated the American box office. However, there were a few exceptions. *Crouching Tiger, Hidden Dragon* was the first Asian action film to become a 'cross-over' success, making it the highest-grossing foreign language, subtitled film ever released in the United States. The French comedy *Amelie* earned $33 million domestically, and became the highest-grossing French-language film ever in the United States.

Documentary films became commercially successful and were well represented at award shows from Cannes to the Academy Awards. Michael

Moore's *Bowling for Columbine* became the highest-grossing documentary of all time, soon to be surpassed by Moore's own controversial, *Fahrenheit 9/11*. Al Gore's *An Inconvenient Truth* grossed over $24 million, and *March of the Penguins,* budgeted at $8 million, earned $78 million, making it the highest-grossing nature documentary.

Furthermore, horror films quickly became one of the most profitable genres of the decade because of their low production costs, and the ability to retell a familiar story without high-salaried movie stars. Though critics derided these films, the youth market came back to theaters in droves.

Steven Spielberg's *Jaws* is often cited as the first $100 million movie in domestic theatrical rentals. In this decade, $200 million was the new bar for a blockbuster; the $100 million mark was only significant when *Spider-Man* became the first film to pass the $100 million level in a single weekend. *Pirates of the Caribbean: At World's End* became the most expensive picture ever made at $300 million, though many "event" films were budgeted at over $200 million. For only the fifth time in film history, a movie reached $1 billion in revenue at the box office: James Cameron's *Avatar.*

The decade saw the creation of new successful franchises, sequels, reboots... and fantastic tales, based on books by J.R.R. Tolkien and J.K. Rowling, CGI-animated characters, or action thrillers. *The Lord of the Rings: The Two Towers, Star Wars Episode II: Attack of the Clones,* and the number one film of the year, *Spider-Man,* were three of the four top grossing films in 2002.

The most successful franchises in movie history still remain: *Star Wars, Harry Potter, James Bond, Batman, Lord of The Rings, Indiana Jones, Pirates of the Caribbean, X-Men, Twilight,* and *The Fast and Furious.*

The Walt Disney Co. bought longtime partner Pixar Animation Studios Inc. for $7.4 billion releasing seven highly successful animated films: *Monsters, Inc.; Finding Nemo; The Incredibles; Cars; Ratatouille; WALL•E;* and *Up.*

There were fewer A-list star-driven hits due to the rise of pre-established franchises and the emergence of often younger or unknown stars. Films and their sequels, such as *The Hangover, Transformers, Star Trek, Harry Potter,* and *Twilight* were all box office hits without big name stars on the marquee.

The highest-grossing actress of the decade was Emma Watson for her role in six *Harry Potter* films, which earned $5.4 billion. Co-star Daniel Radcliffe was the highest average-grossing box-office star in a leading role in the decade, averaging about $285 million per *Harry Potter* domestically.

The Academy Awards

2000

Best Picture: ***Gladiator***
Best Actor: Russell Crowe (*Gladiator*)
Best Actress: Julia Roberts (*Erin Brockovich*)
Best Supporting Actor: Benicio del Toro (*Traffic*)
Best Supporting Actress: Marcia Gay Harden (*Pollock*)

2001

Best Picture: ***A Beautiful Mind***
Best Actor: Denzel Washington (*Training Day*)
Best Actress: Halle Berry (*Monster's Ball*)
Best Supporting Actor: Jim Broadbent (*Iris*)
Best Supporting Actress: Jennifer Connelly (*A Beautiful Mind*)

2002

Best Picture: ***Chicago***
Best Actor: Adrien Brody (*The Pianist*)
Best Actress: Nicole Kidman (*The Hours*)
Best Supporting Actor: Chris Cooper (*Adaptation*)

2003

Best Picture: ***The Lord of the Rings: The Return of the King***
Best Actor: Sean Penn (*Mystic River*)
Best Actress: Charlize Theron (*Monster*)
Best Supporting Actor: Tim Robbins (*Mystic River*)
Best Supporting Actress: Renee Zellweger (*Cold Mountain*)

2004

Best Picture: ***Million Dollar Baby***
Best Actor: Jamie Foxx (*Ray*)
Best Actress: Hilary Swank (*Million Dollar Baby*)
Best Supporting Actor: Morgan Freeman (*Million Dollar Baby*)
Best Supporting Actress: Cate Blanchett (*The Aviator*)

2005

Best Picture: ***Crash***
Best Actor: Philip Seymour Hoffman (*Capote*)
Best Actress: Reese Witherspoon (*Walk the Line*)
Best Supporting Actor: George Clooney (*Syriana*)
Best Supporting Actress: Rachel Weisz (*The Constant Gardener*)

2006

Best Picture: ***The Departed***
Best Actor: Forest Whitaker (*The Last King of Scotland*)
Best Actress: Helen Mirren (*The Queen*)
Best Supporting Actor: Alan Arkin (*Little Miss Sunshine*)
Best Supporting Actress: Jennifer Hudson (*Dreamgirls*)

2007

Best Picture: ***No Country for Old Men***
Best Actor: Daniel Day-Lewis (*There Will Be Blood*)
Best Actress: Marion Cotillard (*La Vie en Rose*)
Best Supporting Actor: Javier Bardem (*No Country for Old Men*)
Best Supporting Actress: Tilda Swinton (*Michael Clayton*)

2008

Best Picture: ***Slumdog Millionaire***
Best Actor: Sean Penn (*Milk*)
Best Actress: Kate Winslet (*The Reader*)
Best Supporting Actor: Heath Ledger (*The Dark Knight*)
Best Supporting Actress: Penelope Cruz (*Vicky Cristina Barcelona*)

2009

Best Picture: ***The Hurt Locker***
Best Actor: Jeff Bridges (*Crazy Heart*)
Best Actress: Sandra Bullock (*The Blind Side*)
Best Supporting Actor: Christoph Waltz (*Inglourious Basterds*)
Best Supporting Actress: Mo'Nique (*Precious*)

Casting Trivia Quiz

1. Russell Crowe won an Oscar for his role as Maximus in **Gladiator**. The role was originally offered to:
   - a. Hugh Jackman
   - b. Mel Gibson
   - c. Kevin Costner
   - d. Christian Bale

2. Hugh Jackman became Wolverine in the **X-Men** series, but someone else was the original choice to play this role:
   - a. Edward Norton
   - b. Russell Crowe
   - c. Keanu Reeves
   - d. Mel Gibson

3. Willem Dafoe played the dual role of Norman Osborn and the evil Green Goblin in **Spider-Man** but the role was first offered to:
   - a. Jim Carrey
   - b. Nicolas cage
   - c. John Malkovich
   - d. All of the Above

4. Halle Berry won a Best Actress Academy Award for her portrayal of Leticia Musgrove in **Monster's Ball**. The role was first turned by:
   - a. Vanessa Williams
   - b. Angela Bassett
   - c. Whitney Houston
   - d. All of the Above

5. The role of banker Patrick Bateman, played by Christian Bale, in **American Psycho** was first offered to:
   - a. Jake Gyllenhaal
   - b. Ewan McGregor
   - c. Leonardo DiCaprio
   - d. Tim Robbins

6. Denzel Washington played the role of Creasy in **Man on Fire.** This actor turned down the role:
   - a. Robert De Niro
   - b. Mel Gibson
   - c. Russell Crowe
   - d. Arnold Schwarzenegger

7. Josh Brolin was cast in **No Country for Old Men** in the lead role of Llewelyn Moss after this actor turned it down:
   - a. Brad Pitt
   - b. Heath Ledger
   - c. Sean Penn
   - d. Keanu Reeves

8. George Clooney cleaned up the messes made by his law firm in ***Michael Clayton***. The role was originally offered to:
   - a. Leonardo DeCaprio
   - b. Denzel Washington
   - c. Christian Bale
   - d. Tom Berenger

9. Renee Zellweger won the lead role in ***Bridget Jones's Diary*** after this actress turned the role down:
   - a. Nichole Kidman
   - b. Toni Collette
   - c. Emily Watson
   - c. All of the Above

10. In ***Casino Royale***, Daniel Craig became the new James Bond. This actor turned the role down:
    - a. Hugh Jackman
    - b. Ewan McGregor
    - c. Gerard Butler
    - d. All of the Above

11. Matt Damon was cast as Jason Bourne in ***The Bourne Identity*** after this actor turned down the role:
    - a. Russell Crowe
    - b. Sylvester Stallone
    - c. Tom Hardy
    - d. Brad Pitt

12. In ***The Gangs of New York,*** Daniel Day-Lewis was brilliantly cast as Bill 'The Butcher" Cutting after this actor turned it down:
    - a. Tom Hanks
    - b. Russell Crowe
    - c. Hugh Jackman
    - d. Robert De Niro

13. In the film ***Kiss Kiss Bang Bang,*** Val Kilmer's role as private investigator Guy Perry was first offered to:
    - a. Bruce Willis
    - b. Mark Wahlberg
    - c. Harrison Ford
    - d. Tom Hardy

14. Hilary Swank won an Oscar for playing the role of ill-fated boxer Maggie in Clint Eastwood's ***Million Dollar Baby***. This actress was first attached:
    - a. Sandra Bullock
    - b. Katie Holmes
    - c. Halle Berry
    - d. Jodie Foster

15. Jack Nicholson was memorable as the mobster Frank Costello in Martin Scorsese's ***The Departed*** but Scorsese's first choice was:
    - a. Robert De Niro
    - b. Al Pacino
    - c. Liam Neeson
    - d. Harvey Keitel

AMERICAN PSYCHO (2000)

Bateman: When I see a pretty girl walking down the street I think two things. One part of me wants to take her out and talk to her and be real nice and sweet and treat her right.

McDermott: And what did the other part think?

Bateman: What her head would look like on a stick.

Plot

A wealthy NYC investment banking executive hides his psychopathic ego from his co-workers and friends.

CASTING

Who Starred as Patrick Bateman?
Christian Bale

Turned Down the Role of Patrick Bateman
Leonardo DiCaprio • Edward Norton • Brad Pitt
Ewan McGregor • Billy Crudup

WHO Trivia

Producer Edward R. Pressman purchased the film rights to Bret Easton Ellis's novel in 1992 with Johnny Depp expressing an interest in the lead role, and David Cronenberg set to direct. It took a number of years before Cronenberg dropped out. Director/Writer Mary Harron was brought in, and she decided to cast Christian Bale in a verbal "good faith" deal.

Development looked like it was finally moving forward following six years of rejection by Hollywood studios when Lion Gate Films acquired worldwide distribution rights in 1997. After having waited for a year, Bale and Harron were aiming to begin filming in 1998. However, the studio didn't think Bale was famous enough, and pursued Edward Norton and Leonardo DiCaprio for the lead role.

Norton turned down the role, but DiCaprio was in provided Pressman replaced Herron with director Oliver Stone. When Stone and DiCaprio could not agree on the film's direction, DiCaprio decided to drop out and make *The Beach*.

Bale remained committed, turning down other movie roles and auditions for nine months, confident DiCaprio would depart. Herron and Bale were eventually brought back under the agreement that the budget would not exceed $10 million for what was to become a cult film favorite.

CHARLIE'S ANGELS (2000)

Charlie: Once upon a time, there were three very different little girls... who grew up to be three very different women. But they have three things in common: They're brilliant, they're beautiful and they work for me... My name is Charlie.

Plot

A trio of elite private investigators who, with the latest in high-tech gadgets, martial arts techniques, and a vast array of disguises, unleash their state-of-the-art skills on land, sea, and air.

CASTING

Who Starred as Alex Munday?
Lucy Liu

Turned Down the Role of Alex Munday
Angelina Jolie • Thandie Newton • Nia Long

WHO Trivia

Drew Barrymore bought the rights to Charlie's Angels prior to the movie being made. A decision that earned her an estimated $40 million.

Milla Jovovich, Alyssa Milano, and Julia Roberts were the forerunners for the parts of Natalie, Dylan, and Alex.

Before Drew Barrymore decided she wanted to play the role of Dylan, she considered Jennifer Jason Leigh, Demi Moore, and Kate Winslet.

Angelina Jolie turned down the role of Alex, admitting she was not a fan of the original television series. Thandie Newton was then cast, but had to drop out when weather caused delays in shooting *Mission Impossible II*. Nia Long turned down the role to make *Big Momma's House*.

Before Lucy Liu was cast in the role of Alex, the following were considered: Victoria Beckham, Penelope Cruz, Jodie Foster, Liv Tyler, Uma Thurman, Gwyneth Paltrow, Jada Pinkett Smith, Halle Berry, and Catherine Zeta-Jones.

Before Cameron Diaz was cast in the role of Natalie, the following actresses were considered: Reese Witherspoon, Renee Zellweger, Jenny McCarthy, and Kristin Davis, who was starring in *Sex and the City*.

GLADIATOR (2000)

Maximus: You ask me what I want. I, too, want to stand before the Emperor as you did.

Proximo: Then listen to me. Learn from me. I wasn't the best because I killed quickly. I was the best because the crowd loved me. Win the crowd, and you'll win your freedom.

Maximus: I will win the crowd. I will give them something they have never seen before.

Plot

A former Roman general sets out to exact revenge against the corrupt emperor who murdered his family and made him a slave.

CASTING

Who Starred as Maximus?
Russell Crowe

Turned Down the Role of Maximus
Mel Gibson

WHO Trivia

Director Ridley Scott's first choice to play Maximus was Mel Gibson, but he turned down the role because he thought he was too old to play the part.

Before Russell Crowe was hired, Scott had Tom Sizemore, who he had worked with on *Black Hawk Down*, audition. Scott then considered Antonio Banderas and Hugh Jackman before Russell Crowe was cast as Maximus.

The young actor who played Maximus' son, Giorgio Cantarini, also played Roberto Benigni's son in *Life Is Beautiful*. Ironically, Crowe and Benigni both won the Academy Award for Best Actor.

Jude Law was seriously considered for the role of Commodus, played by the very vexed Joaquin Phoenix.

Oliver Reed who played Proximo died three weeks before principal photography ended. Since he was a key character, a clause in the movie's insurance coverage would have allowed the filmmakers to re-shoot all of Reed's scenes with another actor, and the insurers would pay the estimated $25 million. However, Scott did not want to cut Reed from the movie, so he had the script re-written; a body double and computer-generated images (CGI) were used to complete the film.

X-MEN (2000)

Professor Xavier: Mutation: It is the key to our evolution. It has enabled us to evolve from a single-celled organism into the dominant species on the planet.

Plot

In a world where mutants, evolved super-powered humans, exist and are discriminated against, two groups form for an inevitable clash.

CASTING

Who Starred as Wolverine?
Hugh Jackman

Turned Down the Role of Wolverine
Russell Crowe • Dougray Scott

Who Starred as Storm?
Halle Berry

Turned Down the Role of Storm
Angela Bassett

Who Starred as Rogue?
Anna Paquin

Turned Down the Role of Rogue
Natalie Portman

Who Starred as Jean Grey?
Famke Janssen

Turned Down the Role of Jean Grey
Peta Wilson • Helen Hunt

WHO Trivia

Russell Crowe was director Bryan Singer's first choice to play Wolverine, but he turned it down because he felt the role was too similar to the role he played in *Gladiator*. He recommended Hugh Jackman, an unknown actor at the time. Singer decided to cast Dougray Scott.

Part of Dougray Scott's contract included a sequel, but the real reason he backed out was scheduling conflicts with *Mission Impossible II*. Based on a successful audition, Hugh Jackman was then cast three weeks into filming.

During the casting process, Keanu Reeves, Mel Gibson, Aaron Eckhart, Edward Norton, Gary Sinise, Jean-Claude Van Damme, Viggo Mortensen, and Bob Hoskins were all considered for the role of Wolverine.

Sir Patrick Stewart was the first actor to be cast as a mutant in the role of Professor X. Singer Michael Jackson wanted this role badly, since he was a big fan of the comic book.

Christopher Lee and Terence Stamp were considered for the role of Magneto before Singer cast Ian McKellen.

Peta Wilson was offered the role of Jean Grey, but had to film the fourth season of *La Femme Nikita* instead. Helen Hunt also turned it down.

Selma Blair, Lucy Lawless, and Maria Bello were all considered for the role before Famke Janssen got the part.

Ben Affleck, Matt Damon, Ethan Hawke, Edward Burns, and D.B. Sweeney were all considered for the role of Cyclops, before Thomas Jane was offered the role, but Jane turned down the role. Finally, Jim Caviezel was cast as Cyclops, but backed out due to scheduling conflicts with *Frequency,* and was replaced by James Marsden.

Angela Bassett was the studio's first choice to portray Storm, but she turned down the role when the studio wouldn't meet her quote. Before Halle Berry was cast, Janet Jackson, Mariah Carey, and Jada Pinkett Smith were considered.

After Natalie Portman turned down the role of Rogue, Sarah Michelle Gellar, Katie Holmes, Kirsten Dunst, Alicia Silverstone, Drew Barrymore, and Christina Ricci were all considered until Anna Paquin dropped out of the lead role in *Tart* to take the role of Rogue.

When early production began, James Cameron was considering a deal to produce the film with his then-wife, Kathryn Bigelow, directing.

Cameron and Bigelow seriously considered Bob Hoskins as Wolverine, Michael Biehn (who Cameron had worked with on *The Terminator*) as Cyclops, Christopher Lee as Magneto, and Angela Bassett as Storm.

The deal fell apart when Stan Lee piqued James Cameron's interest to make a Spider-Man movie with Biehn as Peter Parker. Cameron chose to pursue that idea and dropped the *X-Men* project.

BRIDGET JONES'S DIARY (2001)

Richard: So, why do you want to work in television?

Bridget: I've got to leave my current job because I've shagged my boss.

Richard: Fair enough. Start on Monday. We'll see how we go. And, incidentally, at 'Sit Up, Britain', no one ever gets sacked for shaggin' the boss. That's a matter of principle.

Plot

A British woman is determined to improve herself while she looks for love in a year in which she keeps a personal diary.

CASTING

Who Starred as Bridget Jones?
Renee Zellweger

Turned Down the Role of Bridget Jones
Toni Collette • Nicole Kidman • Emily Watson
Kristin Scott Thomas

WHO Trivia

Toni Collette had to turn down the role because she was in a Broadway musical at the time. Nicole Kidman, Kristen Scott Thomas and Emily Watson then turned down the role.

Also considered for the role were: Cameron Diaz, Helena Bonham Carter, Amanda Donohoe, Miranda Richardson, Tilda Swinton, and Rachel Weisz. Kate Winslet was also considered, but was thought to be too young.

The casting of Renee Zellweger initially caused quite a controversy with fans of the book who were outraged that the very British Bridget was going to be played by an American actress. That quickly changed after Zellweger's performance and Academy Award nomination.

To prepare for the role, Zellweger gained 25 pounds, and then actually worked at a British publishing company for a month. Zellweger adopted an alias as well as a posh accent and wasn't recognized by anyone.

On her desk at the publishing company was a picture of her then-boyfriend, Jim Carrey. Her co-workers just assumed Carrey was her celebrity crush.

MONSTER'S BALL (2001)

Hank Grotowski: I wanna take care of you.
Leticia Musgrove: Good. Cuz' I need to be taken care of.

Plot
After a family tragedy, a racist prison guard reexamines his attitude while falling in love with the African-American wife of the last prisoner he executed, leading to confusion and new ideas for the unlikely lovers.

> ### CASTING
>
> **Who Starred as Leticia Musgrove?**
> Halle Berry
>
> **Turned Down the Role of Leticia Musgrove**
> Vanessa Williams • Angela Bassett • Whitney Houston
>
> **Who Starred as Sonny Grotowski?**
> Heath Ledger
>
> **Turned Down the Role of Sonny Grotowski**
> Wes Bentley

WHO Trivia
This film was floating around the studios for six years. At one time, Sean Penn was on board to direct, and Robert De Niro was to star as Buck Grotowski. Finally, when the film went into production, producer Lee Daniels decided to cast Billy Bob Thornton in the role of Buck, and hire Marc Forster to direct.

Thornton was paid $500,000 for the role of Buck, but to his surprise, received an additional check for $2 million after the film became a hit.

Halle Berry received overwhelming acclaim for her performance. Among other awards, Berry won the Academy Award for Best Actress, earning her the distinction of being the first African-American woman to win an Oscar in that category.

Not wanting to do full frontal nudity, Vanessa Williams, Angela Bassett, and Whitney Houston all turned down the role of Leticia.

Wes Bentley was initially cast in the role of Sonny Grotowski, but dropped out at the last minute. Health Ledger replaced him. Jeffrey Wright and Don Cheadle turned down the supporting role of Lawrence Musgrove, ultimately played by Sean 'Diddy' Combs.

TRAINING DAY (2001)

Alonzo: I run shit here. You just live here! Yeah, that's right, you better walk away! Go on and walk away, 'cause I'm gonna burn this motherfucker down... King Kong ain't got shit on me!

Plot

On his first day on the job as a Los Angeles narcotics officer, a rookie cop spends an intense 24-hour period with his new boss, a rogue detective.

CASTING

Who Starred as Detective Alonzo Harris?
Denzel Washington

Turned Down the Role of Detective Alonzo Harris
Bruce Willis

Who Starred as Officer Jake Hoyt?
Ethan Hawke

Turned Down the Role of Officer Jake Hoyt
Eminem

WHO Trivia

Before director Antoine Fuqua was hired, David Guggenheim was set to direct with Samuel L. Jackson as Detective Alonzo Harris and Matt Damon as rookie officer Jake Hoyt.

When Denzel Washington accepted the lead role, Guggenheim was replaced with Fuqua per Washington's request. Washington's performance garnered him his second Academy Award for Best Actor.

Prior to Washington accepting the role, Bruce Willis had turned it down. Gary Sinise and Tom Sizemore were also considered.

Rapper Eminem was offered the role of Jake Hoyt, but turned it down to stay available for the film *8 Mile*.

Tobey Maguire was seriously considered for the role of Hoyt. He gained weight for the role, and even followed undercover narcotics officers in Los Angeles around for two months. When Ethan Hawke, Fuqua's first choice for the role, was finally available for the new shooting schedule, Tobey Maguire was dropped and Hawke was hired.

THE BOURNE IDENTITY (2002)

Bourne: You could wait...

Marie: Um, with you, you would probably just forget about me if I... stayed... here.

Bourne: How could I forget about you? (laughs) You're the only person I know.

Plot

A man, picked up by a fishing boat, bullet-ridden and suffering from amnesia, attempts to regain his memory by discovering clues to his identity that seem to indicate he is an assassin.

CASTING

Who Starred as Jason Bourne?
Matt Damon

Turned Down the Role of Jason Bourne
Brad Pitt • Russell Crowe • Arnold Schwarzenegger
Tom Cruise • Sylvester Stallone

Who Starred as Marie Kreutz?
Franka Potente

Turned Down the Role of Marie Kreutz
Sarah Polley

WHO Trivia

Director Doug Liman approached a wide range of actors for the lead role of Jason Bourne, including Brad Pitt, who turned it down to star in *Spy Game*.

Liman then offered the role to Russell Crowe, Arnold Schwarzenegger, Sylvester Stallone, and Tom Cruise. They all turned it down.

Before signing Matt Damon to play Jason Bourne, Damon had to turn down the leading role in Frank Darabont's *The Majestic*. Jim Carrey was cast.

Damon, who had never played such a physically demanding role, underwent three months of extensive training in Eskrima. Eskrima is a Fillipino form of martial arts that emphasizes weapon-based fighting with sticks, knives, and various improvised weapons in addition to "hand to hand" techniques.

CHICAGO (2002)

Velma:	Me and Roxie would just like to say thank you!
Roxie:	Thank you! Believe us, we could never have done it without you!
Roxie and Velma:	*(singing)* And all... that... jazz!! (spoken) That jazz!

Plot

Two death-row murderesses develop a fierce rivalry while competing for publicity, celebrity, and a sleazy lawyer's attention.

CASTING

Who Starred as Roxie Hart?
Renee Zellweger

Turned Down the Role of Roxie Hart
Toni Collette • Catherine Zeta-Jones

Who Starred as Billy Flynn?
Richard Gere

Turned Down the Role of Billy Flynn
John Travolta • Hugh Jackman

WHO Trivia

The film rights to the Broadway hit show were originally bought in the 1970s. Bob Fosse was then involved in the project. Goldie Hawn and Liza Minnelli were announced as the stars, with Frank Sinatra or Prince playing Billy Flynn, but Fosse's death ended that attempt at a film version.

The 1996 smash Broadway revival renewed interest, and Nicole Kidman and Madonna were cast. The project again went on hold when Madonna withdrew and Kidman chose to do *Moulin Rouge* instead.

In 2001, Rob Marshall took over; he gave the lead to Renee Zellweger after Catherine Zeta-Jones, who Marshall wanted to play Roxie, told him she wanted to play Velma because she wanted to sing the song, *All That Jazz*.

The role of Billy Flynn was offered several times to John Travolta before going to Richard Gere. This made the fourth time that Travolta turned down a role Gere eventually accepted. Kathy Bates turned down the role of Mama Morton, which went to Queen Latifah. Whoopi Goldberg was also considered for it.

GANGS OF NEW YORK (2002)

"The Butcher": You. Whatever your name is... what is your name?
Amsterdam: Amsterdam, sir.
"The Butcher": Amsterdam? I'm New York. Don't ever come in here empty handed again. You gotta pay for the pleasure of my company.

Plot

In 1862, Amsterdam Vallon returns to New York City to seek revenge against Bill "The Butcher" Cutting for his father's death.

CASTING

Who Starred as Bill "The Butcher" Cutting?
Daniel Day-Lewis

Turned Down the Role of Bill "The Butcher" Cutting
Tom Hanks

Who Starred as Jenny Everdeane?
Cameron Diaz

Turned Down the Role of Jenny Everdeane
Sarah Michelle Gellar • Gwyneth Paltrow
Emily Watson • Catherine Zeta-Jones

WHO Trivia

Writer/Director Martin Scorsese wrote the first draft of the script in 1977. Scorsese planned to cast Dan Aykroyd as Amsterdam Vallon and John Belushi as "The Butcher" Cutting. These plans fell apart when Belushi died.

A cast reshuffle had Mel Gibson as Vallon, Willem Dafoe as "The Butcher," and Tuesday Weld as Jenny. The film never happened.

In 1999, after Miramax bought the script and put the film into production, Scorsese cast Sarah Michelle Gellar as Jenny, but she had to back out because of scheduling conflicts with *Buffy the Vampire Slayer*. Scorsese then wanted to cast Sarah Polley in the role, but the studio wanted a more "bankable star." Cameron Diaz was cast after Catherine Zeta-Jones, Gwyneth Paltrow, and Emily Watson turned down the role.

UNFAITHFUL (2002)

Connie Sumner: Edward... did you hurt him? You did, didn't you?
Jesus, Edward. Talk to me. Tell me what you did.
Edward Sumner: No. You tell me what you did.

Plot
The marriage of a couple living in suburban New York City goes dangerously awry when the wife indulges in an adulterous affair with a stranger she encounters by chance.

CASTING

Who Starred as Edward Sumner?
Richard Gere

Turned Down the Role of Edward Sumner
Robert Redford

Who Starred as Connie Sumner?
Diane Lane

Turned Down the Role of Connie Sumner
Cameron Diaz • Claire Forlani • Kristin Davis
Jodie Foster • Sarah Michelle Gellar • Alyssa Milano
Gwyneth Paltrow • Meg Ryan • Brooke Shields
Hillary Swank • Kate Winslet • Reese Witherspoon

Who Starred as Paul Martel?
Olivier Martinez

Turned Down the Role of Paul Martel
Brad Pitt

WHO Trivia
The role of Connie Sumner was a casting nightmare from the very beginning. Kristin Davis turned it down because she was tied up with the hit television show, *Sex and the City*. Jodie Foster turned it down, choosing instead to replace Nicole Kidman in *Panic Room*. Sarah Michelle Gellar was approached, but due to a locked contract with her television show, *Buffy the Vampire Slayer,* she couldn't accept the part. Alyssa Milano had to turn it down due to scheduling conflicts with her television show, *Charmed*. Reese Witherspoon was then offered the part, but the producers wouldn't meet her asking price. Meg Ryan, Cameron Diaz, Claire Forlani, Hillary Swank, Kate Winslet, Gwyneth Paltrow, and Brooke Shields all turned down the role. Eventually, Diane Lane was cast.

COLLATERAL (2004)

Vincent:	There's no good reason, there's no bad reason to live or to die.
Max:	Then what are you?
Vincent:	I'm indifferent.
Max:	I can't drive you around while you're killing folks. It ain't my job!
Vincent:	Tonight it is.

Plot

A cab driver finds himself the hostage of an engaging contract killer as he makes his rounds from hit to hit during one night in Los Angeles.

CASTING

Who Starred as Vincent?
Tom Cruise

Turned Down the Role of Vincent
Russell Crowe • Colin Farrell • Edward Norton

Who Starred as Max Durocher?
Jamie Foxx

Turned Down the Role of Max Durocher
Adam Sandler • Edward Norton

WHO Trivia

The film lay dormant on DreamWorks' development slate for three years until Russell Crowe became interested in playing Vincent and the project started getting some Hollywood heat. Crowe then brought Michael Mann in after Martin Scorsese, Steven Spielberg, and Spike Lee all passed on directing the movie. Ironically, when it came time to commit, Crowe couldn't because he was preparing for *Eucalyptus*, a doomed Australian film starring Nicole Kidman.

After Colin Farrell and Edward Norton both turned down the role of Vincent, Michael Mann offered it to Tom Cruise, who loved the idea of playing a villain. Edward Norton also turned down the role of Max the cab driver. Eventually the role went to Adam Sandler, who later dropped out due to scheduling conflicts with *Spanglish*. Jamie Foxx replaced him.

Val Kilmer was cast as Detective Fanning, but had to pull out last minute due to scheduling conflicts with *Alexander*. Mark Ruffalo took over the role.

MAN ON FIRE (2004)

Samuel: Your resume is quite impressive. Sixteen years of military experience, extensive counter-terrorism work. I'm surprised anyone could afford you... What's the catch?

Creasy: I drink.

Samuel: How does that affect you?

Creasy: Coordination, reaction time. Top professionals try to kidnap your daughter I'll do the best I can... but the service will be on par with the pay.

Samuel: What if amateurs try?

Creasy: I'd probably kill 'em.

Plot

In Mexico City, a former assassin swears vengeance on those who committed an unspeakable act against the family he was hired to protect.

CASTING

Who Starred as John Creasy?
Denzel Washington

Turned Down the Role of John Creasy
Robert De Niro • Tom Cruise
Will Smith • Bruce Willis

WHO Trivia

The novel *Man on Fire*, written in 1980 by A.J. Quinnell, was first adapted in 1987 and starred Scott Glenn as Creasy.

Director Tony Scott decided to remake it in 2003. Scott offered the role of John Creasy to four actors with whom he had previously worked: Robert De Niro in *The Fan*, Bruce Willis in *The Last Boy Scout*, Will Smith in *Enemy of the State*, and Tom Cruise in *Top Gun*, and *Days of Thunder*. They all turned him down.

Eventually, Denzel Washington was cast in the role of Creasy because of a fortuitous trip to a doctor where Washington ran into Scott in the waiting room. The two men started to chat about the film, and the rest is history.

Prior to his death, Marlon Brando was the original choice to play Rayburn. Christopher Walken was originally cast in the role of lawyer Jordan Kalfus.

After Brando died, Walken wanted to play Rayburn to break away from always playing bad guys. Scott agreed, and cast Mickey Rourke as Kalfus.

MILLION DOLLAR BABY (2004)

Maggie: Working the bag, boss.
Frankie: I'm not your boss and that bag's working you.

Plot
An under-appreciated boxing trainer, with an elusive past and a quest for atonement, agrees to help an amateur female boxer achieve her dream of becoming a professional.

CASTING

Who Starred as Maggie Fitzgerald?
Hilary Swank

Turned Down the Role of Maggie Fitzgerald
Sandra Bullock

Who Starred as Frankie Dunn?
Clint Eastwood

Turned Down the Role of Frankie Dunn
Morgan Freeman

WHO Trivia
Producer Al Ruddy had a tough time finding backers due to the controversial subject matter of the film - euthanasia. After a few years of searching, Ruddy realized he had to have talent attached to the film to find the money he needed. He signed Sandra Bullock to play boxer Maggie Fitzgerald. Ruddy then approached Morgan Freeman to play the role of Frankie Dunn, but Freeman wanted to play Eddie "Scrap-Iron'" Dupris. Ruddy signed him on.

Ruddy took the project out again, and eventually found Clint Eastwood, who read the script and said, "It's a downer, but it's glorious," and agreed to play Frankie Dunn. While screenwriter Paul Haggis was scheduled to direct, Eastwood asked to direct it as well, and Haggis agreed to step aside.

Bullock was now committed to *Miss Congeniality 2: Armed & Fabulous,* opening the door for Hilary Swank to be cast in what was to become her second Oscar-winning role.

BATMAN BEGINS (2005)

Henri Ducard: What do you seek?
Bruce Wayne: I seek the means to fight injustice. To turn fear
                   against those who prey on the fearful.

Plot
After training with his mentor, Batman begins his fight to free crime-ridden
Gotham City from corruption.

CASTING

Who Starred as Batman/Bruce Wayne?
Christian Bale

Turned Down the Role of Batman/Bruce Wayne
Josh Harnett

Who Starred as Alfred?
Michael Caine

Turned Down the Role of Alfred
Anthony Hopkins

WHO Trivia
When Christopher Nolan was putting together his cast for 2005's *Batman
Begins,* the shortlist for the new Dark Knight was apparently whittled down
to three names. Christian Bale was one of them, of course, and he would
eventually take the role, playing Batman across a trilogy of films. Cillian
Murphy was in the running for the role of Batman, but would instead take
the role of Dr. Jonathan Crane.

Josh Hartnett's career included passing on playing the roles of Batman,
Spider-Man and Superman. The perception that Hartnett was resisting doing
blockbuster movies wasn't entirely correct. "It wasn't about not doing big
studio films. At the time, what I was interested in doing were tiny films,
such as *Mozart And The Whale,* a true story about two characters with
Asperger's Syndrome who fall in love. It was more a question of what I
wanted to do as opposed to what I didn't want to do. I always try to look
at things that way."

Liam Neeson was cast as Henri Ducard/Ra's Al Ghul, after Viggo Mortensen
turned down the role.

CASINO ROYALE (2006)

James Bond: The name's Bond... James Bond.

Plot

Armed with a license to kill, Secret Agent James Bond sets out on his first mission as 007.

CASTING

Who Starred as James Bond?
Daniel Craig

Turned Down the Role of James Bond
Hugh Jackman • Ewan McGregor • Gerard Butler

Who Starred as Vesper Lynd?
Eva Green

Turned Down the Role of Vesper Lynd
Ashley Judd • Miranda Richardson

WHO Trivia

Pierce Brosnan expressed an interest in making *Casino Royale*, but was considered too old, and his $30 million price tag too expensive.

Producer Michael G. Wilson claimed there was a list of over 200 names being considered to play the next James Bond. Hugh Jackman had to turn down the role due to other commitments. Both Ewan McGregor and Gerard Butler turned down the role saying they didn't want to be typecast.

Director Martin Campbell said Henry Cavill, who went on to play Superman in *Man of Steel*, almost got the part, but was deemed too young.

From the beginning, producer Barbara Broccoli's first choice for the next James Bond was Daniel Craig after seeing him in *Layer Cake* in 2004.

After Ashley Judd and Miranda Richardson turned down the role of the next "Bond Girl," Vesper Lynd, a number of actresses auditioned. Vera Farmiga was considered too old, Keira Knightley was considered too young, and Eva Longoria was considered "too Latin." Also auditioning for the role: Olivia Wilde, Audrey Tautou, Michelle Pfeiffer, and Charlize Theron.

THE DEPARTED (2006)

Frank Costello: The only one that can do what I do is me. Lot of people had to die for me to be me. You wanna be me?

Billy Costigan: I probably could be you, yeah. Yeah, I know that much. But I don't wanna be you, Frank. I don't wanna be you.

Frank Costello: Heavy lies the crown.

Plot
An undercover cop and a mole in the police department attempt to identify each other while infiltrating an Irish gang in South Boston.

CASTING

Who Starred as Bill Costigan?
Leonardo DiCaprio

Turned Down the Role of Billy Costigan
Tom Cruise • Brad Pitt

Who Starred as Colin Sullivan?
Matt Damon

Turned Down the Role of Colin Sullivan
Brad Pitt

Who Starred as Frank Costello?
Jack Nicholson

Turned Down the Role of Frank Costello
Al Pacino

Who Starred as Sgt. Sean Dignam?
Mark Wahlberg

Turned Down the Role of Sgt. Sean Dignam
Ray Liotta • Denis Leary

Who Starred as Queenan?
Martin Sheen

Turned Down the Role of Queenan
Robert De Niro

WHO Trivia

The Departed has a pretty incredible cast, but it's fascinating to consider how many other actors were almost part of the movie.

In January 2003, producer Brad Grey, and actor/producer Brad Pitt bought the rights to remake the Hong Kong film, *Infernal Affairs*. They changed the name to *The Departed*. Originally the master plan was to have Pitt as Colin Sullivan and Tom Cruise as Billy Costigan. When Cruise wasn't interested, Pitt was considered for both roles.

In March 2004, it was announced that Martin Scorsese would be directing, the film would be set in Boston, and that Leonardo DiCaprio and Brad Pitt were slated to star. Pitt later declined, saying a younger actor should play the role, and decided to be a producer instead. Matt Damon, who grew up in Boston, was suggested for the part of Sullivan; he was cast immediately.

Director Martin Scorsese's first choice to play Frank Costello was Al Pacino, but he turned down the role. Scorsese then asked Jack Nicholson if he wanted to play Costello. Nicholson liked the idea; however, wanted the film to be "something a little more" than the usual gangster film. Screenwriter William Monahan came up with the idea of basing the Frank Costello character on the legendary Irish-American gangster Whitey Bulger.

The casting of Sgt. Sean Dignam was also very interesting. Ray Liotta was offered the role, but had to reluctantly decline due to other commitments. Denis Leary was then offered the role, but he too had to turn it down due to scheduling conflicts with his television show *Rescue Me*.

Finally, after Ethan Hawke was considered, the role was offered to Mark Wahlberg, but he did not necessarily want to play a supporting role to DiCaprio and Damon. He acquiesced after his agent chastised him for turning down an icon like Scorsese, and after a meeting with Scorsese, who told him he could do what he wanted with the part. For his performance, Wahlberg received a nomination for Best Supporting Actor.

Two other well-known actors turned down roles. Robert De Niro turned down the role of Capt. Queenan, to appear in *The Good Shepherd*, and Mel Gibson turned down the role of Capt. Ellerby because he was starting production on *Apocalypto*. The role of Capt. Queenan was played by Martin Sheen, and the role of Capt. Ellerby by Alec Baldwin.

Scorsese also originally wanted to cast a known actress for the part of Madolyn. He considered Kate Winslet, Emily Blunt, Hilary Swank, and Jennifer Aniston before settling on the unknown, Vera Farmiga.

ENCHANTED (2007)

Giselle: Why are you staring at me?
Robert Philip: I don't know. It's... it's like you escaped from a Hall-mark card or something.
Giselle: Is that a bad thing?

Plot

A princess from the 2D-animated world of Andalasia is transported by an evil queen to real-world New York City where she meets a lawyer and his daughter who provide her a place to stay until she can find her way home.

CASTING

Who Starred as Giselle?
Amy Adams

Turned Down the Role of Giselle
Jennifer Aniston • Kate Beckinsale • Cameron Diaz
Jennifer Garner • Anne Heche • Uma Thurman

Who Starred as Robert Philip?
Patrick Dempsey

Turned Down the Role of Robert Philip
Val Kilmer • Sean Penn • Keanu Reeves • Charlie Sheen

Who Starred as Prince Edward?
James Marsden

Turned Down the Role of Prince Edward
Russell Crowe

WHO Trivia

Jennifer Aniston, who was playing Rachel on the television show *Friends* at the time, and Cameron Diaz both turned down the role of Giselle because the producers refused to meet their quote. Uma Thurman turned it down to do another project, while Anne Heche turned it down over scheduling commitments. Jennifer Garner turned down the role because she thought that playing a heartbreaking character would blow her career.

Charlie Sheen turned down the role of Robert Philip because he already committed to the television series, *Two and a Half Men*. Russell Crowe turned down the role of Prince Edward because he thought a lighthearted role would destroy his career.

NO COUNTRY FOR OLD MEN (2007)

Chigurh: I think you do. So, this is what I'll offer: You bring me the money and I'll let her go. Otherwise she's accountable, the same as you. That's the best deal you're going to get. I won't tell you, you can save yourself, because you can't.

Moss: Yeah, I'm goin' to bring you somethin', all right. I've decided to make you a special project of mine. You ain't goin to have to look for me at all.

Plot

A hunter stumbles onto a drug deal gone bad, and ends up with a suitcase containing $2 million dollars in it and an implacable assassin pursuing him.

CASTING

Who Starred as Llewelyn Moss?
Josh Brolin

Turned Down the Role of Llewelyn Moss
Heath Ledger

WHO Trivia

The role of Llewelyn Moss was originally offered to Heath Ledger, but he turned it down to spend time with his newborn daughter. Garret Dillahunt was also in the running for the role of Llewelyn. He auditioned five times for it, but instead was offered the part of Wendell, Ed Tom Bell's deputy.

Josh Brolin was not someone the writers/directors Joel and Ethan Coen were interested in casting, so Brolin enlisted the help of Quentin Tarantino and Robert Rodriguez to make an audition reel. His agent eventually secured a meeting with the Coen brothers, and Brolin was given the part.

Brolin broke his shoulder in a motorcycle accident two days after getting the part, but that turned out to be a non-issue since his character is shot in the shoulder very early in the film.

Before filming started, Javier Bardem nearly withdrew from the enigmatic role of Anton Chigurh due to scheduling issues. English actor Mark Strong was put on standby to take over, but Bardem's scheduling issues were resolved.

THE WRESTLER (2008)

Randy: Give this to your son. It's an authentic Randy "the Ram"
            action figure. It's a $300 collector's item.
Cassidy: Really?
Randy: No.

Plot
A faded professional wrestler must retire, and finds his quest for a new life
outside the ring a dispiriting struggle.

CASTING

Who Starred as Randy 'The Ram' Robinson?
Mickey Rourke

Turned Down the Role of Randy 'The Ram' Robinson
Nicolas Cage

WHO Trivia
There are two different versions of the story about how Mickey Rourke
was cast in the lead role. In the first version, Nicolas Cage entered negotiations in October, 2007 to star as Randy "The Ram" Robinson. A month
later, he was out. According to director Darren Aronofsky, Cage dropped
out because he knew that Aronofsky really wanted Mickey Rourke to play
"The Ram." Aronofsky stated that Cage was "a complete gentleman, and he
understood that Aronofsky's heart was with Mickey and he stepped aside."

The second version comes from a magazine interview Cage gave. In it,
he denied Aronofsky's version, stating instead, "I resigned from the movie
because I didn't think I had enough time to achieve the look of the wrestler
who was on steroids, which I would never do."

Rourke claims that, when he was first approached for the lead role, he was
initially reluctant to accept. He said, "I didn't really care for the script. I kind
of thought that whoever wrote the script hadn't spent as much time as I had
around these kind of people, and he wouldn't have spoken the way the
dude was speaking. So, when Darren let me rewrite all my dialogue, and he
put the periods in and crossed the T's, I agreed to sign on."

Abbie Cornish was originally cast as Stephanie, but had to drop out at the
last minute. Evan Rachel Wood replaced her.

THE BLIND SIDE (2009)

Sean Tuohy:	We have something we'd like to ask you.
Michael Oher:	What?
Sean Tuohy:	Well, Leigh Anne and I, we're... well, we'd like to become your legal guardians.
Michael Oher:	What does that mean?
Leigh Anne Tuohy:	What it means, is, is that, we want to know if you would like to become part of this family.
Michael Oher:	I kinda thought I already was.

Plot

The true story of Michael Oher, a homeless and traumatized boy who became an All-American football player and first round NFL draft pick with the help Leigh Anne Tuohy and her family.

CASTING

Who Starred as Leigh Anne Tuohy?
Sandra Bullock

Turned Down the Role of Leigh Anne Tuohy
Julia Roberts

WHO Trivia

Julia Roberts was offered the role of Leigh Anne Tuohy, but turned it down. The studio releasing the film, Warner Bros., then talked about changing the lead role to a man, but that idea quickly dissipated.

The role was then offered to Sandra Bullock, who also turned it down three times because of her concerns about playing the part of a devout Christian. By her own account, Bullock felt she couldn't objectively represent such a person's beliefs on screen. But after a visit with the real Leigh Anne Tuohy, Bullock not only took the role, she also took a pay cut and agreed to receive a percentage of the profits instead, so the film could be made on budget.

During the first weeks of shooting, Bullock thought her acting was so bad she considered dropping out. However, because director John Lee Hancock had worked so hard on the project, she didn't want to ruin everything for him. Bullock stayed on, and won the Academy Award for Best Actress.

When Quinton Aaron, who played Michael Oher, auditioned for the film, he was working as a security guard between acting gigs. After the audition, he offered to work as a security guard on the set if he didn't get the role.

THE HANGOVER (2009)

Phil: The bachelor party — The whole night — Things got outta control, and, uh… we lost Doug.

Tracy: What are you saying, Phil? We're getting married in five hours!

Phil: Yeah. That's not gonna happen.

Plot
Four friends travel to Las Vegas for a bachelor party, only to wake up the next morning not remembering a thing.

CASTING

Who Starred as Phil Wenneck?
Bradley Cooper

Turned Down the Role of Phil Wenneck
Paul Rudd

Who Starred as Dr. Stu Price?
Ed Helms

Turned Down the Role of Dr. Stu Price
Jeremy Piven

Who Starred as Alan Garner?
Zach Galifianakis

Turned Down the Role of Alan Garner
Jack Black

Who Starred as Jade?
Heather Graham

Turned Down the Role of Jade
Lindsay Lohan

WHO Trivia
Josh Lucas, Vince Vaughn, and Josh Hartnett were considered for the role of Phil Wenneck before Bradley Copper was cast. Will Ferrell, Breckin Meyer and Seth Rogen were considered for the role of Dr. Stu Price before Ed Helms was cast. Jonah Hill, Jake Gyllenhaal, and Thomas Haden Church were considered for the role of Alan Garner before Zack Galifianakis was cast.

Lindsay Lohan turned down the role of Jade, the stripper saying the script "had no potential." She later said she regretted the decision.

Bonus Movies

Cast Away (2000)

In the film, Chuck Noland's only companion during the four years that he spends on a deserted island is a volleyball, which he names Wilson.

Wilson was created by screenwriter William Broyles Jr. who while researching for the film, consulted with professional survival experts. Broyles subsequently chose to strand himself for one week on an isolated beach, and forced himself to search for water and food, and obtain his own shelter.

During this time, a volleyball washed up on shore. This was Broyles' inspiration for Noland's inanimate companion.

The Patriot (2000)

Joshua Jackson, Elijah Wood, Jake Gyllenhaal and Brad Renfro were all considered to play Gabriel Martin. However the producers and director narrowed their choices down to Ryan Phillippe and Heath Ledger, with the latter chosen because the director thought he possessed "exuberant youth."

A Beautiful Mind (2001)

Rachel Weisz, then hot from *The Mummy,* reportedly was offered and turned down the role of Alicia Nash. According to director Ron Howard, the four finalists for the part were Claire Forlani, Ashley Judd, Mary McCormack and Jennifer Connelly, with Connelly getting the role. Tom Cruise was considered for the role of John Nash before Russell Crowe was cast.

Heartbreakers (2001)

When the film was first going to be made, it was called *Breakers*, and was going to star Anjelica Huston and Alicia Silverstone. After that fell apart, the film resurfaced with Cher and Jennifer Aniston in the two leading roles. Finally, when the film was made, the title changed to *Heartbreakers*, and the leading roles went to Sigourney Weaver and Jennifer Love Hewitt.

Lara Croft: Tomb Raider (2001)

Denise Richards was considered a "sure thing" for the lead role because of her physical resemblance to the character in the video game series, but she turned it down. Charlize Theron, Uma Thurman, and Liv Tyler also turned down the role of Lara Croft before Angelina Jolie was cast.

Legally Blonde (2001)

Before Reese Witherspoon was cast as Elle Woods, the following actresses turned down the role: Natasha Henstridge, Gwyneth Paltrow, Chloe Sevigny, Tori Spelling and Charlize Theron. Moonie the chihuahua starred as Bruiser Woods.

Moulin Rouge (2001)

Before Nicole Kidman won the role of Satine, Kyra Sedgwick turned it down. Jake Gyllenhaal and Heath Ledger were both considered for the part of Christian before Ewan McGregor was cast.

Spider-Man (2002)

Before Tobey Maguire was cast as Spider-Man, the studio expressed interest in Leonardo DiCaprio, Freddie Prinze Jr., Heath Ledger, and James Franco, who was then cast as Harry Osborn, Peter's best friend.

Nicolas Cage, Jim Carrey, Robert De Niro, John Malkovich, and John Travolta all turned down the role of Norman Osborn/Green Goblin before Willem Defoe was cast.

Finding Nemo (2003)

After watching a cut of the film, director Andrew Stanton replaced William H. Macy with Albert Brooks to play Nemo's father Marlin; the recasting was thought to have saved the film. It was Brooks who liked the idea of Marlin being a clownfish who isn't funny, and recorded outtakes of telling very bad jokes to sell the idea to Stanton.

Although Stanton originally envisioned Dory as male, he was inspired to cast Ellen DeGeneres after he watched an episode of Ellen in which she "changed the subject five times before finishing one sentence."

Mean Girls (2004)

Lindsay Lohan first read for Regina George. However, the casting team felt that Lohan was closer to their image of another character, Cady Heron. Lohan feared the "mean girl" role, Regina George, would harm her reputation; she agreed to pay Cady Heron.

Rachel McAdams was cast as Regina George because writer/director Tina Fey thought McAdams, being "kind and polite" in real life, made her perfect for such an evil-spirited character. Amanda Seyfried also read for Regina, but the producers ultimately liked her for the role of Karen Smith, due to Seyfried's "spacey and daffy sense of humor."

Kiss Kiss Bang Bang (2005)

Various studios rejected the original script, *You'll Never Die in This Town Again*, until Warner Bros. agreed to produce the movie with a much larger budget if Harrison Ford agreed to play private investigator "Gay" Perry. After Ford passed, Benicio del Toro and Hugh Grant were considered.

Johnny Knoxville was being considered for the role of Harry Lockhart when Susan Levin, who worked as producer Joel Silver's assistant, suggested her boyfriend, Robert Downey Jr., for the role. Downey Jr., was eventually cast. Levin also suggested Val Kilmer, long interested in making a comedy, to play "Gay" Perry.

Michael Clayton (2007)

Denzel Washington turned down the role of Michael Clayton; a decision he later regretted. George Clooney was then cast as Michael Clayton, the "fixer" for the law firm of Kenner, Bach, and Ledeen. Clayton's main job was to clean up messes for the firm.

Knocked Up (2007)

Anne Hathaway, originally cast in the role of Alison, dropped out due to creative reasons. Writer/Director Judd Apatow attributed Hathaway's disagreement with his plan to use real footage of a woman giving birth. Jennifer Love Hewitt and Kate Bosworth auditioned for the part after Hathaway dropped out. Katherine Heigl was Apatow's final choice.

The Curious Case of Benjamin Button (2008)

When Steven Spielberg was attached to direct in the mid 1990s, Tom Cruise was attached to play the lead. Then, when Ron Howard was set to direct in 1998, John Travolta was going to play the lead role. Ten years later, when the film was finally made, Brad Pitt played the role of Benjamin Button.

Taken (2008)

Jeff Bridges was first cast as Bryan Mills, but he dropped out and Liam Neeson accepted the part. Neeson expected the film to bomb, but he signed on in order to spend four months in Paris and learn karate while playing the kind of role he had rarely been offered in the past. Ironically, not only was the film a massive hit for Neesom, but also created a new on-screen persona for him as an action hero.

Inglorious Basterds (2009)

Writer/Director Quentin Tarantino originally wanted to cast Leonardo DiCaprio in the role of Hans Landa. However, that was not possible. Eventually, Tarantino cast Christoph Waltz in the role.

Tarantino asked Adam Sandler to play the role of Donny Donowitz, but Sandler declined due to schedule conflicts with *Funny People.*

Nastassja Kinski was approached for the role of Bridget von Hammersmark, but a deal could not be reached. Tarantino cast Diane Kruger in the role instead.

Simon Pegg was originally set to play Lieutenant Archie Hicox, but was forced to pull out of the project because of scheduling conflicts. Michael Fassbender replaced him.

Rod Taylor, effectively retired from acting, came out of retirement when the role of Winston Churchill was offered to him.

Mickey Ward • Dicky Eklund • Abraham Lincoln • Maya, CIA Analyst
Dan, CIA Intelligence Officer • Django • Dr. King Schultz • Ace Woody
Pat Solitano Jr. • Tiffany Maxwell • Lt. Matt Kowalski • Dr. Ryan Stone
Nick Dunne • Amy Dunne • Sabastian Wilder • Mia Dolan • Lee Chandler
Elton John • King George VI • Aron Ralston • Evelyn Salt • Mark Zuckerberg
Eduardo Saverin • Gil Pender • John Steed • Emma Peel • Jean Valjean • Javert
Fantine • Catwomen/Selina Kaye • John Blake/Robin • Rod Woodroof
Dr. Eve Saks • Hugh Glass • John Fitzgerald • Joy Newsome • Jack Newsome
Elio Perlman • T'Challa/Black Panther • Freddie Mercury • The Joker
Mickey Ward • Dicky Eklund • Abraham Lincoln • Maya, CIA Analyst

2010s

Dan, CIA Intelligence Officer • Django • Dr. King Schultz • Ace Woody
Pat Solitano Jr. • Tiffany Maxwell • Lt. Matt Kowalski • Dr. Ryan Stone
Nick Dunne • Amy Dunne • Sabastian Wilder • Mia Dolan • Lee Chandler
Elton John • King George VI • Aron Ralston • Evelyn Salt • Mark Zuckerberg
Eduardo Saverin • Gil Pender • John Steed • Emma Peel • Jean Valjean • Javert
Fantine • Catwomen/Selina Kaye • John Blake/Robin • Rod Woodroof
Dr. Eve Saks • Hugh Glass • John Fitzgerald • Joy Newsome • Jack Newsome
Elio Perlman • T'Challa/Black Panther • Freddie Mercury • The Joker
Mickey Ward • Dicky Eklund • Abraham Lincoln • Maya, CIA Analyst
Dan, CIA Intelligence Officer • Django • Dr. King Schultz • Ace Woody
Pat Solitano Jr. • Tiffany Maxwell • Lt. Matt Kowalski • Dr. Ryan Stone
Nick Dunne • Amy Dunne • Sabastian Wilder • Mia Dolan • Lee Chandler
Elton John • King George VI • Aron Ralston • Evelyn Salt • Mark Zuckerberg
Eduardo Saverin • Gil Pender • John Steed • Emma Peel • Jean Valjean • Javert
Fantine • Catwomen/Selina Kaye • John Blake/Robin • Rod Woodroof
Dr. Eve Saks • Hugh Glass • John Fitzgerald • Joy Newsome • Jack Newsome
Elio Perlman • T'Challa/Black Panther • Freddie Mercury • The Joker
Mickey Ward • Dicky Eklund • Abraham Lincoln • Maya, CIA Analyst
Dan, CIA Intelligence Officer • Django • Dr. King Schultz • Ace Woody
Pat Solitano Jr. • Tiffany Maxwell • Lt. Matt Kowalski • Dr. Ryan Stone
Nick Dunne • Amy Dunne • Sabastian Wilder • Mia Dolan • Lee Chandler
Elton John • King George VI • Aron Ralston • Evelyn Salt • Mark Zuckerberg
Eduardo Saverin • Gil Pender • John Steed • Emma Peel • Jean Valjean • Javert
Fantine • Catwomen/Selina Kaye • John Blake/Robin • Rod Woodroof
Dr. Eve Saks • Hugh Glass • John Fitzgerald • Joy Newsome • Jack Newsome
Elio Perlman • T'Challa/Black Panther • Freddie Mercury • The Joker
Mickey Ward • Dicky Eklund • Abraham Lincoln • Maya, CIA Analyst
Dan, CIA Intelligence Officer • Django • Dr. King Schultz • Ace Woody

Hollywood's New Business Model

The new decade brought Hollywood a new business model - a switch from the once profitable sale of DVDs to video on-demand services and the digital delivery of movies over the Internet. Various options were developed to increase home entertainment media sales, including: storing and watching movies in the "Cloud;" digitizing personal DVD collections; different price points depending on how soon a digital copy was available after the theatrical release; and the creation of specific movie Apps where additional content could accompany an available film.

Sony Pictures Entertainment, 20th Century Fox, Universal Pictures, and Warner Brothers made a deal with DirecTV to release films two months after their theatrical release, but before their DVD release. This distribution system was immediately viewed as a possible threat to bricks-and-mortar theaters, especially the smaller movie chains that had just committed to expensive upgrades to accommodate digital and 3-D projection.

During the decade, home digital streaming of video content continued to boom and topple traditional DVD and Blu-Ray revenues, which decreased by $3 billion between 2009 and 2013. The rise of new subscription services and competition for market share from new and powerful players such as Netflix and Amazon, offering original movies, produced dramatic changes in the industry.

Disney's purchase of Twentieth Century Fox for $52.4 billion was one of the biggest showbiz mergers of all time. The merger was part of Disney's plan to acquire more content for a future launch in 2019 of its own subscription streaming service that could compete with Netflix.

Throughout the decade, attendance had been mostly down at movie complexes. Many factors impacted attendance: rising ticket prices, over-familiarity with sequels and remakes, more viewing options, inadequate sound and images in multiplexes, overcrowded weekends, inconsiderate theater patrons, and the glut of other diversionary technological gadgets.

However, foreign box office revenues climbed to an all-time high with six major Hollywood studios reporting $13.53 billion in overseas ticket sales to start the decade. This was an all-time record, which helped to cushion the blow of shrinking domestic revenues and declining DVD sales.

The decade saw the end of celluloid film - no more celluloid with sprocket holes and gear-driven projectors. By mid-decade, the phase-out from 35 mm to digital was almost complete for the 40,000 U.S. movie screens, making it cheaper to produce and ship film prints, and created digital prints of higher quality with superior copyright protection.

Although there was a spike in the number of women filmmakers in the 2010s, the number of major studio films directed by women continued to be exceedingly low. Females usually directed romantic comedies or documentaries, while Hollywood traditionally employed men to make the bigger action and super-hero films.

One exception was *Wonder Woman*, directed by Patty Jenkins, which became the biggest blockbuster ever directed by a woman. And for the first time in 60 years, the three top-grossing films of 2017 featured women in lead roles: Daisy Ridley in *Star Wars: The Last Jedi,* Emma Watson in *Beauty and the Beast,* and Gal Gadot in *Wonder Woman.* Still, there continued to be an ongoing wage disparity in Hollywood, in which men were making a lot more money than women.

Another significant event occurred toward the end of the decade - the MeToo movement was born. This movement called attention to the lack of diversity in filmmaking and to sexual abuse and harassment within the industry. The result was that more women executives were put into decision-making positions. Correspondingly, as it applied to casting, more films with female leads were being made.

With a new decade on the horizon, and the power of Netflix and Amazon growing, the "old guard" of major studios realized that they would have to change the way they think and do business to survive and compete in the fast-paced, ever-changing, film industry.

The
Academy Awards

2010
Best Picture: ***The King's Speech***
Best Actor: Colin Firth (*The King's Speech*)
Best Actress: Natalie Portman (*Black Swan*)
Best Supporting Actor: Christian Bale (*The Fighter*)
Best Supporting Actress: Melissa Leo (*The Fighter*)

2011
Best Picture: ***The Artist***
Best Actor: Jean Dujardin (*The Artist*)
Best Actress: Meryl Streep (*The Iron Lady*)
Best Supporting Actor: Christopher Plummer (*Beginners*)
Best Supporting Actress: Octavia Spencer (*The Help*)

2012
Best Picture: ***Argo***
Best Actor: Daniel Day-Lewis (*Lincoln*)
Best Actress: Jennifer Lawrence (*Silver Linings Playbook*)
Best Supporting Actor: Christoph Waltz (*Django Unchained*)
Best Supporting Actress: Anne Hathaway (*Les Miserables*)

2013
Best Picture: ***12 Years a Slave***
Best Actor: Matthew McConaughey (*Dallas Buyers Club*)
Best Actress: Cate Blanchett (*Blue Jasmine*)
Best Supporting Actor: Jared Leto (*Dallas Buyers Club*)
Best Supporting Actress: Lupita Nyong'o (*12 Years a Slave*)

2014
Best Picture: ***Birdman or (The Unexpected Virtue of Ignorance)***
Best Actor: Eddie Redmayne (*The Theory of Everything*)
Best Actress: Julianne Moore (*Still Alice*)
Best Supporting Actor: J.K. Simmons (*Whiplash*)
Best Supporting Actress: Patricia Arquette (*Boyhood*)

2015
Best Picture: ***Spotlight***
Best Actor: Leonardo DiCaprio (*The Revenant*)
Best Actress: Brie Larson (*Room*)
Best Supporting Actor: Mark Rylance (*Bridge of Spies*)
Best Supporting Actress: Alicia Vikander (*The Danish Girl*)

2016
Best Picture: ***Moonlight***
Best Actor: Casey Affleck (*Manchester by the Sea*)
Best Actress: Emma Stone (*La La Land*)
Best Supporting Actor: Mahershala Ali (*Moonlight*)
Best Supporting Actress: Viola Davis (*Fences*)

2017
Best Picture: ***The Shape of Water***
Best Actor: Gary Oldman (*Darkest Hour*)
Best Actress: Frances McDormand (*Three Billboards Outside Ebbing, Missouri*)
Best Supporting Actor: Sam Rockwell (*Three Billboards Outside Ebbing, MO*)
Best Supporting Actress: Allison Janney (*I, Tonya*)

2018
Best Picture: ***Green Book***
Best Actor: Rami Malek (*Bohemian Rhapsody*)
Best Actress: Olivia Colman (*The Favourite*)
Best Supporting Actor: Mahershala Ali (*Green Book*)
Best Supporting Actress: Regina King (*If Beale Street Could Talk*)

2019
Best Picture: ?
Best Actor: ?
Best Actress: ?
Best Supporting Actor: ?
Best Supporting Actress: ?

Casting
Trivia Quiz

1. Before Christian Bale won an Oscar for playing drug-addicted Dicky
   Eklund in *The Fighter*, this actor turned down the role:
   - a. Jake Gyllenhaal
   - b. Eminem
   - c. Bradley Cooper
   - d. Miles Teller

2. Before Jessica Chastain was cast in the role of CIA Analyst, Maya in
   Zero Dark Thirty, the role was turned down by:
   - a. Emma Stone
   - b. Rooney Mara
   - c. Amy Adams
   - d. Kate Winslet

3. Jamie Foxx plays Django in *Django Unchained*. The role was first
   offered to:
   - a. Denzel Washington
   - b. Cuba Gooding, Jr.
   - c. Will Smith
   - d. Terrence Howard

4. In *Silver Linings Playbook*, the leading female role of Tiffany, played
   by Jennifer Lawrence, was originally turned down by this actress:
   - a. Anne Hathaway
   - b.. Amy Adams
   - c. Blake Lively
   - d. Natalie Portman

5. Sandra Bullock who played Dr. Ryan Stone in *Gravity* wasn't the first
   choice for the role. This actress turned the role down:
   - a. Angelina Jolie
   - b. Marion Cotillard
   - c. Natalie Portman
   - d. All of the Above

6. Though Rosamund Pike plays the title role of the disappeared wife Amy
   Dunne in *Gone Girl*, this actress originally bought the film rights to
   both produce and play the role:
   - a. Jennifer Aniston
   - b. Reese Withertspoon
   - c. Jennifer Garner
   - d. Margot Robbie

7. In *La La Land*, Emma Stone won an Oscar playing struggling actress
   Mia. The role was originally offered to:
   - a. Emma Watson
   - b. Amy Adams
   - c. Anne Hathaway
   - d. Jennifer Lawrence

8. Casey Affleck won an Oscar playing a grieving husband and father in **Manchester By The Sea,** but the role was originally to have been played by:
   - a. Ben Affleck
   - b. Matt Damon
   - c. Matthew McConaughey
   - d. Robert Downey Jr.

9. Chadwick Boseman plays the role of T'Challa in **Black Panther**. Originally, this role was going to be played by this actor:
   - a. Will Smith
   - b. Wesley Snipes
   - c. Michael B. Jordan
   - d. None of the Above

10. Rami Malek won an Academy Award playing the role of Freddie Mercury in **Bohemian Rhapsody**, but the role was first offered to:
    - a. Sacha Baron Cohen
    - b. Ryan Gosling
    - c. Joseph Gordon-Levitt
    - d. Ryan Reynolds

11. Leonardo DiCaprio won an Oscar for his role in **The Revenant,** but the role was originally intended for:
    - a. Christian Bale
    - b. Kevin Costner
    - c. Sean Penn
    - d. Samuel L. Jackson

12. The role of Nick Dunne in **Gone Girl** was played by Ben Affleck. It was originally going to be played by this actor:
    - a. Jon Hamm
    - b. Seth Rogan
    - c. Ryan Reynolds
    - d. Matt Damon

13. In **Silver Linings Playbook,** Bradley Cooper played Pat Jr., a role that was turned down by this actor:
    - a. Mark Wahlberg
    - b. Ryan Gosling
    - c. Christian Bale
    - d. Matt Damon

14. Elton John was played by Taron Egerton in the autobiographical film, **Rocketman**. This actor turned down the role due to scheduling conflicts:
    - a. James McAvoy
    - b. Daniel Radcliffe
    - c. Thomas Hardy
    - d. Justin Timberlake

15. Originally, the lead role in the film, **Salt**, starring Angelina Jolie, was turned down by:
    - a. Tom Cruise
    - b. Matt Damon
    - c. Rooney Mara
    - d. Marion Cotillard

THE FIGHTER (2010)

Dicky Eklund: Hey Mick... Do you think I knocked down Sugar Ray Leonard?

Micky Ward: Yeah, sure I do. You were the pride of Lowell. You were my hero, Dicky.

Dicky Eklund: I was. I was.

Plot

The story of "Irish" Micky Ward, a fledgling boxer who tries to escape the shadow of his more famous but troubled older boxing brother and get his own shot at greatness.

CASTING

Who Starred as Dicky Eklund?
Christian Bale

Turned Down the Role of Dicky Eklund
Brad Pitt • Matt Damon • Eminem

WHO Trivia

Mark Wahlberg, besides being one of the producers, was going to play the role of Micky Ward. He actually began training for it in 2005. Throughout various production delays, he continued to train every day, so he would be ready for filming, which finally began in 2009.

Brad Pitt and Matt Damon were attached at one time to play Dicky Eklund, but both backed out due to scheduling conflicts when the film was finally ready to go into production.

In his capacity as one of the film's producers, Wahlberg then went to rapper Eminem and offered him the role. He declined to work on his music.

Not sure where to turn next, Wahlberg accidently ran into Christian Bale at the elementary school both their daughters attended, and told him about the film. After reading the script, Bale signed on to play Dicky Eklund.

Bale was also the one who suggested David O. Russell as the director, after Martin Scorsese, Darren Aronofsky, and Peter Berg turned down the job.

LINCOLN (2012)

Abraham Lincoln: Abolishing slavery by constitutional provisions settles the fate for all coming time. Not only of the millions now in bondage, but of unborn millions to come. Two votes stand in its way. These votes must be procured.

Plot

As the American Civil War continues to rage, America's president struggles with many inside his own cabinet on the decision to emancipate the slaves.

CASTING

Who Starred as Abraham Lincoln?
Daniel Day-Lewis

Turned Down the Role of Abraham Lincoln
Liam Neeson

WHO Trivia

Director/Producer Steven Spielberg had *Lincoln* in development for 12 years. Liam Neeson, who was attached to play Abraham Lincoln since the project began, decided to drop out. According to Neeson, he felt he was too old to play the part after waiting so many years for the project to get the go-ahead.

Daniel Day-Lewis originally turned down the role of Abraham Lincoln sending Steven Spielberg the following letter:

"Dear Steven. It was a real pleasure just to sit and talk with you. I listened very carefully to what you had to say about this compelling history, and I've since read the script and found it - in all the detail of which it describes these monumental events and in the compassionate portraits of all the principle characters - both powerful and moving. I can't account for how at any given moment I feel the need to explore one life as opposed to another. But I do know that I can only do this work if I feel almost as if there's no choice; that a subject coincides inexplicably with a very personal need and a very specific moment in time. In this case, as fascinated as I was by 'Abe,' it was the fascination of a grateful spectator who longed to see a story told rather than that of a participant. That's how I feel now in spite of myself, and though I can't be sure this won't change, I couldn't dream of encouraging you to keep it open on a mere possibility. I do hope this makes sense Steven. I'm glad you're making the film. I wish you the strength for it and I send both my very best wishes and my sincere gratitude to you for having considered me. Daniel."

ZERO DARK THIRTY (2012)

Maya, CIA Analyst: I'm going to smoke everyone involved in this op and then I'm going to kill Osama bin Laden.

Plot

The chronicle of the ten-year manhunt for terrorist leader Osama bin Laden after the 9/11 attacks, and his death at the hands of Seal Team 6.

CASTING

Who Starred as Maya, CIA Analyst?
Jessica Chastain

Turned Down the Role of Maya, CIA Analyst
Rooney Mara

Who Starred as Dan, CIA Intelligence Officer?
Jason Clarke

Turned Down the Role of Dan, CIA Intelligence Officer
Joel Edgerton

WHO Trivia

After Rooney Mara, originally cast as CIA analyst Maya, dropped out, Jessica Chastain was offered the role, which was declined by her agents. Producer Megan Ellison, who had worked with Chastain on *Lawless,* gave Chastain's private phone number to director Kathryn Bigelow so she could personally offer her the role. When she did, Chastain accepted.

Joel Edgerton was originally cast as Dan, CIA Intelligence Officer, but had to drop out due to scheduling conflicts. When the conflicts were resolved, Edgerton was able to return to the film as the Seal Team 6 Team Leader.

At one point, Tom Hardy, Idris Elba, and Guy Pearce were considered for different roles. None of them appeared in the film.

James Cameron, ex-husband of Kathryn Bigelow, was in negotiations to direct the film but dropped out to work on *Avatar 2,* which is now scheduled to come out in 2021. Writer Mark Boal said he wrote the screenplay with Kathryn Bigelow in mind to direct.

DJANGO UNCHAINED (2012)

Django: What's a bounty?
Schultz: It's like a reward.
Django: You kill people? And they give you a reward?
Schultz: Certain people, yeah.
Django: Bad people?
Schultz: Ah, badder they are, bigger the reward.

Plot

With the help of a German bounty hunter, a freed slave sets out to rescue his wife from a brutal Mississippi plantation owner.

CASTING

Who Starred as Django?
Jamie Foxx

Turned Down the Role of Django
Will Smith

WHO Trivia

Writer/Director Quentin Tarantino wrote the role of Django with Will Smith in mind. Will Smith's agents and manager all wanted him to do it, but he ultimately declined. Cuba Gooding Jr. lobbied for the role of Django, but Tarantino would not consider him. According to Gooding, the biggest disappointment in his career.

Tarantino did consider Denzel Washington, but deemed him too old. Tarantino also considered Idris Elba, Chris Tucker, Terrence Howard, and Tyrese Gibson before offering the role of Django to Jamie Foxx.

Tarantino immediately cast Christoph Waltz in the role of Dr. King Schultz.

Kevin Costner was in negotiations to play Ace Woody, a Mandingo trainer and Calvin Candie's right-hand man, but Costner dropped out due to scheduling conflicts. Kurt Russell replaced him, but also had to drop out. Eventually, the role of Ace Woody was not recast; instead, it was merged with the character, Billy Crash, played by Walton Goggins.

Fun Fact: Jamie Foxx rode his own horse, Cheetah, in the film.

SILVER LININGS PLAYBOOK (2012)

Tiffany: Why did you order Raisin Bran?
Pat: Why did you order tea?
Tiffany: Because you ordered Raisin Bran.
Pat: I ordered Raisin Bran because I didn't want any mistaking it for a date.
Tiffany: It can still be a date if you order Raisin Bran.
Pat: It's not a date. So, how's your thing going -- dancing thing?
Tiffany: It's good. How's your restraining order?

Plot
A former teacher, who after a stint in a mental institution, moves back in with his parents and meets a mysterious girl with problems of her own.

CASTING

Who Starred as Pat Solitano Jr.?
Bradley Cooper

Turned Down the Role of Pat Solitano Jr.
Mark Wahlberg

Who Starred as Tiffany Maxwell?
Jennifer Lawrence

Turned Down the Role of Tiffany Maxwell
Anne Hathaway

WHO Trivia
Writer/Director David O. Russell initially intended to make the film with Vince Vaughn and Zooey Deschanel, but went on to make *The Fighter* instead.

When the film finally went into production, Mark Wahlberg, who worked with Russell on *The Fighter,* was set to work with him for the fourth time but had to drop out after delays in production created a scheduling conflict.

Russell originally planned to work with Bradley Cooper on an adaptation of the films, *Pride and Prejudice* and *Zombies*. Impressed with Cooper's performance in *Wedding Crashers*, citing his "good bad-guy energy" and unpredictability, Russell cast him as Pat Solitano Jr.

After Anne Hathaway, cast as Tiffany Maxwell, dropped out over creative differences with Russell and conflicts with *The Dark Knight Rises,* Russell decided to cast Jennifer Lawrence in the role.

GRAVITY (2013)

Lt. Kowalski: Gotta admit one thing. Can't beat the view. So, what do you like about being up here?
Dr. Ryan Stone: The silence. I could get used to it.
Lt. Kowalski: Terrific.

Plot
A medical engineer and an astronaut must work together to survive after an accident leaves them adrift in space.

CASTING

Who Starred as Lieutenant Matt Kowalski?
George Clooney

Turned Down the Role of Lieutenant Matt Kowalski
Robert Downey Jr.

Who Starred as Dr. Ryan Stone?
Sandra Bullock

Turned Down the Role of Dr. Ryan Stone
Angelina Jolie • Marion Cotillard
Blake Lively • Natalie Portman

WHO Trivia
Co-Writer/Director Alfonso Cuarón offered the role of Dr. Ryan Stone to a number of actresses before Sandra Bullock was cast in October 2010.

Earlier in the year, Angelina Jolie was in contact with Warner Bros. to star in the film, but conflicts involving her film *In the Land of Blood and Honey*, and a possible *Salt* sequel, led Jolie to end her involvement with *Gravity*, leaving Warner Bros. with doubts the film would get made.

In June 2010, Marion Cotillard was offered the role, but turned it down to accept a role in *Inception*. A month later, Blake Lively turned it down due to scheduling conflicts. Alfonso Cuarón then decided he wanted Salma Hayak to play the role but the studio refused, saying no one would believe a Mexican astronaut.

In September 2010, Cuarón received approval from Warner Bros. to offer the role to Natalie Portman, but she also had to decline because of scheduling conflicts. Warner Bros. then approached Sandra Bullock.

GONE GIRL (2014)

Nick Dunne: When I think of my wife, I always think of the back of her head. I picture cracking her lovely skull, unspooling her brain, trying to get answers. The primal questions of a marriage: What are you thinking?... How are you feeling?... What have we done to each other?

Plot

The mysterious disappearance of a woman becomes the focus of an intense media circus, while her husband sees the spotlight turned on him when it's suspected he may not be innocent.

CASTING

Who Starred as Nick Dunne?
Ben Affleck

Turned Down the Role of Nick Dunne
John Hamm

Who Starred as Amy Dunne?
Rosamund Pike

Turned Down the Role of Amy Dunne
Reese Witherspoon

WHO Trivia

In June 2012, Reese Witherspoon obtained the film rights from writer Gillian Flynn for her novel, with the idea she would play Amy Dunne.

However after meeting with David Fincher, the director, and listening to his vision of the film, Witherspoon realized she wasn't the right person to play the female lead, but decided she would stay on as a producer.

Fincher considered Charlize Theron, Emily Blunt, Rooney Mara, Olivia Wilde, Natalie Portman, and Abbie Cornish for the role of Amy Dunne before casting Rosamund Pike.

Fincher wanted Jon Hamm to play Nick Dunne, but he had to turn down the role due to commitments for *Mad Men*. He then considered Seth Rogan and Ryan Reynolds before offering the role to Ben Affleck.

LA LA LAND (2016)

Mia: It's pretty strange that we keep running into each other.
Sebastian: Maybe it means something.
Mia: I doubt it.
Sebastian: Yeah, I didn't think so.

Plot
While navigating their careers in Los Angeles, a jazz pianist and an actress fall in love.

CASTING

Who Starred as Sebastian Wilder?
Ryan Gosling

Turned Down the Role of Sebastian Wilder
Miles Teller

Who Starred as Mia Dolan?
Emma Stone

Turned Down the Role of Mia Dolan
Emma Watson

WHO Trivia
There are two stories as to why Miles Teller, who was originally going to portray Sebastian, did not play the role.

In the first story, Teller, having worked with director Damien Chazelle on *Whiplash,* walked away after contract negotiations broke down. In the second, Chazelle decided he wanted to make his characters somewhat older, with more experience struggling to make their dreams, rather than younger newcomers just arriving in Los Angeles. This made Miles Teller too young for the role, and he departed as a favor to Chazelle.

Coincidentally, Emma Watson turned down the role of Mia in *La La Land* due to scheduling conflicts with *Beauty and the Beast*, while Ryan Gosling turned down the lead role of the Beast in *Beauty and the Beast*, to appear in *La La Land*.

To get the character of Sebastian right, Gosling learned to tap dance and play the piano.

MANCHESTER BY THE SEA (2016)

Lee:	I don't understand.
Dr. Muller:	Which part are you having trouble with?
Lee:	Well, I can't be his guardian.
Dr. Muller:	Well, your brother provided for your nephew's upbringing. I think the idea was that you would relocate.
Lee:	Relocate to where? Here?
Dr. Muller:	Well, it was my impression you had spent a lot of time here.
Lee:	I'm just a back-up.

Plot

A brooding, irritable loner is named guardian to his 16-year-old nephew after his older brother dies, returning him to the place an unspeakable tragedy occurred years before.

CASTING

Who Starred as Lee Chandler?
Casey Affleck

Turned Down the Role of Lee Chandler
Matt Damon

WHO Trivia

In 2011, Matt Damon, "concerned about Kenneth Lonergan being in horrible limbo," wanted to do something nice for his friend, so he pitched him an idea for a script about an emotionally crippled handyman who is thrust into taking care of his teenage nephew after his father dies. Damon thought the themes would be right up Lonergan's dark alley.

Damon and John Krasinski had brainstormed the idea, thinking Krasinski would star and Damon would direct. Both actors became occupied with other projects while Lonergan worked on the screenplay for three years. After Damon read a rough draft of the script, he insisted Lonergan should direct it, he would star in it, and Krasinski would became an Executive Producer.

Pre-production began in September 2014. However, Damon would not have a break in his schedule for another year. In early December, it was announced Casey Affleck would replace Damon in the lead role. Damon said "I wouldn't give this role up to anybody but Casey Affleck."

ROCKETMAN (2019)

Bernie Taupin: Don't you want to just sing without this ridiculous paraphernalia?

Elton John: People don't pay to see Reg Dwight!... They pay to see Elton John!

Plot
A musical fantasy about Elton John's breakthrough years.

CASTING

Who Starred as Elton John?
Taron Egerton

Turned Down the Role of Elton John
Tom Hardy

WHO Trivia
Elton John and husband David Furnish had tried to produce a film based on Elton John's life for almost twenty years. The earliest dated back to 2001, when the film initially started at Walt Disney Studios with Justin Timberlake to star as a young Elton John. In an article written for The Guardian, John said that he struggled to get the project off the ground due to studios wanting the film to be toned down to a PG-13 rating instead of an R-rating.

In March 2013, Focus Films got involved and hired Michael Gracey to direct, with Tom Hardy cast to play John. Filming was planned to start in 2014, however, creative differences between John and Focus, along with budget issues, caused him and Furnish to take the project elsewhere.

No further development on the film was announced until July 2017, when it was announced Hardy was dropping out of the project due to his busy schedule. Before Taron Egerton was cast, James McAvoy and Daniel Radcliffe were considered for the lead role.

Taron Egerton had worked with Elton John in *Kingsman: The Golden Circle,* and developed a great relationship with him. John's advice to Egerton was not to copy him too much; instead to make his own version. Egerton, who recorded songs for the films, *Eddie the Eagle* and *Sing,* does his own singing in the film.

Bonus Movies

The King's Speech (2010)
Colin Firth won an Oscar for Best Actor for the role of King George VI. Written with Paul Bettany in mind, but wanting to spend more time with his family, Bettany turned the role down The producers considered Ralph Fiennes and Robert Downey Jr. before offering the role to Hugh Grant who also turned it down; later said to be "kicking himself" with regret.

127 Hours (2010)
Cillian Murphy was Danny Boyle's first choice to play Aron Ralston before James Franco was cast.

Salt (2010)
Originally, the film was titled *Edwin A. Salt* with Tom Cruise in the lead role. After Cruise dropped out, the role was rewritten for a female lead, renamed *Salt,* and Angelina Jolie was cast.

The Avengers (2012)
Mel Gibson turned down the role of John Steed and Gwyneth Paltrow turned down the role of Emma Peel for the film based on the successful television series. Ralph Fiennes and Uma Thurman played the roles.

Les Misérables (2012)
Prior to production, director Tom Hooper was approached by Hugh Jackman who was interested in playing the role of Jean Valjean. Jackman was to star alongside Paul Bettany as Javert, but Bettany was placed by Russell Crowe.

Anne Hathaway eventually won the role of Fantine, but not before Amy Adams, Jessica Biel, Marion Cotillard, and Kate Winslet were considered.

The Dark Knight Rises (2012)
A number of actresses, including: Natalie Portman, Keira Knightley, Kate Mara, Jessica Biel, Blake Lively, and Lady Gaga auditioned for the role of Catwoman/Selina Kyle. Anne Hathaway was eventually cast.

Chloe Grace Moretz and Jennifer Lawrence auditioned for the role of Jen, Selina Kyles's sidekick, played by Juno Temple. Ryan Gosling was considered for the role of John Blake, played by Joseph Gordon-Levitt.

Dallas Buyers Club (2013)

Before Matthew McConaughey, who played Rod Woodroof, came onto the project and was able to get the financing in place, a number of actor/director duos tried to get the film made. In the mid 1990s, Woody Harrelson and Dennis Hopper were attached, followed by Brad Pitt and Marc Foster, and finally Ryan Gosling and Craig Gillespie.

Hilary Swank was cast in the role of Dr. Eve Saks, but dropped out due to scheduling conflicts; Jennifer Garner replaced her.

The Revenant (2015)

Development of David Rabe's script, *The Revenant,* began in August 2001, with producer Akiva Goldsman acquiring the rights to a then-unpublished novel, with Samuel L. Jackson in mind to star. The development stalled until 2010, when a new adaptation of the novel was written. John Hillcoat was then set to direct the film, and Christian Bale was to star as Hugh Glass, until Hillcoat left the project in October 2010.

In August 2011, Alejando G. Inárritu came on board to direct. Inárritu wanted Leonardo DiCaprio to play Hugh Glass and Sean Penn to play John Fitzgerald. Sean Penn was cast, but had to drop out due to scheduling conflicts. Penn was replaced by Tom Hardy. DiCaprio turned down the lead role in *Steve Jobs* to do this film.

Black Panther (2018)

In June 1992, Wesley Snipes announced his intention to make a film of *Black Panther.* Snipes suggested that Africa had been poorly portrayed in previous Hollywood films. Snipes thought that the lead noble character in *Black Panther* would highlight the majesty of the continent as well as portray the antithesis of "African stereotypes."

In 1994, Snipes initiated development of the film with Stan Lee and Columbia Pictures. Eighteen months later, Lee indicated he was not pleased with the scripts for the project. In 1997, *Black Panther* was listed as part of the Marvel Comics film slate with Snipes attached. In August, corporate problems at Marvel put everything on hold.

By 2002, the production was resurrected, and David S. Goyer was set to direct. However, Goyer suggested that Snipes' starring in both *Black Panther* and *Blade: Trinity* "might be overkill." For unknown reasons, the film was delayed again.

Finally in 2015, the film went into pre-production. Ryan Coogler was the new director; Chadwick Boseman was cast as T'Challa/Black Panther. Boseman was chosen over John Boyega who went on to star in three *Star Wars* movies in the new *Star Wars*.

Bohemian Rhapsody (2018)

Sacha Baron Cohen was the original choice to play Freddie Mercury with Stephen Frears to direct. When Frears left the project, the deal with Cohen fell apart. Rami Malek was eventually cast as Mercury.

Casting Trivia Quiz Answer Guide

The 1930s
1(b) 2(a) 3(a) 4(b) 5(b) 6(d) 7(b) 8(c)
9(d) 10(a) 11(b) 12(a) 13(d) 14(a) 15(d)

The 1940s
1(d) 2(c) 3(b) 4(d) 5(b) 6(d) 7(b) 8(a)
9(d) 10(d) 11(a) 12(a) 13(c) 14(c) 15(d)

The 1950s
1(a) 2(d) 3(c) 4(d) 5(c) 6(a) 7(a) 8(b)
9(a) 10(a) 11(a) 12(b) 13(c) 14(c) 15(d)

The 1960s
1(c) 2(d) 3(a) 4(d) 5(b) 6(a) 7(c) 8(d)
9(a) 10(a) 11(c) 12(c) 13(c) 14(c) 15(d)

The 1970s
1(d) 2(d) 3(b) 4(d) 5(a) 6(a) 7(d) 8(a)
9(c) 10(c) 11(a) 12(d) 13(a) 14(c) 15(d)

The 1980s
1(d) 2(d) 3(b) 4(b) 5(a) 6(c) 7(d) 8(b)
9(a) 10(d) 11(a) 12(a) 13(a) 14(d) 15(b)

The 1990s
1(d) 2(b) 3(a) 4(c) 5(a) 6(d) 7(c) 8(a)
9(a) 10(c) 11(a) 12(d) 13(b) 14(d) 15(b)

The 2000s
1(c) 2(b) 3(d) 4(d) 5(c) 6(a) 7(b) 8(b)
9(d) 10(d) 11(d) 12(a) 13(c) 14(a) 15(b)

The 2010s
1(b) 2(b) 3(c) 4(a) 5(d) 6(b) 7(a) 8(b)
9(b) 10(a) 11(a) 12(a) 13(a) 14(c) 15(a)

Movie Index

1930s

Bringing Up Baby, 11
Captain Blood, 17
Dracula, 17
Frankenstein, 17
Golden Boy, 18
Gone With the Wind, 12-13
Hunchback of Notre Dame, The, 18
It Happened One Night, 9
King Kong, 17
Lost Horizon, 17
Mr. Smith Goes to Washington, 18
Public Enemy, 17
Adventures of Robin Hood, The, 10
Stagecoach, 14
Topper, 17
Wizard of Oz, The 15
Wuthering Heights , 18

1940s

All the Kings Men, 38
Arsenic and Old Lace, 32
Casablanca, 31
Double Indemnity, 33
Easter Parade, 40
Gaslight, 39
Gentleman's Agreement, 36
His Girl Friday, 27
It's a Wonderful Life, 35
The Killers, 40
Laura, 39
The Lost Weekend, 40
Maltese Falcon, The, 30
Mildred Pierce, 34
Mrs. Miniver, 39
National Velvet, 39-40
Philadelphia Story, The, 28

Rebecca, 29
Saboteur, 39
Sergeant York, 39
Stranger, The, 40
Treasure of Sierra Madre, The, 37
Yankee Doodle Dandy, 39

1950s

African Queen, The, 70
A Star is Born, 60
A Streetcar Named Desire, 52
All About Eve, 49
Annie Get Your Gun, 70
Ben-Hur, 67
Born Yesterday, 50
Bridge on the River Kwai, The, 65
Cat on a Hot Tin Roof, 66
Dial M for Murder, 61
East of Eden, 71
From Here to Eternity, 55
Giant, 63
Gigi, 72
Guys and Dolls, 71
High Noon, 53
Man Who Knew Too Much, The, 72
Man With the Golden Arm, The, 72
Mr. Roberts, 62
North by Northwest, 68
On the Waterfront, 59
Rebel Without a Cause, 71
Rio Bravo, 73
Roman Holiday, 57
Shane, 58
Singing in the Rain, 54
Some Like It Hot, 69
South Pacific, 72
Stalag 17, 71

2000s

The information contained in this book has been compiled from over a dozen sources, including websites, books, and magazine articles.

A three-source verification system was utilized for accuracy.

With that said, this book is about Hollywood and the film business which can be a bit crazy at times. So, if you think we have something wrong, or that we missed something that should be in the book, please contact us at: starringwhobook@gmail.com

The End

Made in the USA
Lexington, KY
24 November 2019

57617396R00179